Social Media Metrics

FOR

DUMMIES®

Social Media Metrics

FOR

DUMMIES®

by Leslie Poston

WILEY

John Wiley & Sons, Inc.

Social Media Metrics For Dummies®

Published by
John Wiley & Sons, Inc.
111 River Street
Hoboken, NJ 07030-5774

www.wiley.com

WILEY

About the Author

Leslie Poston co-authored *Twitter For Dummies,* contributed to the *Social Media ProBook,* wrote *The Grande Guide to Social Media Advertising,* and has written many other books, magazine articles, ebooks, and blog articles for companies like John Wiley & Sons, Inc., Eloqua, Jess3, Media Bullseye, Mashable, TechnoBuffalo, TechBlorge, MacBlorge, and Profy.

Leslie is the Founder and CEO of Magnitude Media, an emerging media and business consultancy. She works with businesses of all shapes and sizes as your emerging media specialist and business growth source. Whatever your size, from individual or SMB to international corporation, she can help you.

Leslie's worked with a variety of companies, including, but by no means limited to: Hewlett-Packard, Left Bank Films, Fight It Out, LIM College, Hatchling Studios, Indian Head Resort, Hayward & Company, Company C, boutique wineries, exciting restaurants, musicians of all sizes, regulated industry businesses, and much, much more.

Leslie is also a sought-after speaker, headlining at MIDEM in Cannes, France as well as leading talks and workshops at events such as Book Expo America.

A firm believer in translating online relationships and successes into the offline world, Leslie has also founded Social Media Breakfast New Hampshire, PodCamp NH, and the nationwide Strong Women in Tech initiative. She has served on several boards of directors, including Portsmouth Public Media. She lives a stone's throw from Boston in the beautiful seacoast city of Portsmouth, NH. When Leslie isn't writing or consulting, she enjoys playing piano, singing, listening to live music, and cooking or seeking out great whiskies, wines and fantastic food.

Dedication

To my social media friends and colleagues, thank you for your support in writing this book and for sharing your case studies — variety breeds authenticity.

To John, Dave and Max Barber a special thank you. You've made so much possible with your support over the years.

Author's Acknowledgments

I'd like to thank everyone who allowed me to use any case studies, screen shots, or anecdotes in the making of this book. I know so many smart and kind people, and I couldn't have made such a rich book without the addition of your perspectives.

Publisher's Acknowledgments

We're proud of this book; please send us your comments at http://dummies.custhelp.com. For other comments, please contact our Customer Care Department within the U.S. at 877-762-2974, outside the U.S. at 317-572-3993, or fax 317-572-4002.

Some of the people who helped bring this book to market include the following:

Acquisitions and Editorial

Project Editor: Kelly Ewing

Acquisitions Editor: Amy Fandrei

Technical Editor: Michelle Wolverton

Editorial Manager: Jodi Jensen

Editorial Assistant: Leslie Saxman

Sr. Editorial Assistant: Cherie Case

Cover Photo: © iStockphoto.com / Alex Slobodkin

Cartoons: Rich Tennant (www.the5thwave.com)

Composition Services

Project Coordinator: Katherine Crocker

Layout and Graphics: Jennifer Creasey, Joyce Haughey

Proofreader: The Well-Chosen Word

Indexer: Valerie Haynes Perry

Publishing and Editorial for Technology Dummies

    Richard Swadley, Vice President and Executive Group Publisher

    Andy Cummings, Vice President and Publisher

    Mary Bednarek, Executive Acquisitions Director

    Mary C. Corder, Editorial Director

Publishing for Consumer Dummies

    Kathleen Nebenhaus, Vice President and Executive Publisher

Composition Services

    Debbie Stailey, Director of Composition Services

Contents at a Glance

Table of Contents

Introduction

. . . .

*S*ocial media metrics is simply a fancy name for tracking whether or not the things you do on social media platforms are working for you and giving you a measurement against which to fine-tune your efforts to make sure that you aren't wasting your time.

If you've been on Twitter, Facebook, Google+, or any other social network, if you've written a blog or started a website, run an ad online, or done anything else related to being a "social business" online, you've probably wondered how to tell which efforts are working and which ones are just throwing your effort into the wind.

Engaging and conversing on social networks and social platforms can be frustrating. It can take up a lot of time to try to hear every person who talks to you on every site that's out there. Figuring out how to listen to the things that are relevant and respond to them in way that works and increases your bottom line is key to your success on the social web and on social mobile platforms.

About This Book

What would you say if I told you that by the end of this book, you'd feel like all your efforts online had a purpose? What if I said you'd not only see the purpose of your efforts, but be able to measure these efforts and adjust them to consistently maximize the value you're getting out of them?

Skeptical of what you can achieve online? Thinking that the online business arena doesn't give you enough room to market your product or service? I show you how to use the social aspects of the web to achieve not only more return on your efforts but a higher quality return and a more loyal customer base.

You can say and do so much in the social space, and all of it — every single thing — can be measured and analyzed. In fact, the things you do online can be measured and analyzed in far greater detail than many of your traditional marketing efforts ever could. What's the ROI of a television ad? It's hard to determine precisely. But you can track the ROI of a YouTube video, for example, from minute to minute down to the nth detail.

Conventions Used in This Book

In this book, I stick to the following conventions to help with readability:

- ✔ Whenever you have to enter text, it is shown in **bold** so that it's easy to see.

- ✔ `Monofont` text denotes an e-mail address, website URL, or social media handle.

- ✔ Twitter handles are always preceded with a @ sign, like `@dummies`, Google+ by a + sign, like `+leslie poston`, and so on.

- ✔ Social media pages and features — such as Settings or Replies — are called out with capital letters.

- ✔ Numbered lists guide you through tasks that must be completed in order from top to bottom.

- ✔ You can read bulleted lists in any order you like (from top to bottom, bottom to top, or in any way you'd like).

I've been on social media for quite a while, and I have a good sense of what's out there and how people are using it; but social media is a living, breathing, and constantly changing community dynamic. The services may change their feature set, its privacy features, or change direction overnight, which will change the way that people use it. As things change, keep in touch with me on social media (`@leslie`, `+leslie poston`, and so on) for the latest on my thoughts about metrics.

What You're Not to Read

This book is written for the beginner to intermediate social media metrics user. If you already have social media metrics accounts for you or your business on a variety of social sites and platforms, you can probably skip the chapters on how to sign up and get moving, though you may find it useful to review the sections for a refresher.

If you're a business and have already gotten rolling on some analytics, you can probably safely ignore many of the starting chapters and start checking out Parts III and V.

If you're a pro and could have probably written this book, feel free not to read anything and use this book to make art and recycle it when you're done.

Foolish Assumptions

In this book, I make the following assumptions:

- ✔ You are at least 13 years of age.
- ✔ You have access to a computer and the Internet (and know how to use it!).
- ✔ You have a working e-mail address you can access.
- ✔ You have a Google account so that you can play with some free Google toys.
- ✔ You have a smartphone (if you want to use a mobile metrics application).
- ✔ You can at least copy and paste basic HTML or JavaScript if called for.
- ✔ You can read.

How This Book Is Organized

Like other *For Dummies* books, each chapter is self-contained and can be read in any order you'd like. However, I've organized the book into seven parts that can, when read in order, give you a strong understanding of social media metrics.

Part I: Metrics? What the Heck is That?

Part I introduces you to the very basics of metrics and how to understand what they can tell you. In the chapters that follow, I show you how to pump up your efforts and squeeze the most metrics juice out of your time online. By the time Part I closes, you'll be able to navigate the metrics landscape easily.

Part II: Navigating the Measurement Jungle

After you're familiar with the basics of metrics and measurement, I show you how to start decoding all the various clues your metrics will give you about how well your time online in being spent. Whether you want to know the demographics of people reading your blog or the income levels you reach on Facebook or Twitter, your metrics can tell you. This book makes it easy to figure out who you're reaching online and how.

Part III: Putting Your Metrics on Steroids

After you can speak the language of metrics and know how and where you can get the most use out of the reports your metrics give you, you can dive into the deeper layers of measurement. Want to export metrics to a spreadsheet that will update in real time so that you can show stakeholders what's working? Want to know from minute to minute what time of day you move the most product and why, or how to amplify sharing? Metrics can, and will, tell you everything you need to know to get your business cranking.

Part IV: Keeping Your Finger on the Pulse of Living Breathing Metrics

In Part IV, the book talks about the big picture and what metrics can do for your growth online and offline. It also covers ways you can branch out past the online world and into the offline, traditional marketing, using your online metrics to discover how your traditional advertising dollars are working for you as well, and how you can expand their usefulness.

Part V: Taking the Deep Dive into Advanced Metrics

In this part, the book outlines the tips, tricks, and ninja secrets of metrics that the metrics gurus use to stay on top of everything they do online. If you want to know how the metrics rock stars can keep track of the infinite number of details metrics bring in and use them to eliminate wasted time and effort, this part is your guide to the secrets of the metrics masters.

Part VI: Predicting Future Metrics

As with everything else online, metrics and measurement tools, tips, tricks, and techniques are in a constant state of flux. I use this part of the book to help you figure out how to see the future, or at least the near future, so that

you can be prepared for the latest and greatest in metrics that may not have
even been invented yet. This part ends with a working knowledge of how to
tell which shiny objects are going to be important and how to leverage them
when the time is ripe.

Part VII: The Part of Tens

The final part is typical of every *For Dummies* book. In these chapters, I provide
you with highlights of my ten favorite metrics tools, ten favorite use cases, and
even some other applications and techniques that have the same or similar
functionality as the chosen favorites that you can check out.

Icons Used in This Book

Icons are fantastic at pointing out important things for you to look at, remember,
and absorb. In the following list, I go over the icons I use throughout the book
to guide you on your metrics journey.

The tip icon points out helpful information that's likely to improve your
experience.

The Remember icon marks interesting or useful facts that you'll need to
remember while you're learning metrics.

The Warning icon highlights potential danger. When I use this icon, I'm letting
you know that you should proceed with caution.

Where to Go from Here

If you haven't even thought about metrics, amble on over to Chapter 1 and start
reading, and I'll get you up to speed in no time. If you've been measuring your
efforts for a while and have a good command over where the bang for your buck
is but would like a better idea of how to amplify what your metrics are telling
you, head on over to Part III where I shift metrics into high gear. If Part III is
old hat for you, Part V goes over some interesting business, personal, and
not-for-profit stories that can help you grow as a metrics pro.

Occasionally, we have updates to our technology books. If this book does have technical updates, they will be posted at

```
dummies.com/go/socialmediametricsfdupdates
```

Lastly, social media itself is a living, breathing series of web applications or platforms that change from time to time. From the time I started writing this book to the time I completed it, there have been about a dozen changes in the interfaces of social media platforms, including complete layout overhauls. While everything may change around a bit, the basics of social media will likely always be the same. Once you get an idea for how the services work and how metrics integrates into them, it'll be pretty easy for you to find anything that may have moved since the publication of this book.

With that, I'll see you online.

Finally, the author Leslie Poston is not an employee, representative, or shareholder in any particular metrics service mentioned. The opinions here represent what has worked for her, her networks and clients, but not necessarily the social media world at large.

Part I
Metrics? What the Heck Is That?

The 5th Wave

By Rich Tennant

"He saw your laptop and wants to know if he can check his Facebook traffic."

In this part . . .

You may find getting started with metrics and measuring how social media is working for you a little intimidating. That's because so many solutions are available, and you can track what you are doing in so many different ways.

In this part, I cover the basics of what metrics are and what I mean by measurement of social media. I go over analytics and tracking and show you what each component of your overall metrics looks like. I help define metrics for you.

Chapter 1

Social Metrics Aren't Scary; They Just Measure Value

*U*sing social media metrics, you can measure results generated from social media and other online activities or see where results are missing. An understanding of these measurements lets you adjust your approach to social media as you go, as well as make improvements that can help you achieve your goals. These metrics may take time to set up, but a good foundation will save you time and money later on.

If you've ever run a radio spot, a television ad, or even an old-school Yellow Pages ad, then you know how difficult it is to gauge the success of those ads — that is, how much business you received from those efforts. Good social media metrics and online tracking can give you these answers. It can tell you to the penny where you need to be spending your time and money and give you constant feedback on your customers' wants and needs — pretty neat, right?

Figuring Out the Metrics and Measurement Thing

You may have heard of the term *social media metrics* but have no idea what they actually are. The term *metrics* can mean several things, but generally speaking, a metric is a measurement that allows you to quantify and evaluate something. Social media metrics, then, are simply measurements that help you understand if what you're doing in social media is working for you or for your customers — or not — in a very detailed and concrete way.

The easiest way to think of metrics is to think of them as a way to figure out *if* what you're doing online is working for you, *how* it is (or isn't) working for you, and as a road map that shows you how you can tweak and adjust what you're doing online to work *better*. Don't worry if the idea of using metrics seems intimidating. I'm not talking quantum physics here — just spreadsheets and reports and data crunching. If *I* can do it, so can *you*.

Because you're reading this book, you probably already know what social media is — you just want to find out how to measure the various aspects of social media and to improve the ways you use this technology. This means you've graduated from a beginner's level of social media engagement and now see the potential social media has for you. In fact, if you've already installed Google Analytics somewhere, even if you aren't really using it yet, or if you've investigated things like Klout scores, Twitter Grader measurements, or some other type of assessment value, however silly that value may be, it tells me you want to do more. That's good news!

Metrics measure what happens to the content and the conversations you create online on social networks, blogs, and websites. Each piece of content you generate, whether it is a simple comment, a long blog post, a new website, an app, or a status update, is designed to get some kind of response.

Response, however, is a hard concept to measure, so it helps to break it down into more concrete terms:

- ✔ **Attention:** Attention is a loose way of describing how people see, and how *long* people see, your content. You see this reflected in time spent on a web page, how many minutes a tweet continues to be retweeted or replied to, how long a status update stays in Facebook's Most Interesting section of the newsfeed, how long a comment thread is, how long the duration of shares lasts on Google Plus, and more.

- ✔ **Reach:** Reach sounds impressive, but it really just refers to how far your content travels and for how long. As a measurement, reach indicates a combination of quality content, high attention levels, and connectivity to appropriate influencers. A post with a decent reach value gets reshared dozens of times on various social networks and is commented on and discussed as well, especially over the course of hours, days, or months. New attention to your post's content through these shares indicates good reach as well.

- ✔ **Influencers:** I can describe influencers in many ways, but for the purpose of this book, influencers are people who share or interact with your content and by doing so inspire others to share and interact with it as well. Influencers can often affect actual sales and lead generation, so they can improve your bottom line if you find the right ones to target.

- ✔ **Interest:** Related to attention, interest helps make content both sticky and shareable. For example, 14 consecutive posts about your lunch may appeal to a small audience, but you would receive a failing grade on the interest measurement scale. Content about your lunch in Italy on your speaking tour, however, may have a much higher interest score. Being picky about the content you generate and creative in how and where you share it will increase interest overall.

- ✔ **Views:** As you explore the world of analytics, you'll notice several different types of metrics called *views*. A view can be the first time someone looks at something you shared, or it can be each time a person visits your page. You often see views described as "unique," "repeat," and more.

- ✔ **Actions:** Actions is my catchall term for the way people interact with your sites and content. Sharing links, subscribing to newsletters, requesting quotes, leaving comments, clicking links, leaving reviews, and downloading files are all actions.

- ✔ **Community:** Successful online businesses develop a community around their social media activity. Measuring community may be difficult, but it's not impossible. Increasing this metric can help you with your overall success. A solid community often encourages your customers to act as a champion of whatever you do — every business needs as many champions as they can get to succeed in a tight economy!

- ✔ **Listening:** Keeping your ear to ground is the most important metric of all. If you aren't listening to what people are saying about your brand, and where they are saying it, you can't modify your business plans accordingly to make sure that your online efforts convert into sales.

Don't bother obsessing over individual metrics like page views. Sure, having a site with hundreds of thousands of views looks great, but if your visitors aren't clicking links, engaging with the site, buying your products or services, or sharing any of your content, you won't get anywhere. Cast a wide metrics net instead and evaluate many different aspects of your return on investment to see what works for you.

Applying Metrics to Business Use

Metrics, measurements, spreadsheets, link tracking, campaigns, goals — it can all be a little overwhelming. In fact, it took me a long time to get over my fears — especially my fear of math — when I first started in consulting. When I figured out that some simple bits of code, a few spreadsheets, and a handful of other tools and tricks make everything easy, I never looked back. My goal is to make metrics feel that easy for you as you apply them to your business.

One of the first challenges a business has is to figure out where to apply metrics. The most likely answer, of course, is everywhere you can. That's quite a task, however, especially if you've never used metrics, so the following sections describe some key measurements.

Your website

Your business website is the most important location for your metrics. It's the one place online that you completely own.

Third-party sites like Facebook and others own the data you place there. Not only do you get only the metrics the third party site tells you are important and nothing more, they can take the photos, notes, and other content you put on their servers and use it to make money! Now why would any savvy business want that to happen?

If you've put all your eggs into the Facebook, Tumblr, or Google free-site basket, I highly recommend you put down this book long enough to get a hosting account and at least set up a self-hosted version of a WordPress blog. (WordPress uses an open-source content agreement and allows users to retain ownership of their own material.) Post everything related to your business on your own website first so that you own it and then link out elsewhere to share.

Your *domain name* is your Internet calling card for your business — the address where folks will go to find you. Think of it as the online version of your brick-and-mortar store or office. Pick a good name that is easy to remember! Once you have a domain, you need hosting (a place to put your web files). Web hosting is cheap these days! For $5 to $20 each month, you can get an account on Bluehost, Go Daddy, DreamHost, Rackspace, or any one of a dozen or so reputable web hosts. After you have hosting, a simple blog can get you started.

Your e-mail

E-mail is going to be a backbone of your online marketing and business. The great news is that nowadays you can apply metrics to your e-mail, too. Using an e-mail service provider, you can track who opens which e-mail, who reports you for spam instead of simply unsubscribing, what the reader clicks, how long they spend on each page, where they share your e-mail info, and so much more. E-mail has certainly come a long way since the days of "You've got mail."

Your images

You can apply metrics to any photos or image files you upload. In fact, Google rolled out an image search function this year that finds what you need by searching the picture (graphic) itself, not words.

Image search results have been a leading traffic generator for websites for the past several years. It pays to pay attention to the details when you're placing your content online and planning to track how it works for you.

Don't forget your titles, tags, captions, and other helpful file data. (And of course, make sure that you check the copyright details of images before use!)

Social networks

Many social networks, such as Facebook, Google+, YouTube, SlideShare, Twitter, and LinkedIn, offer varying levels of insights, metrics, and statistics for you to use right on their sites. This data allows you to get at least a rudimentary snapshot of how your content and engagement is doing for you online.

Some of these metrics are only superficial. However, you can go deeper with these data sets from simplistic and incomplete methods like Klout or HubSpot's Graders, to third-party services like ShortStack in tandem with Google Analytics, or something more robust that you put in place yourself.

Traditional collateral

Don't forget to track your traditional collateral. That's right — use online tools like hashtags and offline tools like good signage to direct traffic you receive offline and track the attention you can bring online from that offline traffic.

Tracking offline traffic and traditional marketing efforts, such as print ads, in-store sales, radio spots, and so on, requires a bit more effort than online metrics, but you can get at least a rudimentary picture of how your traditional marketing is doing by strategic cross promotion and general crossover of key elements and trackable phrases, QR codes, and links.

Getting a Closer Look at Analytics

"Measure Everything — you cannot improve what you cannot measure."

—Peter Stern, CEO of bit.ly and Founder of Datek

`http://eranyc.com/blog`

Social media sites are so unassuming that they make it easy for anyone to use them. This means that folks may find personal success on social media but not have the strong business background necessary to take that success further. I'm here to tell you that while studying metrics can't magically give you business savvy, anyone can learn how to read the data they collect and use it to improve what they are doing online.

Metrics and analytics are fairly interchangeable words both indicating measurement. People have many reasons for wanting to track analytics. Four common reasons include

✔ **Sales generation:** Any good business owner will want to use metrics to track sales and to generate additional sales from their activity online. Metrics are an integral part of the *sales funnel,* which is a way to visualize the sales process for your company that tracks the process from the wide top of the funnel (lead generation) to the narrow bottom (actual sales). In fact, good metrics will turn your sales funnel upside down, making your entire sales process more efficient and getting your business better returns overall.

✔ **Qualifying leads:** Leads, while part of your overall sales process, are an entity all to themselves. By creating separate metrics campaigns to track qualified leads, you'll find you are able to generate more qualified leads in a shorter time frame. What's more, you'll discover when and where you may be wasting effort, enabling you to shift your focus to better lead-generating sites and sources.

✔ **Focus groups:** Focus groups and crowdsourcing are important to your business. *Crowdsourcing* just means asking a group of people to answer a question and help you define an idea or reach a solution, based on the "wisdom of the crowd" philosophy. If you have solid metrics in place, you can get real-time feedback on the ideas, changes, and thought processes behind your brand and its products. Sure, expensive and controlled focus groups still have their place, but online metrics help broaden your reach when you don't need a more formal solution.

✔ **Competitive intelligence:** That's right — competitive intelligence. Metrics can help you spy on your competition. Pretty cool, right? If you're using keyword- and search-based metrics well, you can tell where your competition is headed and what they've been working on. Sometimes you can tell where they're going before they even know themselves. Now that's a stealth trick you want to have in your bag.

✔ **Customer service:** Metrics can also help you take good care of your existing customers. Metrics help you listen in real time to what people are saying about your brand and products, enabling you to respond in a timely fashion and do what you can to give them the best experience possible. If you're really sharp, you can pull some of that competitive intelligence magic in here as well. Listen to your competition's feedback and solve their customer's problems if you can, especially if they're slow due to not listening — that's certainly one way to get the attention of a potential customer.

✔ **Tracking influence:** Tracking influence can get tricky, as influence has to be defined to be useful. Influence may mean number of followers on a service or reshares of content in some campaigns. In other campaigns, someone with fewer followers may wield more influence if the network they've built results in more sales or actions on your campaigns. Before you build out metrics for influence, be sure you outline the definition of what kind of influence you need for your goal.

Every metrics campaign needs a baseline, a snapshot of where you are today, for comparison later. You may as well start putting this metrics stuff into practice right now. Put this book down and make a list of all the social media sites on which your brand has a presence. Not online? Write that down also. Then add detail: List how many fans, followers, page views, outposts, and so on you have today. Take a look at how you measure up. Do a quick search on Google and Facebook to see whether fans or customers have created pages for you, too. Then, when you finish this book and are a metrics whiz, you can see how far you've come.

Discovering the Kinds of Social Metrics Services Out There

So many types of metrics services are out there that it would be impossible to list them all in this chapter. However, here's a quick run-through of the basic types to get you started:

✔ **Single-metrics services providers:** This third-party metric service measures only one thing. One example is Twitter Grader, made by HubSpot, a service that loosely measures exactly what it sounds like — your Twitter account's reach and activity (see Figure 1-1). Another is Klout, a service that measures volume across several networks (Twitter, Google+, Facebook, and more) and then rewards high scorers with small perks sponsored by brands (see Figure 1-2).

Figure 1-1:
Twitter Grader helps you measure your Twitter account's reach and activity.

Figure 1-2:
Klout
evaluates
your volume
across
networks to
arrive at a
score
for your
social-media
performance.

Figure 1-2:
Klout evaluates your volume across networks to arrive at a score for your social-media performance.

More detailed single-metric services like Smarterer measure your individual actual knowledge of a service, such as Twitter, LinkedIn, or even Microsoft Word, in the form of a weighted test and then gives you a badge that you can display that will update as you retake tests and improve your knowledge (see Figure 1-3). That's a concrete measurement of what you know about something delivered in a trackable badge and valuable for companies who want to display that their employees know their stuff and indicate that customers can trust them.

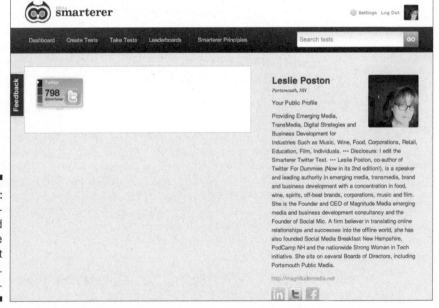

Figure 1-3:
A Twitter-related knowledge badge at Smarterer.com.

TIP

✔ **One-site metrics:** Some sites, such as Facebook or SlideShare, offer their own insights and analytics services that track your metrics and traction on their site. These metrics can be pretty detailed, but because they look at only one site, they can hardly be considered comprehensive.

I cover how to make one-site data part of your overall metrics tracking in Part III.

✔ **Advanced metrics:** With services like Google Analytics, you can track your metrics down the most microscopic result. Not only can you track them online, you can do advanced tricks, such as exporting your metrics to spreadsheets or massaging your data to wring the most information out of it that you can. These advanced techniques are where metrics become truly powerful.

Determining Which Measurements Matter and Which Ones Are Junk

It's human nature to want things to be easy and to take little time. Busy people have important things to do! Be careful, however. Some of the junk metrics available online rely on folks who are looking for a quick fix.

Luckily, you aren't one of those people, or you wouldn't be reading this book right now. The following sections help you separate the measurement pitfalls from the measurement gold mines.

Beware of single-metrics services providers

That is, beware of services like Klout and Grader. Setting aside the scary privacy issues some of these services have (I'm looking at you, Klout — see the upcoming "Safeguard your privacy!" section) any metric that measures only volume or quantity can tell you only one part of the whole story. These metrics work best when considered alongside other metric indicators, such as reach, conversion, sentiment, click-throughs, views, location data, device data, demographics, and more.

Know which measurements are important

Measurements that matter are the ones that tell you clearly what people are doing to interact, engage, and use your stuff online. Are you getting forms filled out, tweets and retweets, comments, newsletter subscriptions, sales,

sales leads, and more? Or are you being ignored in the sea of online brands? Even if you're getting results, you should also be tracking what kind of online person, site, or brand is getting you the most sticky results. Retweets are nice, but not all retweets lead to action. Pay attention to more than how noisy or popular someone is.

Note: *Sticky* refers to content that resonates with the viewer and remains "stuck" in their mind. *Noisy* refers to that online user who just can't seem to tone down the number of updates that they make and who doesn't filter out mundane updates — so they have volume without quality.

Safeguard your privacy!

Many automated metrics services are worth trying, but some are dangerous phishing scams. Be careful if you're asked to give a password to use a service — double-check the service's reputation online before handing your password over.

OAuth services (services that ask you to log in to your account on another service, such as Twitter, and then click a button to connect — meaning you don't have to share that password to link the services) are somewhat better in that they don't require your password, but many want too much information about you, and they often demand access to your accounts beyond what they need. Klout is one example: Using it gives the service access to your private messages on sites like Twitter, and to the people in your extended network — even if those people aren't Klout users!

Look beyond follower count

When you're seeking influencers to help spread your message, look beyond follower count. Someone with 50 loyal followers that are fully engaged and invested in their network will often get more results for you than someone with 5,000 people in their network that ignore them and don't engage with their online interactions. Use good metrics to filter out the best influencers and campaign targets for you.

Chapter 2

Sorting It All Out

. . . .

In This Chapter

▶ Aggregating data: The incoming data fire hose, keeping it from eating you alive

▶ Finding the right service

▶ Using metrics with search engines

▶ Dealing with daily metrics

▶ Adjusting on the go: Shift on the fly listening

. . . .

*Y*ou're probably thinking to yourself "How the heck am I going to keep all of these incoming data sets and metrics organized?" Fortunately, tools and techniques can help you sort it all out and keep you from feeling overwhelmed.

For one thing, making metrics a part of your daily routine is one of the most important things you can do to stay on top of the wave of information that will be coming your way. After you've gotten some experience with the different metrics, you discover which ones are important for you to track closely and which you can put on the back burner. Until then, think of checking your incoming metrics data the same way you do e-mail: a task you do two or three times a day, but not something you pay attention to all day long.

Focus and goals play an important role in how you filter your metrics results as well. Every metric tells a different story, and you'll want to give each story different importance at different times depending on what you hope to achieve. "General knowledge about a keyword or brand" is going to be a very different data set than "influence in topics like cottage cheese and raisins."

Whether your goal is to march web visitors down your sales funnel with precision, find new employee prospects that exhibit a great knowledge of your field, handle customer issues with aplomb, or increase your brand's reach, metrics can help. However, each of these goals requires its own set of metrics, its own method of tracking those metrics, and its own adjustment schedule. This chapter shows you how it all works.

Keeping Incoming Data from Eating You Alive

In online marketing circles these days, people toss the term *fire hose* around like candy, but what does it mean? *Fire hose* simply refers to a large amount of unsorted incoming information, often the real-time data generated by individual social media services, such as the "Twitter fire hose" or concepts like the "Real Time Search fire hose."

When you really start to pay attention to metrics and measurement, you discover the incredible variety of information available to you: customer reviews, coworker opinions, statistics, infographics, brand metrics, clicks, hits and views, retweets, shares, updates, purchase data, conversion rates, lifetime click-through rates, costs per click, referral data, favorites, bookmarks, and on and on until your brain wants to scream "STOP!"

The first advice I have for you is borrowed from author Douglas Adams: "Don't panic!" The next piece of advice is to start small. There is nothing wrong with getting your feet wet slowly. Pick one thing to look at first, then another, and eventually, when you're comfortable, you can think about jumping off the high dive.

Practice looking at small metrics first. Think about the last time you popped your own name into Google's search box. (I know you've probably done it at least once!) Searching on your name or brand, called a *vanity search,* is more than just a fun pastime — it's a type of simple metric.

Think about the search results that came up. If you've been doing what you do long enough and well enough, your search results could equal bragging rights if you're in a field where dominating search results indicates topic qualifications. For example, at the time of writing, searching on my name, "Leslie Poston," yielded accurate search results on the first 7 pages of Google, with the first incorrect result occurring on page 8, and no other errors occurring until page 11. This means I could conceivably tell someone to "Google me" with confidence.

That's a pretty solid and simple metric showing how long I've been doing what I do and how prolifically I'm currently indexed by search engines on a wide variety of sites. Why do I say "currently"? Because search engine algorithms change all the time, so queen for today could be court jester tomorrow if I don't use more complex metrics tracking to keep my sites rising to the top of the search heap.

Using search operators

When searching on sites like Google, Yahoo!, or Bing, *search operators* can help you make your search more relevant. For example, putting a phrase in quotes tells the search engine to keep those words together, meaning you get more accurate results. Adding a hyphen (-) before a word, like -green, removes that word from search, narrowing it further.

You can choose from many types of search operators, all of which will improve your search results. For more ideas, try typing the term "search operator" into your favorite search engine. You can also find an explanation of *Boolean search operators* — that is, logic-based operators such as AND and OR — at www.internettutorials.net/boolean.asp.

Finding the Right Metrics Service

What do I mean by service? A *metrics service* is any program, site, or software that helps you keep track of your metrics. You probably have heard of several: Google Analytics, Facebook Insights, Google+ Ripples, Klout, Twitter Grader, Radian6, MediaVantage (formerly DNA 13), CustomScoop, HootSuite Analytics, and hundreds of other sites and services that would take a chapter of their own to list (and still more would have cropped up by publication time — measurement is a hot topic in social media right now).

In the following sections, I take a look at a few of these metrics by type of measurement or service measured. This list is by no means complete! I'm just taking a snapshot of some of the options available to you right now. These simple tools can get you started with basic metrics.

You may see a trend in *freemium* as a service model — where a service offers a free trial or a limited free version of its software with a paid version offering more functionality available. You're not imagining things! It's become quite popular over the last two years, though its success for companies seems to vary.

Twitter

Hundreds of services claim to measure Twitter metrics and influence. In fact, Twitter itself offers metrics if you're a brand that pays to advertise on Twitter via their Promoted Tweets, Promoted Topic, and such. However, most smaller brands have trouble swallowing the official Twitter promotion price tag. Until Twitter's new á la carte affordable ads, which are similar to AdWords, become the norm, you can try a few of these services:

✔ **Twitter Grader** (`http://tweet.grader.com`), made by Boston company HubSpot, is a simple metric to measure your amplification and traction on Twitter (see Figure 2-1). It doesn't dig very deep, but it will give you a quick snapshot of how you're doing in your main topic or locality versus others who are similar to you.

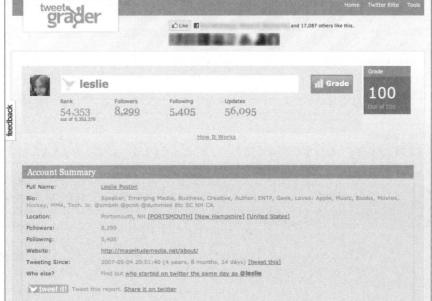

Figure 2-1: The Twitter Grader website.

✔ **Twitter Score** (`http://twitterscore.info`) is also a single metric score system without much depth. Because Twitter Score is another snapshot service for a quick picture, you'll need to use other metrics to get a complete idea of the influence or knowledge of the company or person you're looking at.

✔ **Twitalyzer** (`www.twitalyzer.com`) pulls some great metrics from Twitter and from other measurement services and then arranges them into a visually pleasing and easy-to-understand grid (see Figure 2-2). This setup is a great way get a look at how you're doing on Twitter and compare your potential reach to your actual reach.

✔ **TweetLevel** (`http://tweetlevel.edelman.com`) by Edelman is not a service that I found especially accurate as far as influencers and topics. In fact, it made some of the same errors as Klout (only measuring volume and not going deep enough under the surface), which makes me give it a "use with a grain of salt" rating. I would use these three metrics services in tandem with each other to get a more complete picture of what you're seeking more info about.

Figure 2-2:
The
Twitalyzer
website.

- ✔ **TweetReach** (http://tweetreach.com) checks only one thing — how far your tweet has travelled — but it's one *very useful* thing. Twitter. com is constantly changing how the service handles things like retweeting and how users see favorites, retweets, and follows, so anything that can give you a better, more consistent picture of how far your tweets go after they are launched is a good tool.

- ✔ **Crowdbooster** (http://crowdbooster.com) doesn't only focus on Twitter; it also pulls in Facebook. However, Crowdbooster is best at analyzing Twitter and telling you the best time of day to tweet and the effectiveness of your last several tweets. It offers a freemium model: free to try for limited accounts and then pay to play for more. In my opinion, the free version is more than enough because the paid version no longer offers detailed reporting.

- ✔ **TweetMeme** (http://tweetmeme.com) focuses more on how topics are perceived by others on Twitter. TweetMeme is useful for keyword and trending topic measurement and can help you fine-tune what you're talking about on Twitter and how you're talking about it to be most effective.

Facebook

Facebook actually has a decent set of on-site metrics for folks who use its Pages. Facebook's metrics don't look to anything shared outside of the site, but they can give you a surprising overview of the demographics of and interest in your brand online. Drawbacks include a lack of tab-specific tracking and no ad-tracking integration. Facebook keeps Page Insights and Ad Insights in different places. If you want to track your tabs or shares outside of your Page, you're going to have to get creative or try Crowdbooster (see preceding section) or other Facebook-related tools, like these:

- ✔ **Booshaka** (`http://booshaka.com`) is another tool offering the free-mium model. Booshaka tells you who the top contributors are to your Facebook Page. This information is useful — if the top contributors are your team and immediate friends, you have some work to do to get the word out about your page!

- ✔ **ShortStack** (`http://shortstackapp.com`) is an app that makes Facebook tabs for you and also measures how they're working. It has a free and a paid version, and even the free version allows you to not only see detailed metrics as they measure them, but to add in Google Analytics, MailChimp Analytics, and more inside each tab for extremely detailed tab monitoring.

- ✔ **Tribemonitor** (`www.tribemonitor.com`) is relatively new and not isolated to Facebook. It's in Dutch, but the charts and graphs are clear and easy to read. If you use Google Chrome as your browser, you can automatically translate any site not in your native language (a nifty trick). Tribemonitor gives you a way to track your Facebook fan base and follow it across other networks as well.

YouTube

YouTube is now owned by Google. This means it has some powerful metrics tools under the hood and that you can integrate with Google Analytics (see Figure 2-3). (If you feel like I mention Google Analytics a lot, it's because I do. Google Analytics can be a powerful, affordable, and versatile weapon in your metrics arsenal.)

To find the YouTube Insight analytics program for your videos, look at `www.youtube.com/t/advertising_insight`.

Not too many third-party tools, though, measure YouTube effectively at an affordable price. However, TubeMogul (`http://tubemogul.com`), the video uploading service, does offer analytics. It starts with limited stats for free, and then you can access more advanced stats with a paid subscription.

SlideShare

SlideShare is the popular slide-sharing service where people and brands can post their slide decks for viewing online. The company has since added video and documents to its file formats, so you can post your actual speaking videos and sales documents as well. SlideShare becomes more useful by the day.

Although you can post your slides, documents, and videos for free, if you want analytics from SlideShare directly — yep, you guessed it! — you'll have to buy a paid plan. Luckily, analytics start at about $20 if you're a business with a robust channel that needs to know how you're doing on the network, and this paid plan also allows you to overlay a lead capture form on each document (not something that has anything to do with metrics, but a cool feature nonetheless).

No great third-party tool focuses on SlideShare well enough currently to mention here, though I'm sure one will eventually come along, as metrics remains a hot topic. Meanwhile, you can use Google Analytics to track things like SlideShare stats.

LinkedIn

LinkedIn is the social network known for its business focus. Whether you're an individual looking to network or a company that has a page and/or group, LinkedIn can be a valuable social tool. If you have a page for your company, a group, or a personal pro account, LinkedIn also has some pretty detailed metrics for each function (see Figure 2-4). LinkedIn is also rolling out metrics on events in the coming months, and I'm sure they'll be offering insights site-wide before too long.

Figure 2-3:
YouTube
Analytics.

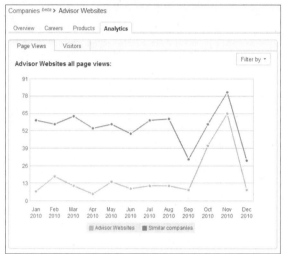

Figure 2-4: LinkedIn Analytics.

If you don't have a pro account, you can still see limited personal metrics using the Who's Viewed My Profile metric. However, you have to have portions of your profile set as "viewable" to do so. You also don't need a pro account to see your business page insights or the basic group statistics.

As with SlideShare, there are not really any wonderful tools for measuring LinkedIn. A few services, such as HootSuite, link to it and track some basic things, but few free or freemium services go in depth. However, thanks to the magic of Google search optimizers and shortcuts, you can get some data from Google searches, Google Alerts, and Google Analytics that will be helpful to you.

Google+

That's right: Big Daddy Google has its own social network now, tied in to many of its other services (As if you needed one more place to keep track of your brand, right?). The happy news here is that amazing statistics come built right in. One of my favorites is their Ripples metric, which tells you per post how the *shares* (people who found your content valuable enough to reshare to their network) and *plus-ones* (similar to a Facebook like, but with more depth) grew (see Figure 2-5). When you get someone like Chris Penn or Chris Brogan with hundreds of interactions, the Ripples graph gets very interesting very quickly. I especially like how you can animate the way a post grew in reach. What a great (and addictive) visual tool.

Third-party tools for Google+ include the following:

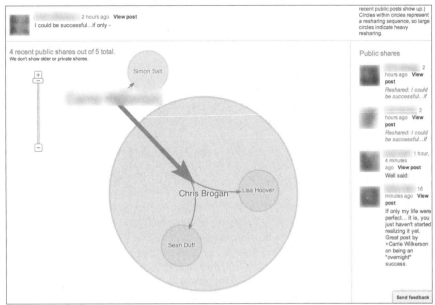

Figure 2-5:
Google+
Ripples.

- ✔ **FindPeopleOnPlus** (`http://findpeopleonplus.com`): Google+ has a lot of great features and great analytics built right in, but falls oddly short on searching for new users. Because search is Google's bread and butter, I'm betting it fixes that problem soon. Until that time, FindPeopleOnPlus shows you users by keyword and category in a clean list, along with assigning a number to the influence on Google+ that seems to be based on the karma of being plussed and shared often more than on your number of followers. That's a number I can support.

- ✔ **SocialStatistics** (`http://socialstatistics.com`): SocialStatistics, on the other hand, is strictly a popularity contest. If follower counts matter to you (they shouldn't, by the way), then you'll like this simple stat service for a quick look at someone's rank on the service by follower count.

Multiple service simple metrics

Some third-party services claim to measure multiple social sites and services, with varying degrees of success. Here's s a brief list of that type of metrics service:

- ✔ **PeerIndex** (`www.peerindex.com`): PeerIndex is attempting to be a competitor to Klout, and succeeding. While still too basic to be truly useful, PeerIndex does a much better job than Klout of making rankings and statistics it pulls contextual, so you know what is feeding your number. PeerIndex also has somewhat less invasive privacy practices than Klout, though, like Klout, it also does a little too much digging into the networks of people connected to you who aren't signed up for the service yet. PeerIndex works with several other sales tools, such as Rapportive, which can come in handy when you need a quick peek at someone's activity online before making that sales call.

✔ **Crowdbooster:** I cover Crowdbooster in the section "Twitter," earlier in this chapter, but it's a nifty tool to grab the metric of when your tweets, Facebook updates, and Page updates have the most traction in a day.

If seeing brand new services, such as Google+, makes you nervous (after all, maybe you just got on Twitter and Facebook — how can you be expected to be everywhere yet?), take a deep breath. Think of this book as a roadmap to your future to use at your own pace. Perhaps give the new shiny toys enough notice to log in and claim your brand name so that no one else can and put up some basic content. Then you can go back to learning at your own pace until you're ready. You don't need to stress out or overextend yourself.

Remember, I touched on only a handful of tools here to get you started thinking of social media as something you can measure (and measure in new and intriguing ways). None of the metrics tools I list are intended to be used as stand-alone solutions, by any means. In fact, no one tool really rules when it comes to metrics. You need to have at least two, and maybe more, in place to get the complete picture that measures all the different ways you can see impact and reach online.

Working with What You Find

After you start playing around with different basic metrics and third-party tools, you're probably starting to notice data coming in — data that you now have to sort and understand. In fact, piles and piles of data are out there to sort and sift through. How do you know where to start digging in?

The simplest way to begin is to create a spreadsheet to track each goal you have. That way, you can track your successes and make use of data-sorting, web-saving, and annotating tools like Evernote (http://evernote.com) and other tools like it to start sorting your incoming feeds. Use your browser bookmarks and folders to keep online tools straight.

If I have to have you choose between a document, which most folks are familiar and comfortable with, and a spreadsheet for tracking your goals, I'd tell you to go with a spreadsheet. Some people already use them extensively, and that's great! For those of you who don't use them yet because they seem too "math-y" or because you think you might not "do it right," it's high time you got comfortable with them. Using your goals is a good start.

To get started tracking your goals in spreadsheets, follow these steps:

1. **Title the spreadsheet with your goal or objective for your social interaction for the coming week.**

2. **Make a column for each of the sites you want to engage (Twitter, Facebook, and so on).**

3. **Go to the various services described earlier in this chapter and start keying in your goal as the metric to track.**

   For these steps here, assume that brand awareness is your goal. *Brand awareness* is your brand's online presence, and its general level of client, peer, and fan engagement are the metrics you track.

4. **Do your vanity search and plug the response you get into your spreadsheet.**

   Make sure that you keep track of the dates you do this search. (If you're unfamiliar with a vanity search, see Chapter 1.) If you haven't ever tracked the results of any of these services, you're creating your baseline. Dating the results, or creating a new spreadsheet tab for each week, helps you compare the metrics in a simple way across time. If you're handy with Excel or Google Spreadsheet formulas, you can pull your data into graphs and pivot tables as you go, creating dynamic results tracking.

5. **Choose another platform, such as Twitter, and do some metrics hunting for your brand and handle using the search feature and other tools specific to those sites or platforms.**

   For example, if you're tracking Twitter, use the Twitter-related tools listed in the earlier section on Twitter.

6. **Track the results in your spreadsheet for each platform.**

   How engaged are the people in your network? Are they ignoring you or talking to you and sharing or interacting with you online?

   For purposes of your baseline, for each service, track the number of your followers, subscribers, friends, circlers, or fans, along with the number of people you follow, fan, subscribe to, or circle. Record these values in your spreadsheet.

   Although this metric is the least important overall in terms of depth of information, it does provide a quick way to gauge brand growth over time.

   Congratulations! You've just made your first basic metrics tracking spreadsheet.

As you get better at tracking metrics, you'll find that you'll leave behind a lot of these simple metrics services in favor of automating your spreadsheets using more advanced tools. Starting here, however, gives you the practice you need to successfully fine-tune your results and understand what you're seeing.

By the time you finish this book, you won't much need those simple metrics services that track only one thing. (You need to drop by only once in a while, to take the measure of how your brand or goals are perceived by folks who haven't gotten more advanced or who don't know you can get more advanced.)

If you're a whiz at databases and think spreadsheets are old hat, you can use the spreadsheet techniques described here to build brand metrics databases on your own.

Using Metrics and Search

One area (of many) where metrics will prove to be invaluable to you is in search. Whether you need to improve what you're searching for to get better results or improve how you appear when folks search for you, your brand, or your brand's topics — metrics data can help you.

To get a better idea of what I mean, take a look at one of Google's most useful tools, the Google Insights tool.

First, look at Google Insights for Search (www.google.com/insights/search), which allows you to compare search patterns, brands, and keywords across regions, time periods, categories, and properties (see Figure 2-6). By using your metrics data and this tool, you can get a good idea of the traction your brand has (or your competitor's brand has — don't forget this metrics stuff is a useful tool to evaluate your competitors as well).

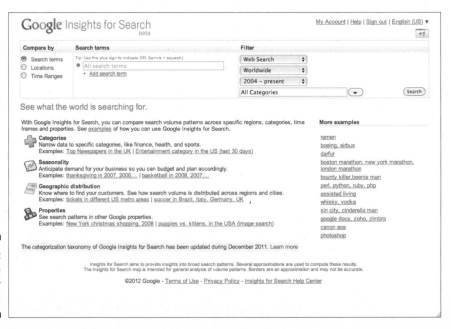

Figure 2-6:
Google
Insights for
Search.

Next, take a gander at Google's real time Insight tool, Think With Google. It does exactly what it sounds like — gives you a snapshot of metrics for search in real time. To see what the Think With Google wheel looks like, just head to `www.thinkwithgoogle.com/insights/tools/real-time-insights` and choose your poison.

One of the most useful real time metrics on the Google wheel is the What Are People Looking For segment, which takes you over to the AdWords Keyword Tool (or you can get there directly if you click this somewhat long link: `https://adwords.google.com/o/Targeting/Explorer?__u=1000000000&__c=1000000000&ideaRequestType=KEYWORD_IDEAS#search.none`). Just a few of the things you can use the AdWords Keywords Tool to accomplish are

- ✔ Hone your SEO (search engine optimization)
- ✔ Write better blog post titles that get better search results
- ✔ Write more relevant content on social networks
- ✔ See where your brand keywords fall on the spectrum of popularity
- ✔ Adjust your focus when you have a marketing campaign

If you're starting to see how metrics and search can help you be better at business overall, you're on your way to becoming a metrics whiz kid!

As you can probably tell, while it's never good to put all your eggs in one basket, Google stuff is going to be a basket that holds a lot of your eggs. To get the most out of all of the many Google toys and tools, you'll want a Gmail account. It's totally free, so go grab one now if you don't already have one!

Tracking Daily Metrics

> *"Data analysis is not easy. It takes years to get good at it, and once you get good at it, you realize how much more there is to learn. That is part of the joy. You are always learning. You are always growing."*
>
> —Avinash Kaushik,
> Digital Marketing Evangelist, Google

These words are words to live by. This book sets you on your way, but then it's up to you to keep learning and modifying what works and what doesn't. In the case of metrics, the art is in the tweaking and testing.

Metrics that are *not* important to look at daily include

- The number of people who connect with you or your brand on various social media services
- How many people visited your blog in the last few hours
- How many people unfollowed you on Twitter
- The page rank of your site

You can probably tell where I'm going with this one. While it's good to *know* the stats by day, week, month, and year for all those metrics so that you can do comparisons and grow, it's not healthy for you or for your bottom line to actually look at those stats every single day.

Don't fall into the trap of paying more attention to number crunching than to generating good content, good engagement, good products, and good services. Track your metrics daily and weekly, but only study them weekly or monthly. You can adjust what you're doing over time for greater effect as metrics tell you more about your own story, but you shouldn't get lost in the data or have it become a time sink that keeps you from doing your job well.

A better way to approach your tracking is to look at daily patterns over time. Tracking daily patterns helps you know whether you get the most bang for your buck on Mondays and Thursdays, for example, and helps you focus your overall efforts. It gives you snapshots of when your customers and fans are looking for what you offer online.

By not looking at your metrics in real time every day, you also avoid the common pitfall of metrics as distraction. Just like everything else in the shiny world of social media, metrics can be distracting. Watching those charts, graphs, and spreadsheets change right before your eyes is a little bit addictive, so do yourself a favor and put yourself on a metrics diet by scheduling your check-ins just like you would schedule time to check your e-mail or return phone calls.

Metrics become more important to see daily when they affect an ongoing, time-sensitive goal. At times, checking metrics every day becomes important. During those periods, where you're proving and adjusting a time-sensitive goal, you'll still want to set up a schedule.

Having a schedule makes it easier to read your metrics in the most accurate way for your goal without getting distracted. One interesting thing to remember is to pay attention to the metrics history during these campaigns as well. *You can't know where you're going, if you don't look at where you've been.* How can you measure growth without your baseline, after all?

When making your spreadsheets and including daily metrics, remember that at some point you'll want to visualize your data or help someone else visualize your data. Most often you can use charts or graphs to represent your findings. When making your spreadsheets, always keep in the back of your mind that you'll have to translate the data into something with an *x*- and *y*-axis (as one example) and that both axes must be defined to have clear representation.

Adjusting on the Go: Shift on the Fly Listening

Many things are, to quote Stephen Colbert, "truthy" about metrics. One of these things is the frequency at which incoming data can shift and dramatically change — *shift on the fly* or as you go, if you will. Another is the way tracking metrics can create a sea change in your overall strategy, causing a need for you to be able to shift on the fly as well.

When you're operating in shifting conditions, your strategy needs to use your metrics to accommodate those shifts. And if your strategy is strong and you have practiced metrics enough to trust your gut when you need to, it will include a plan of action for changing the metrics when they aren't working well or telling you what you need to know.

Metrics may not always tell you what you want to hear. When a metric gives you an answer you don't like, it doesn't mean that metric isn't working. It's your data trying to help you do something better. Remember to look at your data with an open mind and a willingness to change.

One way to adjust to shifting conditions is to calibrate your metrics. Know that date ranges and goals are important in looking at data. Depending on what answer you seek or the goal you want to achieve, it's important to select the right the date range or other criteria.

If you need to measure performance over a long period of time, look at data by month and week, not by days stretched out over a period of months. Narrowing your focus gives you better answers to the questions "What is this data telling me?" and "What can I do to improve my results using it?" And knowing the answers to those questions increases the success of your goals and campaigns every time.

Chapter 3

A Tour of a Few Free or Freemium Analytics Solutions

- -

In This Chapter

▶ Exploring Google Analytics

▶ Working with Clicky

▶ Tracking both online and offline sources with CustomScoop

▶ Surveying other free or freemium tools

- -

*I*n Chapter 2, I show you some basic, single-function free or freemium solutions for each platform. In this chapter, I take a look at some of the free or freemium solutions that can track metrics across a variety of platforms, sites, and social media services. Free services are those that are always free and have no other paid layers to upgrade to. Freemium services are those that have a free trial or a free version of their service or tool with a paid layer available with added features that you can upgrade to.

Each of these free or freemium solutions offers varying degrees of user control and data customization. As your knowledge increases, you can expand each one, though some are more flexible than others. In this chapter, I discuss a small variety of solutions that address a wide array of challenges. Some touch on similar points, but all have slightly different main focus points.

This chapter describes the tip of the iceberg for free or freemium services. With so many to choose from it can seem overwhelming. Just remember that you want your metrics to cover a wide range of goals, sources, and keywords.

Avoid things like Klout or Buffer as solo solutions. If you want to use these types of single metric or limited source solutions, make sure you have other, more comprehensive metrics in place or you run the risk of missing key information.

If you've been using a single metric solution up until this point and feeling like you are treading water on your ROI (return on investment), you'll be excited to finally see a complete set of metrics. If metrics are new to you, by avoiding putting all of your eggs in one basket you are going to get a better, more rounded picture of your successes and for where and what you need to improve.

The Big Daddy: Google Analytics 101

Google Analytics (see Figure 3-1) is incredibly versatile, so much so that I could easily fill an entire book on its features and uses. However, because I don't have room for that, I'll stuff a single section full of key points to get you started quickly.

The first thing you need to know to use Google Analytics is that you need to have a Google account to do so. In fact, having a Google account isn't a bad idea, anyway — it allows you access to a variety of free Google tools that will enhance your online experience. But for now, we're focused on one: Google Analytics. The easiest way to get a Google account is to either set up a Gmail account (free) or a Google+ account (free).

Figure 3-1:
Google
Analytics.

Google Analytics offers a lot of hidden features — features that can really improve your metrics-reading skill set. I can't cover them all here, but did you know Google offers classes, too? Sign up to qualify for the Google Engage for Agencies program or one of their other free course series to get certified as a pro Googler! It helps you make your business better, and it looks great on your resume. Look for it in the help section of your Google Analytics account or AdWords account.

Installing Google Analytics

If you don't already have Google Analytics working for you on your blog or site, you can quickly and easily install it. Installation takes only a minute and is completely painless.

The process is slightly different depending on whether you're installing on your blog or your website. The next two sections provide the details.

First, grab your Google Analytics ID and write it somewhere. It's easy to find. Just log into Google Analytics and from your dashboard and click the gears icon. You should see your ID next to your URL on the page that comes up. It's the number that starts with UA-.

Installing Google Analytics onto your blog

WordPress is by far the most popular blog solution right now, and the most accessible (and free), so I focus on that. If you have a WordPress installation on your own hosted blog or site, a quick and simple plug-in does all the installation dirty work for you. To use it, simply do the following:

1. **Log in to your WordPress blog.**

2. **In the left column of your dashboard, click Add Next next to the word Plugins heading.**

3. **In the Search For Plugins area of the new window that opens, type** Google Analytics for WordPress.

4. **In the search results, look for the plug-in authored by Joost de Valk.**

5. **Click the words Install Now below the plug-in title (Google Analytics for WordPress).**

6. **Confirm that you want to install the plug-in.**

7. **After the Installation indicator lets you know that you're finished, click the words Activate Plugin.**

8. **Follow the instructions for setting up the plug-in.**

   You must enter your website Analytics ID (the number on the Google Analytics Dashboard that starts with a **UA-** next to your site URL).

   You're all set and ready to start crunching data from your WordPress blog!

If you're already familiar with using an FTP program to upload files directly to the WordPress Plugins folder on your server for installation, you can skip these steps and go right to the source to download the plug-in file: `www.google.com/analytics/apps/about?app_id=456001`. From there, you simply upload the files into the `Wp-Content/Plugins` folder on your FTP server. After that, the files will automatically appear in your WordPress dashboard under the Plugins menu on the left. Simply navigate to the plug-in and select the blue Activate This Plugin link.

Installing Google Analytics onto your (non-WordPress) website

If you don't have a blog like WordPress, Joomla, or Drupal, but want Google Analytics on your website, you can make that happen with a simple cut and paste. Just follow these steps:

1. **Open the HTML source code file for your website footer.**

2. **Separately, head over to your Google Analytics dashboard.**

   This is the same Google Analytics account you set up in Chapters 1 and 2, if you've worked through those chapters.

   In the same window where you find your Google Analytics ID, you also find some JavaScript code.

3. **Copy the JavaScript code in its entirety.**

   It looks like this:

```
<script type="text/javascript">
var _gaq = _gaq || [];
_gaq.push(['_setAccount', 'UA-xxxxxx-xx']);
_gaq.push(['_trackPageview']);
(function() {
var ga = document.createElement('script'); ga.type =
      'text/javascript'; ga.async = true;
ga.src = ('https:' == document.location.protocol ?
      'https://ssl' : 'http://www') + '.google-
      analytics.com/ga.js';
var s = document.getElementsByTagName('script')[0];
      s.parentNode.insertBefore(ga, s);
})();
</script>
```

Did you navigate away from the window that showed the code you need to copy over at Google Analytics? Don't worry! You can get back to it. Log in to your Google Analytics dashboard. In the list of websites, find the one that you're installing Analytics on and click the word Edit in blue to the right of that row. In the window that opens, click the words Check Status in the upper right. That brings the Paste This Code window back up for you.

4. **In your text editor, paste the code you copied in Step 3 into your HTML, just before the `</body>` tag.**

5. **Save and upload the new HTML file.**

   After you save and upload the file and check for tracking, Google Analytics begins gathering data for you to put to work.

After you install Google Analytics your analytics data will appear in your dashboard in about 48 hours. After you see data, the fun begins! You can check immediately to see whether the code is working, however, by logging back into your Analytics account and looking for the OK symbol to appear in the tracking area — upper right. If it isn't working, you see an exclamation point inside a yellow triangle and should try again.

Using Google's Analytics Overview

Your Overview in Google Analytics will become your home away from home for metrics on your website, Facebook, and many other tools and sites that offer ways to work with this versatile Google tool (see Figure 3-2). Your Overview is your gateway to all the data from the websites in which you've installed Google Analytics.

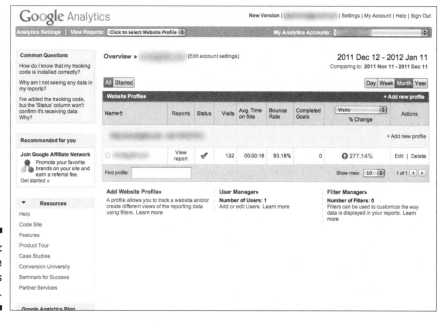

Figure 3-2: The Google Analytics Overview.

The sections of the Google Analytics Overview are as follows:

✔ **Dashboard/Website Profiles:** This is where you will find a list of all websites you've opened Analytics accounts for.

I recommend only opening your own analytics on websites that are yours, and opening client analytics websites under their own account. At this time, account ownership can't be transferred, so the owner of the website itself should be the owner of the website's analytics account. Of course, if a person owns multiple websites, those websites should all be in that person's Overview for one-stop maintenance.

✔ **Name:** This column holds the website URL and Google Analytics code in bold on the top line; the account installation link appears below it in regular type with a star next to it. The star simply gives you a way to "favorite" a site, just like you'd use it to mark things as favorites in other Google tools, like Gmail. Marking a site as a favorite is helpful if you own many websites and want to be able to sort them by most viewed.

✔ **Reports:** Under this column, you will find the blue View Report link for each website. This link is how you access the actual data coming in for that site.

✔ **Status:** A green check mark indicates that all is well with the analytics code running on that site. If you see a yellow triangle with an exclamation mark, you need to go into the settings for the site to figure out what is wrong or try replacing the code.

✔ **Visits:** This section reveals how many people have come to visit your site in a certain period, generally a week.

✔ **Avg. Time on Site:** This area measures the average time a visitor spends on your site per visit and tells you the average time on site for all visitors during the time period. Sites that are *sticky* have longer visit times than the average website — they're designed well, so people want to spend more time interacting with the site. That's a good thing.

✔ **Bounce Rate:** This area simply measures how quickly someone who came to your site leaves without visiting any other pages than the one they clicked in on. The lower the percentage here, the better you're doing at keeping folks interested in your site.

✔ **Completed Goals:** This area requires going in to your site reports by clicking View Reports and setting goals to track different landing pages and campaigns. A site with no goals set for that time period will show 0 here.

✔ **% Change:** This quick snapshot tells you whether you're improving in any one of the previous four columns over the time period. A significant increase would merit a day-by-day look at the site to see what encouraged the improvement, and a significant drop might warrant some troubleshooting.

✔ **Actions:** This column allows you to add new profiles for each site, edit the analytics for the site, or delete the site.

Digging into the dashboard

Clicking the blue View Reports link in your Overview takes you to your site's dashboard, where you can drill down through your content, backlinks, visitor data, referring sites, and entry and exit page data, among other things. It also is the place where you'll set goals and campaigns and work with real time stats (see Figure 3-3).

When you first access your dashboard, assuming Analytics has been gathering data on your site for at least a week or so, you will see a wavy line graph. This graph represents your overall visits for the time period. Most days, you can ignore this graph — unless you see a significant dip or spike. When that happens, you should investigate so that you can find out how to adjust your site or blog to fix the issue (or to do more of whatever it was that piqued folks' interest).

Many of the features of Google Analytics are straightforward and will become clear with trial and error. A few of these features are worth discussing in the following sections, however, because they are building blocks to some of the more advanced stuff later on.

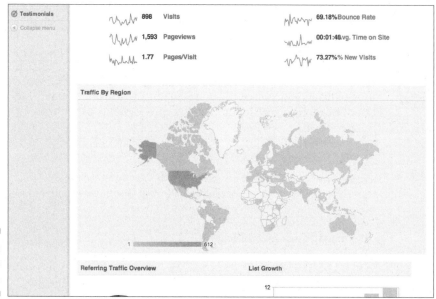

Figure 3-3:
A WordPress dashboard.

Bounce rate

Bounce rate is the percentage of visitors who left your site after arriving at your entrance *(landing)* page (see Figure 3-4). A high bounce rate percentage isn't necessarily bad — it depends on your website and your intentions with that site. Say, for example, that you want people visiting your site to immediately perform a call to action, such as calling your toll-free telephone number. If most people are actually making that call, you'd end up with a high bounce number. However, because you're getting those calls, the bounce number is irrelevant — you're seeing a return on your call to action as you intended.

On the other hand, if you want folks to mosey around your site and look at many pages, you want your bounce rate to be low. (The Average Time On Site metric contributes to this reading also.) If you aren't getting the results on your site goals that you intended, you can use this metric (and the Average Time On Site metric) to monitor how well your adjustments work.

If you click through to Content / Site Content / Pages on the dashboard, you will see which pages on your site are leading the pack in page views. You can also sort these pages by Bounce Rate — just by clicking on the Bounce Rate column. Does a popular page have a high bounce rate? If so, why? Is it because folks are satisfied with what they found there and took action, such as calling a toll-free number? Then you don't need to do a thing. If not, and if you'd prefer that visitors stay and browse around awhile, you'll want to do more digging and adjust your content based on what you find.

 Bounce rate can also indicate how pages are performing for your sales funnel. If the page is designed to move people to a sales page or a sales process, a low bounce rate is an indicator that the page is doing its job. Check your sales figures to be sure. In fact, if the page is doing its job and you have low sales, your bounce rate tells you that your sales copy or some other aspect may need improvement.

Traffic Sources

Traffic Sources is one of my favorite Google Analytics metrics. In fact, while different metrics are important to different people for very different reasons, I love seeing where my traffic is coming from!

This metric does two things:

- ✔ It tells me where my biggest fans or my biggest returns on content investment are — something key to know in social media.
- ✔ It tells me how relevant my site is in search results.

The All Traffic metric in Traffic Sources gives us a great snapshot of our best referrers. Frequent referrals from a site coupled with a low bounce rate means you have connected with the right influencer or influencing site for the goal you are trying to achieve with that page. Good job!

Traffic Sources also tells you what type of visitor the sources send over. If Facebook sends a lot of referrals but has a high bounce rate, perhaps you can either pull back on your Facebook efforts or adjust them to go to another page. Or perhaps you can even change the landing page content to make it more sticky (the landing page is the page you link to on other sites that you want visitors from that site to land on).

Use a different landing page for different visitors or traffic sources. The contacts you make on Twitter are very different than the contacts you make on Facebook or LinkedIn or even via Google Search. Don't overlook "snackable" content shared to discovery sites like StumbleUpon.com either — very easy to make share-worthy landing pages peppered with humor or interest items.

Keywords

Click Search / Organic in the Traffic Sources section, and you will find Keywords. Keywords are the meat and potatoes of good blogging. Writing keyword-rich content that sounds natural isn't easy, but the Keyword tracker in Google Analytics can help you get better at it. Even if you're not a blogger, the Keywords tracking feature in Google Analytics tells you which words are driving the most folks to your site. More importantly, by tracking keywords along with the Bounce Rate, Average Time on Site, and the Traffic Source metrics, you can identify which visitors leave your site frustrated and change those Landing Pages to help them better.

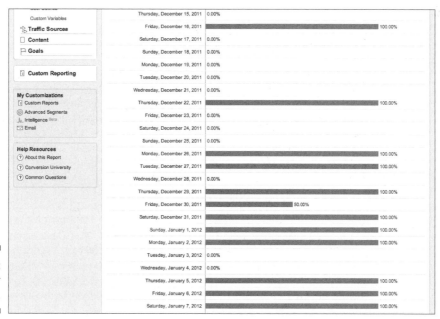

Figure 3-4:
Tracking your bounce rate.

Segmentation

The Segmentation metric helps you answer the secondary questions that crop up as you get the basic questions answered through metrics. Analytics can tell you how many visitors came to your site, but segmentation answers the follow-up questions of "How many were from the United States?" or "How many of the visitors from the United States used a Macintosh running Safari to browse the site?"

Campaigns

Click through to Traffic Sources / Incoming Sources / Campaigns to get to your Campaigns information. Campaigns are how the metrics gurus always know so precisely how folks are getting to the site. By attaching different campaign parameters to different banner ads or other calls to action on your site via links, you can create a trackable link (these are a mile long, by the way). If you then shrink down the link with your favorite URL shortener (see Chapter 7) and share this link on sites like Twitter, Facebook, and LinkedIn — sites that are normally hard to track — you can discover the smallest details of who gets to your site from where and to what content. Pretty cool for a free service, isn't it?

Campaigns are complex, and I am not going to take you to the deep end on this topic (Yet! I do in Chapter 14) but wanted to note it as one of the metrics in Google Analytics that you should pay attention to.

Get Clicky with It

Clicky (www.getclicky.com) is a fun yet useful freemium service that offers a variety of plans for tracking real-time metrics on your website. The free plan lets you track one website up to 3,000 page views a day and gives you access to real-time analytics on referrers, site visitors, segmentation, searches, and more. Clicky isn't customizable like Google Analytics is, but if you want something that is prepackaged and set to run with minimal input from you, Clicky may be just what you need (see Figure 3-5).

One of my favorite features of Clicky is the Spy feature. Much like Woopra, it lets you spy on people as they use your site in real time. (For more on Woopra, see the section "Looking at Other Free or Freemium Tools," later in this chapter.) This feature can give you invaluable user data on how people navigate your site. Do they go where you want them to from each landing page? How long do they stay? Do they find what they need? Unlike Woopra, Clicky doesn't drain your bandwidth, so while you lose the cool Woopra chat feature, you don't lose time waiting for the information to load for you.

Spend some time watching your site's real-time visitors. Their activity tells you more about how well your site was designed faster than almost anything else. You can pinpoint design successes and mistakes and improve your site dramatically.

The other features of Clicky tell you similar metrics to those in Google Analytics, but without a few of the customization options Google Analytics has. Like Google Analytics, Clicky offers segmentation, which allows you to dig more deeply into your metrics to find out better answers to questions about your site demographics and use cases.

Clicky has a variety of apps and plug-ins you can use, including a Chrome plug-in, a Windows dashboard, WordPress and Drupal widgets, and code you can manually integrate into your sites and apps to get even more data fed to your Clicky metrics account. (Heck, it even has code for older sites like MySpace). The folks at Clicky have made it very easy to put Clicky everywhere you need it to be.

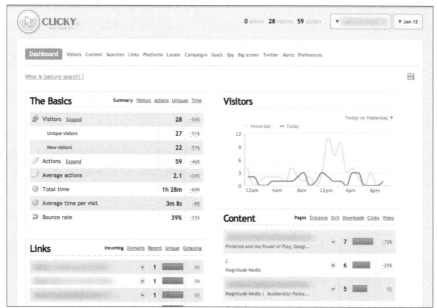

Figure 3-5: Clicky.

Get the Scoop with CustomScoop

Not all metrics are created from online sources. How do you track online and offline sources well? A few companies offer this service, such as MediaVantage (formerly DNA 13), but CustomScoop (www.customscoop.com) offers it at a great price — a free trial/tiered plan pricing combo that most folks will find within reach of their budget (see Figure 3-6).

CustomScoop not only has comprehensive software to bring you automated metrics tracking, it also has real people that help you look for more metrics from more sources. This intriguing combination definitely allows for a wider variety of results.

Focused on campaigns, keywords, and news monitoring, CustomScoop is a solution that works well for brand management, but it can also be applied to personal brand and individual search metrics. Used in tandem with a tool like Google Analytics, CustomScoop can amplify the metrics you track and broaden your brand's reach.

CustomScoop as a tool allows you a larger picture of how effective your message is and what trends are in your industry. It's a bit more outward facing than traditional metrics.

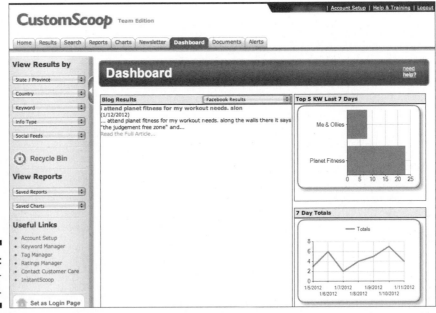

Figure 3-6: Custom-Scoop.

Looking at Other Free or Freemium Tools

Many free or freemium tools are available to you to track your analytics. Each tool has strengths and weaknesses, and few are as versatile as the completely free Google Analytics. A few worthy of mention are

- **Mint:** If you're looking for a PHP-based tool that you can customize and build on, take a look at Mint (`www.haveamint.com`). This tool creates a lovely widget-style interface that looks at all segments of data on your blog. It pulls in real-time statistics as well as statistics over time, makes backups for you, and offers you an API to make it more complex if you know PHP or have someone in-house who does.

- **Woopra:** Woopra (`www.woopra.com`) is a fun tool, but a bandwidth hog. It works as a plug-in on your blog and not only tells you statistics in real time using visually pleasing graphs and colors, it lets you scare the heck out of unsuspecting site visitors by allowing you to suddenly start chatting them. Another drawback, besides bandwidth use, is Woopra's addictive nature. It's hard to walk away from the ever-changing visual graphs. Sites like Clicky or Google Analytics, which have less "bling," can be easier to view daily without derailing your productivity.

- **Bit.ly:** Bit.ly (`https://bitly.com`) is actually an URL shortener that gives you analytics on your site links when sharing, allows custom links, and other features. Bit.ly is fairly simplistic, it's free, and it picks up the slack when you need to track a link from a site that the other analytics programs might not catch. A good URL shortener with analytics is an essential part of your metrics arsenal (see Figure 3-7).

- **Gist:** Similar to *Rapportive* (also a good tool) Gist (`www.gist.com`) helps you make sales by tracking information about your contacts. Not so much a straight-up numerical metrics tracker, Gist is still useful to pull in information and track activity metrics on people you follow and need to do business with. Gist and Rapportive both integrate with Gmail and other e-mail programs, putting your activity metrics at your fingertips. Currently, Gist is free, though it may move to a freemium model at some point.

- **PeopleBrowsr:** A freemium service with a variety of possible metrics, PeopleBrowsr (`www.peoplebrowsr.com`) is both social media engagement platform and analytics tool. It also is trying to compete with Klout and other services to become a widely used credential service. The user interface is a bit messy for some, but the statistics and metrics are worth giving it a trial run.

- **ThinkUp:** ThinkUp (`www.thinkupapp.com`) requires a more advanced knowledge of server installation than any of the other tools. I mention ThinkUp early on, however, because it's an *open-source tool* (that is, a tool that's free and can be modified to suit people's needs) that does some very intensive monitoring and measuring of your social metrics. I highly recommend getting to know ThinkUp if you have web hosting and aren't afraid to look under the hood (see Figure 3-8).

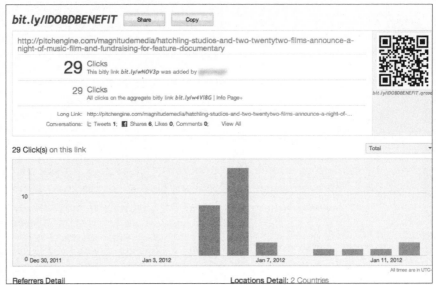

Figure 3-7:
Bit.ly.

Figure 3-8:
ThinkUp.

Avoid things like Klout or Buffer as solo solutions. If you want to use these types of single metric or limited source solutions, make sure that you have other, more comprehensive metrics in place, or you run the risk of missing key information.

If you've been using a single metric solution up until this point and feel like you're treading water on your ROI (return on investment), you'll be excited to finally see a complete set of metrics. If metrics are new to you, by avoiding putting all of your eggs in one basket, you're going to get a better, more rounded picture of your successes and for where and what you need to improve.

This chapter just describes the tip of the iceberg for free or freemium services. With so many options to choose from, you may feel overwhelmed. Just remember that you want your metrics to cover a wide range of goals, sources, and keywords.

Chapter 4

Measuring Everything

*Y*ou may find yourself wondering what you should measure. I say measure everything and then sift through the data to get to the meat of the information. Social media changes so fast and has such a human element at its core that the only way to get results you can use is to absorb and track everything possible.

Measuring the seemingly fickle and unpredictable behavior of people online can seem like a chore at first, but it's actually quite interesting. If you've ever seen birds fly in formation, then you know that everything eventually follows a pattern, and that the leaders (influencers, if you will) often self-select mid-stream. Metrics help you track not only specific, linear data sets but also that type of malleable data online.

Measuring everything includes measuring the offline efforts you're making for your brand. This measurement requires some finesse. Using links, hashtags, keywords, familiar icons referring to your social profiles, and specific landing pages on your website for each medium of advertising or contact, as well as having the customers self-select which campaign brought them in, will all contribute to your measurement efforts. Increasing the scope of what you measure requires clear calls to action and tracking.

In this chapter, I show you some of the ways you can start measuring everything.

Capturing Data with a Wide Net

The first step to being able to measure everything is to cast a wide net. This step involves several layers of action on your part, including excellent branding offline and online, comprehensive search engine optimization (SEO) and social media optimization (SMO) tactics, great web design that includes clear calls to action, a lean, focused business plan, and clear, measurable goals.

Becoming familiar with tools like keywords and with how people use the web and, more specifically, your website, will be invaluable to the process. Keeping up with changes in search engine tactics will help as well — Google has changed how it ranks sites in search results a number of times this year alone. Because search engines are constantly trying to improve results for people using them, you need to know the best practices of each one. If staying current on so many best practices sounds a bit daunting, start with the best-known ones like Google, Bing, and Yahoo!, and then expand from there.

One thing to avoid while casting your wide net is using technology just for the sake of using it because it's new and cool. (For an example, see the nearby sidebar.

Do your due diligence before launching a campaign. Know who and where your audience is, how to measure your results, and how you're offering them value in the process. The trade-off of an easy flow of data for your marketing use is the customer's time, information, and attention. Give them value in exchange if you want to be a beloved brand.

Homing in on hyperlocal metrics

Hyperlocal means tracking social media and marketing metrics right at the point of sale, in your neighborhood, or a customer's precise location. Hyperlocal takes metrics to the next level of accuracy by laser-focusing on where people are interacting with your brand.

The best way to get hyperlocal metrics is to add strong mobile and geolocation components to your marketing campaign and to have geolocation tools enabled on your landing pages. Encourage people to check in to your brick-and-mortar business and to interact with you on- and offline while they're in the store. Best Buy does a great job of getting hyperlocal by using QR Codes and Facebook and foursquare deals and specials to encourage people to become more involved with its in-store shopping experience through interactive purchasing and on-site research.

Don't use technology just because it's cool

QR Codes are neat, and with tools like YouScan. me or a great landing page on your website, you can easily get analytics on the codes you send into the wild. If you haven't run across *QR Codes* yet, they're patterned 2-D bar codes that allow you to send information to your customer using a scanning program on a mobile phone.

Progressive Insurance offers a cautionary tale from the 2011 Shazam promotion it ran for its television commercials over the summer and fall. As you watch mascot Flo talk, a graphic pops up on-screen telling you to Shazam for more information.

Though the marketer in me got excited at a new way to track the analytics of television viewing, this campaign involved making assumptions that

✔ Folks would know what Shazam was (a phone app for music discovery, making this the first use of an audio QR Code that I know of).

✔ They would have their smartphone or tablet with them while watching television (and that the code worked on that phone).

✔ They didn't DVR or TiVo the show and fast-forward past the commercials.

✔ They could get the phone booted in time to grab the audio needed to discover the Easter egg Progressive had put on Shazam.

✔ The customer wasn't then annoyed that after all the effort he put into seeing what the icon was about, all they got was a photo of Flo and (if he had an iPhone) a link to a quote — nothing special like a deal or more information in exchange for their time.

I'd love to see audio QR Codes and QR Codes used in a way that was less about "look what technology we have!" and more about actual tracking of customer movement and activity (see figure). This book is designed to make sure that you're using new technology in the right way, and in the most measurable way.

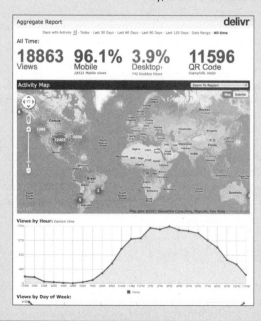

One interesting thing for business is how many people choose to allow location-based tracking, seemingly without thoughts for safety or privacy, simply because it's integrated into their favorite games and applications on their browser and their mobile devices.

If you're not clear yet why getting hyperlocal with your measurement will benefit you, especially if you have a brick-and-mortar component to your brand, focus on samples of the questions hyperlocal metrics can answer for you:

- ✔ How many of my competitors within walking distance from me are getting more shopping traffic on a Saturday?
- ✔ How are folks engaging with the business next door right now, and how can I leverage that to bring them into my store?
- ✔ How many competing restaurants are located within ten blocks of me?
- ✔ How does peak shopping hours traffic compare block to block in my city?
- ✔ What is my market share for my type of business within a mile?
- ✔ What movies get the most check-ins at the theater on my block, and how does that help me target my merchandise to that demographic?

These questions are just a few that location-based data can help you answer.

Hyperlocal isn't restricted to brick-and-mortar stores, either. You can apply the techniques and concepts to online news-paid content sites and other intangible services and information outlets.

One business that is seeing results from a combination of hyperlocal marketing data and putting more control in the hands of store-level managers is Supervalu, a grocery store. Supervalu is empowering its managers with a hyperlocal demographic data dashboard that gives the managers information about the demographic makeup of their store's neighborhood. Then Supervalu gives the managers full control of 50 percent or more of their store's *end caps* (those displays on the ends of aisles and in the middle of walking paths inside a store). The managers are then able to combine the data with their creativity and experience to increase sales at a very local level.

Data is power, and hyperlocal data puts the power at street level for you to grab. Offer your customers and potential customers value in exchange for their location and habits data, such as paying with their phone or receiving a special or tip, and you'll find that people will willingly share with you for that value.

Gathering global metrics

Hyperlocal metrics are important (see preceding section), but global metrics are equally important. Your brand has to be able to step back and view the big picture — to see its impact from a wider worldview. Having a global data set will help you make the fast, sweeping decisions you need to make in business.

What's the difference between local and global measurement? You can fine-tune *local* (or *hyperlocal,* if you get very detailed with your data) measurement right down to the city block a person is on, the store she's standing in, and the purchase she just paid for with her mobile device. You can discover whether that person is male or female and her income level and shopping habits, all within a block-by-block framework, if you want to get that detailed with your data subset.

Global measurement is broader in scope and looks at the patterns and habits of whole regions, areas, and countries. You can get similar drill-down demographic data like gender, age ratio, and online shopping habits, among other things, but global metrics are designed to give you a broader look at a whole data pile that includes broader matching on all data sets.

Global metrics will always be useful. For example, knowing that Twitter is "big in Brazil" is a metric that can help plan using the social tool behind a large campaign that will reach across countries. However, the trends are firmly moving toward hyperlocal and mobile for useful metrics that you can apply to economic growth and recovery.

Knowing What to Do with Metrics

After you've gathered as much metrics information as you can, you're ready to put that data to good use. You can use the information that you find to discover what your competitors are up to (and beat them at their own game!), grow your business, and increase your sales.

With so many options for excelling in competition using what you discover for your metrics, I'm sure you're seeing the value of having metrics in place everywhere possible. If the tool you're using has no metrics capabilities, make sure to utilize your landing pages with Google Analytics to bridge the gap and gather information. If you can have people self-select their own data through mailing list subscription forms and lead gathering opportunities, it will add another layer to your metrics program that will help you get a leg up on the competition.

Pursuing competitive intelligence

One of my favorite ways to use social media metrics is in the pursuit of competitive intelligence. The term competitive intelligence doesn't refer to knowing more about everything than the person next to you and winning a prize, but rather refers to knowing all about what your competing business brands are up to (which makes the prize you "win" a better business). *Competitive intelligence* helps you compete on price, service, perception, attention metrics, audience, reach, and more.

Thanks to social media metrics, you can follow along with your biggest competitor's every move and then decide when to match it, one-up it, or simply ignore it. Gone are the days where you had no idea what your competition was up to until it was already done. Enter the days where your biggest competitors tell you what they are up to, in great detail, every day. The data is yours for the taking, if you know where to look.

Want to know who your competitors talk to most and what they talk about? You can track that information on social media. Want to keep a topic list of your competitors' keywords? Metrics tools, such as free Google Alerts, deliver those lists right to your door. Wondering if your competitor has the massive page views and site results it's claiming? Check them out using any one of a number of sites, tools, extensions, or plug-ins.

One of the most useful browser options for the metrics junkie is Chrome, with Firefox high in the ranking as well. By simply switching your browser from Safari or Internet Explorer or whatever came with your machine and using something different, you get access to a variety of extensions designed to do some subtle spying on other people's website trends and tools. Toss in your Analytics knowledge and search mojo, and you get the kind of statistics and information that people used to pay hundreds of dollars a pop for.

Using metrics to compete

If you've ever watched your competitor try and succeed with a new idea that seems remarkably similar to one you've had in the past, chances are you have a competitor who is well versed in social media metrics and using them to level the playing field for competition. How can you tap into this same pool of information? Easy — listening metrics plus a little self-control.

Instead of crowing about your big idea to all who will listen, try closing your mouth and activating your data-gathering system. Listen to the keywords inherent to your idea. Monitor the keywords as used by others in your field. Fine-tune the listening by location and age, as well as target market. By not speaking your idea out loud, the market for it remains fresh (no one can steal an idea you don't disclose). Combined with the data you've gathered, you have a greater recipe for success.

Social media metrics can reveal quite a bit about your target market before you even release your product. They can tell you things like the most popular color in your demographic, the most used phone or computer, what kind of shoes people wear, what the disposable income levels might be to help you refine pricing, and other tidbits you need to refine your offering.

You can also use on-site metrics from sites like SlideShare plus landing page data to refine your competitive edge in public speaking as well. If you want to get more speaking gigs that lead to better opportunities, you can fine-tune your topics and optimize your presentations using the data you glean from people watching your slides, commenting on them, marking them as favorites, and otherwise engaging with them.

TIP

Use a Chrome extension (see Figure 4-1) like W3Spy, W3Techs, BuiltWith, or Chrome SEO to take a peek under the hood of your competitors' websites. Discover the plug-ins they use, the site rank they have, their keywords, their daily estimated dollar value based on traffic, and more with only a click or two.

Figure 4-1:
A Chrome extension can offer important competitive intelligence.

Competitive intelligence also gives you a chance to move faster than your competition. By having listening metrics in place in addition to data metrics, you'll hear competitor customers first when they have a problem or challenge. By being helpful to them, sometimes faster than your competition, you not only increase the goodwill of your brand, you have a good chance of snagging a new customer when they search for a new provider.

Growing your business

Another set of uses for social media metrics is business growth and knowledge growth. If you want to expand your business reach and sales, social media is a great tool to include in your overall arsenal, and metrics will only amplify your results and speed your growth.

Having the data at your fingertips to show who is interacting with your brand, topics, geographic region, and products in real time or near real time and to extrapolate that data over time is to have the power to know how to target the growth of your business for more effective success. Having the metrics from your social media efforts lets you know when the time is right to make your next move. It also helps you create your roadmap for your future.

Social media metrics also allow you to batch-test small initiatives *(A/B testing)* when you're thinking of launching a new service or product. By A/B testing your campaign or initiative through staggered releases on various social media sites and concentrated influencer sharing, combined with a great landing page targeted to each group that is packed with metrics goodness, a company can save the cost in money and time of a failed launch of a product that is a poor fit for its target market.

One of the companies excelling at applying social media metrics to their customer base is Starbucks. Starbucks is using listening metrics and demographic metrics from its *white label* (company branded) My Starbucks Idea website, Twitter engagement, Facebook page, Gold Card rewards program, and more to fine-tune what it's offering customers and to growing its reach.

Starbucks is applying metrics to a variety of social media platforms and offline programs so that it can offer better quality deals, rewards, products, and promotions to its loyal customers, as well as attract new loyal fans. Starbucks is very adept at leveraging its data to create engaged, enthusiastic fans of the company — and not just coffee drinkers. Some of the engagement types Starbucks is tracking include

- ✔ **In-store:** Rewards Card tracking (see Figure 4-2) allows Starbucks a real-time, geolocation-enabled view of how and what their customers purchase and what the peak times are. Free iTunes songs and apps allow Starbucks to offer value incentives and track redemption. Free Wi-Fi through the Starbucks web portal allows Starbucks to track in-store web surfing and usage.

- ✔ **Online:** Starbucks uses a variety of landing pages and sites to engage and track its customer base online, including My Starbucks Idea, a white label social networking site designed to encourage market research and self-directed focus group activity that generates and tests new ideas for the stores. Starbucks is also active on Facebook, Twitter, and other social media sites and uses hashtags, promoted tweets, promoted trends, tabs, and landing pages to track the engagement people have with its brand there.

- ✔ **Charity:** Starbucks uses *cause marketing,* which attaches a charity donation to a CD sale, wristband purchase, or other purchase, to drive customer behavior. Cause marketing also gives them another metric to track — customer altruism and its effect on purchase behavior.

- ✔ **Mobile:** Starbucks uses geolocation applications, such as foursquare and Facebook Places, to interact with its customers on the go via check-ins on their phone, which activates trackable hyperlocal metrics. Starbucks also is among the first companies to use *augmented reality —* an artificial environment created through the combination of real-world and computer-generated data — in a focused marketing campaign, by creating an Augmented Reality application called Cup Magic for iPhone and Android that people can download. Cup Magic animates the graphics on their red holiday cups, offers rewards, and gives Starbucks another way to engage and track customer behavior.

Using an augmented reality application or QR Code from a company like Starbucks? Be aware that this technology is still in its early stages. It requires a steady hand and patience to capture the images before you see the animation or whatever other virtual experience has been designed. If you're designing an app or code for your company, keep user experience in mind — let them know that a 15-second delay in processing the image may occur. It will keep your customers happy.

Use of good social media metrics and cross platform tools increased Starbucks global same-store sales by 7 percent in the first quarter of 2011. That's a strong argument for how targeted metrics and solid social media implementation can affect a brand in a positive way.

Increasing sales with metrics

The Starbucks example (see the section "Growing your business," earlier in this chapter) is also a snapshot of how to use social media metrics for sales. Another company using social media metrics and cross-platform engagement for sales is Best Buy. Best Buy has brought mobile shopping and social shopping into its in-store experience using QR Codes for each item on its shelves. Customers can scan the QR Codes for each item in the store to get more information, including reviews, which encourages them to buy.

Figure 4-2:
Starbuck's
Rewards
Card
tracking
customer
feedback
website.

Another social media metric used to drive sales is the metric of reach. Hashtags like `#shoplocalsaturday` on Twitter combined with free Facebook ads for Shop Local Saturday drove awareness and sales to local businesses that would not otherwise have been able to afford campaigns to attract seasonal shoppers and compete with Black Friday deals at larger stores. (A *hashtag* is simply a keyword or keyphrase denoted with the # sign on Twitter, Google+, and other services and is used to track a topic.)

If you're using third-party sales drivers like the Shop Local Saturday ads and hashtag, however, you need to have an excellent metric-catching system in place for your business. For example, make sure that you have the following ready, or you may miss measuring the effectiveness of taking part in a collective campaign:

- A landing page set up for the effort
- In-store signage that asks people to self-identify as coming from that hashtag
- Check-in specials in place for mobile tracking that leverage services like foursquare

If your tracking is in place on all possible platforms, however, you can track your customer movements and habits on that targeted marketing day. You can then leverage this data for future price incentives and product movement. You can also use this data to discover peak times for promotion-based shopping habits in your store.

Use signage in your store to encourage customers to opt in to your metrics platforms. If you're on foursquare or Facebook or if you have a deal on your website, put a sign up by the door and by the register. Don't expect people to seek you out everywhere automatically — people often need a nudge.

Identifying Metrics Sources

Figuring out where your data is coming from is key to your success. Some incoming data will be generated by your marketing efforts, but not all. You need metrics tracking in place to capture data from the organic discovery of your brand on and offline as well.

You also need metrics in place to capture data on how your customers are finding you. Are you strong in search engine optimization? Do new people come to you from Google? What about Bing's location-driven search? Is foursquare your main referrer? Do you get traction on Twitter? Having Google Analytics in place will capture this data even if you don't have a specific goal or campaign running.

After you begin collecting this global data on organic discovery of your brand, you can use it to fine-tune your goals and campaigns to reach the best customers for you with the stickiest promotions. Targeted, metrics-based outreach is going to drive more sales and increase your reach.

As organic data on where people are discovering your brand and what is driving that discovery comes in, you can begin to target your message and set new goals. For example, if you find that your mom-and-pop shop gets a lot of foot traffic from Bing's local focused search results, you know you can add in a strong geographic and mobile component to your online branding to get more traction.

To leverage local search results, use foursquare (see Figure 4-3) as a quick and easy tool. It allows you to claim a business page, attach a website and Twitter account and set up deals, tips, and specials to drive customers into your establishment using layered marketing campaigns direct to their mobile phone.

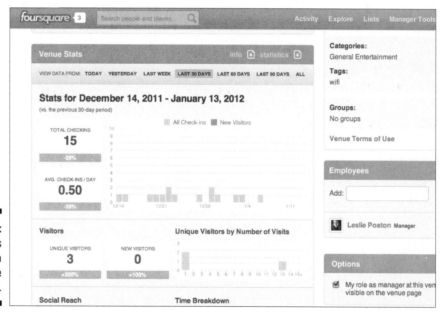

Figure 4-3:
Business metrics on a foursquare venue page.

Part II
Navigating the Measurement Jungle

"Face it, Vinnie—you're gonna have a hard time getting people to subscribe online with a credit card to a newsletter called 'Felons Interactive.'"

In this part . . .

After you master the basics of how social media metrics work, you're going to want to take your metrics tracking even farther and deeper. You can easily get distracted and lost in the process of tracking metrics. In this part, I look at how to overcome the challenges you may face.

I cover the various aspects of driving your metrics, from content generation and conversation tracking to social listening. This part gives you a deeper understanding of how metrics tracking starts at the point where you make something, not after the fact.

Chapter 5

The Six Stages of Metrics Grief: Turning Chaotic Information into a Business Advantage

· ·

In This Chapter

▶ Overcoming denial and isolation

▶ Channeling anger at bad metrics into productive behavior

▶ Handling the depression that comes with a new site that doesn't have many visitors yet

▶ Reaping metrics acceptance and advantages of great landing pages

· ·

*I*mplementing good metrics for your social media efforts and integrating them well into your social media marketing can be a struggle. As with anything, struggle can lead to great things, but it can be mentally draining at first.

The stages of metrics implementation are similar to the stages of grief, but don't worry — there is a light at the end of the tunnel! The path you take to get there will make all the difference in your success.

Foundation is going to be a key element. Google has a learning program for each of its tools: AdSense and AdWords. Simply taking these free courses and reading books that walk you through getting started will give you a strong foundation to build on and a deeper understanding of how keywords and other search criteria work, which will allow you to make your metrics matter more.

The stories told by your metrics data are only as good as the questions you ask your data-gathering service to answer. By understanding what questions your potential customers are asking on the Internet, you can be more helpful and useful to them, even in an organic search result. Understanding data will help you make the conversions you need for a strong business.

In this chapter, I talk about the various elements you may struggle with when implementing your metrics for the first time.

Battling Denial and Isolation

The biggest struggle you'll face when embarking on metrics gathering and analysis is feeling alone and unheard at first. Any new campaign, website, Twitter account, Facebook page, or other item you want to measure starts at zero. This number can make you feel like you're talking into a void, talking to yourself or that you're hidden from view. This feeling can lead to an overall sense of isolation as you look at stagnant metrics numbers.

The typical Google Analytics graph of a website that just launched looks like Figure 5-1.

You can see that this site has had only 21 visitors in one week. If you're looking for the validation of people visiting your site and reading your blog, this metric can be a harsh feeling! What these numbers don't tell you is that increased targeted content will drive up your visits and conversions considerably. Add in social media sharing, and your site traffic will also become much healthier, which will be captured (and trackable) in future graphs.

Figure 5-1:
The Google
Analytics
graph of
a new
website

Make sure that you build your website or blog on a domain that you host or that you pay to host! These days, getting a `.com` for your domain name URL isn't as important as it used to be — you can make do with `.net` and so on, for example — but having your own hosting is very important. It allows you full control over what you do with your site or blog and makes you look professional. Go the extra mile: Make sure that your contact e-mail is on your domain as well. Nothing says "I don't know what I'm doing" or "I don't take this seriously" like a `hotmail.com` or `yahoo.com` address, for example.

Don't be tempted to bomb all your friends with the link to your new site or campaign over and over again in an attempt to feel heard and not be isolated. Broadcasting without balanced sharing and engaging is a turn-off in this age of the social Internet. You have to build your network in such a way that you know they will get the word out without being nagged.

So how can you climb out of isolation? Try a few simple tips to jazz up traffic to your new or recently updated site or blog:

- **Use your own domain for hosting your site or blog.** This gives you the most control over your content and your visitors' experience on your site.

- **Use that same domain for your e-mail accounts.** Using a consistent domain makes you look more professional.

- **Use a platform for your site or blog that you can easily update in the future and that is well supported now.** WordPress is a popular choice for bloggers, as is Drupal. Designing your site in something like HTML5 is future-thinking as well.

- **Remember that titles and title tags are important for both search engines and the folks that visit your site.** Short, catchy titles get the most bang for your buck.

- **Tag and categorize all your content.** Tagging and categorizing also helps search engines find what you've written or recorded and will help visitors navigate your site more easily.

- **Link to give credit, build a network of backlinks, give folks more information, and share and engage.** Visitor preferences differ, but, in general, have links open in a new browser window or tab where possible.

- **Hold off on advertising.** The average site or blog takes a while to build up enough readership to warrant ads. During the audience-building phase, ads will be a total turn-off to your visitors.

- **Be visually pleasing.** Using images and videos in the content on your site or blog breaks up the monotony of text and keeps visitors on your page longer.

- **Pay attention to high traffic days and focus your best content there.** Use the rest of your analytics to focus your content topics and target demographics.

✔ **Measure everything.** By having analytics code everywhere possible, you can track down in the most minute detail how people are using your site or blog and adjust your content, posting times, and conversion goals accordingly. Don't just have the code in the site footer — track inside each post. Use URL shorteners with analytics like Bit.ly where possible. Track everything for better data that you can put to work for you.

✔ **Be sure to back up your site:** You need to protect your installation in case of issues in future — you want to be able to recover your data!

Why focus on your website or blog when this book is supposed to be about social media metrics? Because your website is the only place on the Internet that you own. It's not subject to third-party site rules and regulations, 4,000-page terms of service agreements, or a mysterious shutdown or possible closure. Your data on your site or blog is yours, and your social media efforts should always lead people back to it for the best conversion and tracking. Even your Tumblr "blog" should lead back to your real blog or site — Tumblr.com and mini-blogging sites like it are also third-party sites that you don't have ownership on, even though you'll find that, used correctly, they'll generate substantial traffic for you.

Dealing with Anger

As you begin to measure everything, you may begin to experience frustration with the data you find. You'll notice that sites with less useful information (or, in some cases, completely wrong information) get better site traffic than you.

You'll see that some folks openly "borrow" the ideas and memes others start and build success on the backs of their competitors' hard work. It can make you want to throw in the towel, but don't! Because you are measuring everything, this kind of competitive intelligence simply gives you the edge you need to improve and cultivate a better class of visitor to your site, blog, or social media profiles. Better visitor quality means better conversion rates. Better data means better content and design, which lead to better visitor quality.

Treat social media metrics and web data with the same number-crunching attitude you would statistics or algebra. Sort your data well as it comes in. Utilize spreadsheets and database files where you can to keep ongoing records of data you can categorize and compare against a variety of criteria over time.

So, what *should* get your dander up? Bad, shallow, or useless social media metrics. What's a bad social media metric, you ask? Any metric that only looks at one piece of data or that doesn't openly disclose its criteria for measurement. For example, at the time of writing, Klout is the media darling for social media metrics, but it's largely useless as a measurement of anything — so I killed my Klout account.

Why? Because the number is meaningless without full disclosure of the algorithm used to decipher it and a clear graph of what is being measured. An arrow going up in a graph with no *x* or *y* axis data tells me exactly zero information (see Figure 5-2). Going up as compared to what? Using what criteria to measure it? These are key things to know if you're trying to extrapolate behavior changes and results based on data gathered for conversion — and believe me, true social media ROI lies in conversion rates, not follower counts and noise levels.

If you're using social media and the web well, in a focused manner that is data driven, and your intention is sales or sales leads, you should be seeing increasing numbers of sales and sales leads over time. Through use of good analytics, you'll find that these increased number often have little to do with the number of followers or likes you have or how noisy you are, and more to do with quality content and quality connections leading to a site that is well designed for converting to action.

Bargaining for Quick Solutions

As you embark on tracking your data, beware of one common trap — being distracted by supposed "easy metrics" solutions and fly-by-night page view and follower count schemes and the like. Some solutions (for example, Radian6 or CustomScoop) automate a significant portion of your metrics tracking and can help you track specific things, if you have the means to purchase them. But not all metrics tracking tools are created equal, and easy and fast usually come at a price. Be wary of bargaining with your data and results for quick solutions that may not produce valuable data.

Figure 5-2: Klout score graph showing no *x* or *y* data.

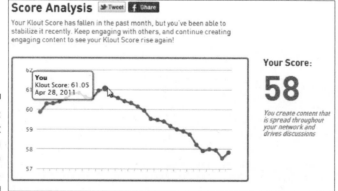

Even if you use Radian6, CustomScoop, Mint (see Figure 5-3), or other solid, proven paid solutions, nothing takes the place of also tracking your own metrics using your own tools, such as Google Analytics. Having multiple tracking solutions in play makes sure that you're getting all types of data through all funnels and don't miss a trick when it comes to ensuring that you're getting the most out of your time and energy spent online.

TIP

If you've already fallen for a quick measurement scheme online, simply back out quickly and install a more effective solution. There is no need to panic. You can use the data you got from the first solution, even if it's slim, as a baseline and go from there with the new, more comprehensive solutions you put in place.

Overcoming Depression

If you've begun tracking metrics and are enjoying the bounty of data you're now able to see, sift through, and use, you may wonder what could possibly cause depression! Easy: data loss.

Say that you have a site issue or somehow lose access to your site or data. Do you have your backup plan in place? I'd recommend having one from the beginning. Actually, I'd recommend having a multilayered backup system just like you have a multilayered metrics system.

Figure 5-3:
Mint is
a more
affordable
PHP solution
tracking
similar data
to Radian6.

Tools like Google Analytics do most of the backing up for you because they are part of the huge Google machine. Even the Google machine has issues now and then, though, such as users getting locked out of accounts or system faltering from heavy use or server issues.

You can get around this headache by using the report feature inside Google Analytics. Send each report to yourself as a `.csv` file via e-mail weekly or daily, and you'll always have a fairly recent copy to work from should something happen and you have to fall back ten and punt.

Every reputable service, paid or free, has some way for you to access your data offline. The best services offer spreadsheet-compatible file formats, but even a PDF can be useful in a pinch. Make sure that you find and set up the backup features in all your metrics sites.

You can also cover your bases if you have analytics on your site or blog by doing a regular backup of your site and the database behind it. I make an effort to back mine up weekly. Some people like to back up more often if they're on a busy server or if they change their content more often. This backup also keeps a copy of your analytics code if you need to do a reinstall, as long as you remember to back up your theme and plug-ins as part of it (this is where the code is located).

Doing a backup may sound difficult, but it isn't. Tools like WordPress allow you to export to an `.xml` file, and there are even plug-ins and other third party solutions that automate backups if you travel a lot or forget to do this kind of task, like BackupBuddy or Backupify (see Figure 5-4). All you have to do is set it and forget it.

Tools like Silentale, Backupify, and an ever-changing array of others are designed to back up social media data. You may not use all this data for analytics, but you should find a reliable backup service anyway, in case you find yourself in a situation where you have to find an old tweet or status update to handle a problem. Be sure to check the service's Terms of Service for information on how it handles privacy and data security. For the services that offer analytics on the data they back up, make sure that you set up the send report feature there as well.

What do you do with the data after you've backed it up? I like to sort mine into folders by date and service or site. I keep one backup for each year (comprehensive) and one each month that I swap out, and one each week. I also keep a daily folder for a few of the more active and least stable services, just in case, and a new backup before any upgrade.

Some services offer no way to back up the data in any form, using any solution. For those services, I capture screenshots using Evernote's ability to save an entire webpage. I do this anytime the data changes significantly. It's a cobbled together solution, but it still allows me to track data changes and make useful notes I can then transcribe into a spreadsheet.

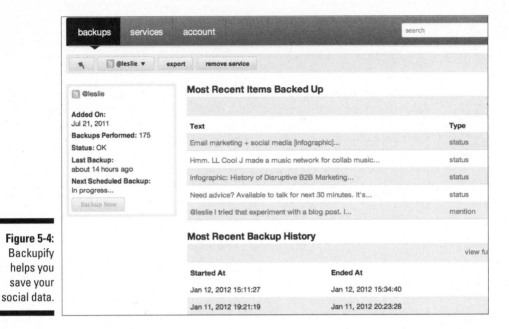

Figure 5-4:
Backupify
helps you
save your
social data.

Reaching a State of Acceptance

As you get into the habit and practice of studying data, you'll begin to not only reach a state of acceptance, but one of happiness. You'll finally feel that your efforts online for yourself and your brand aren't being wasted. That feeling of spinning your wheels or losing control of your time will disappear. Your fear of numbers and spreadsheets will go away as you see how useful the information you're tracking is to your bottom line.

One thing you can do to reach that state of acceptance faster is solidify metrics as part of your daily, weekly, and monthly routine. Spend time each week, especially, studying the data you have gathered and thinking of new ways to put it to work for you (see Figure 5-5).

Play around with spreadsheets, even if you don't think you're good at them yet. Practice moving your data around and study how using different sets of criteria and different ways of seeing the information can give you a fully different picture. You may walk away with two solutions to a tricky problem instead of one just by learning how to adjust the data inside your spreadsheet to answer different questions.

Clicks ⑦	Impr.	CTR ⑦	Avg. CPC ⑦	Cost	Avg. Pos.	Metro Area
1,972	489,911	0.40%	$3.71	$7,324.75	3.5	San Francisc
67	643	10.42%	$3.26	$218.60	4.9	Los Angeles
36	255	14.12%	$3.24	$116.71	4.7	Sacramento-
27	33,931	0.08%	$4.17	$112.63	5.7	
15	172	8.72%	$3.11	$46.65	5.8	San Diego C
13	530	2.45%	$3.21	$41.77	6.3	New York NY
10	41	24.39%	$3.34	$33.37	5.1	Boston MA-M
8	33	24.24%	$3.27	$26.16	4.2	Portland OR
7	60	11.67%	$3.35	$23.47	4.2	Fresno-Visal
7	33	21.21%	$3.23	$22.62	5.1	Eugene OR
7	61	11.48%	$3.06	$21.42	6.5	Monterey-Sal
7	93	7.53%	$2.93	$20.53	6.2	Denver CO
6	46	13.04%	$3.05	$18.29	4.6	Chicago IL
6	9	66.67%	$3.00	$17.99	4	Atlanta GA
6	19	31.58%	$3.00	$17.97	5.4	Miami-Ft. La
5	6	83.33%	$3.43	$17.16	3.8	Philadelphia

Figure 5-5:
Sample data
report.

Use your spreadsheet program's tools, such as pivot tables and graphs or charts, to change the way you see the information. Make basic infographics or slideshow visualization of your data by answering different questions. Pretend you have to present the answer to a visual thinker and work to clarify what it would mean to them. That approach, in turn, will clarify the information to you.

While manipulating the data and massaging it to wring every ounce of data juice out of it, don't modify it! Remember, manipulating data refers only to sorting it or studying it by different criteria, not to altering the data itself. Altered data doesn't help you achieve your goals — only true data can do that.

Chapter 6

Maximizing Listening

*M*easurement tactics differ vastly for a business and an individual using the data for personal use or as a solopreneur. Though each methodology shares some characteristics, tools, and techniques, the goals are often diametrically opposed.

One of the main differences you'll discover is your target audience. Knowing who you are talking to and getting a vision of who is listening is key to creating a base of topics that are helpful, useful, and engaging for your audience. The folks that tune in to an individual are going to be different than the type of audience an organization creates.

That said, any measurement is going to help you see a better return on time spent on social media and your website. Even if you have to mix and match your goals for a bit as you get your measurement legs under you, you're still going to be taking an essential step toward maximum efficiency and return on effort.

The folks I talk with as `@leslie` on Twitter are vastly different than the folks `@ford` talks to, for example, and they have different needs. Tracking analytics can help you pinpoint those needs via click tracking and keywords and fine-tune your content to be the most helpful and engaging.

Having those conversations that aren't targeted, that are just engagement, are still important. In this chapter, I show you how having analytics in place even during the casual conversations you have online can help you focus your efforts for maximum effect when it's time to focus on conversion and lead generation.

Looking at How Individuals Use Metrics

If you're an individual reading this book, then your social media use is going to be vastly more conversational in nature than the average corporation. This is a good thing! There is a solid case for the value of casual engagement. Casual engagement leads to offline referrals, casual word-of-mouth promotion, and the kind of organic, naturally occurring, connections that stem from getting to know someone. You can and will measure these things, but you should be doing it in the background, in order to keep your interactions genuine.

It's still important to be authentic and very much yourself whether you're talking about your personal voice or your brand voice.

Measuring organic relationships

Measuring a truly organic connection is always going to be a mostly manual process. For example, in my individual use of Twitter, I have made thousands of connections. Over the years, I've developed an understanding of people's strengths and weaknesses and special talents. I've gotten to know them well through casual conversation, occasional real-life meetings, and shared projects.

As time has gone on, I've entered them into my customer relationship manager (CRM), which happens to be BatchBook, with a note about what I've discovered. It is not uncommon for me to make introductions between my connections when I see a fit or to send a job someone's way because of what I know about them.

If I get a referral, I ask how they found out about me, enter that connection in my manual tracking, and hope that the people I introduce or refer have done the same. Tracking referrals takes a little effort, but it's worth it because an automated analytics program won't be able to measure these types of individual-driven conversions or results.

You can also track who you are engaging with on an individual level using mobile Evernote photo notes, scanning business card images into a database using your phone and a card reader program, importing conversations to your contacts, tracking your e-mails, and using services like Backupify or interactions via HootSuite plus reporting to keep a log of who said what to whom and when.

HootSuite offers a variety of reports you can purchase, but did you know that HootSuite also has a series of quick free analytics tools you can check out under the Quick Analytics tab? You can use this tool to quickly see how individual URLs are performing or how a particular personal account is doing with retweets and other shares and connections.

Thinking about time of day

If you're an individual, you may wonder when the best time of day for engagement is so that you get the most bang for your buck. Tools like Crowdbooster can tell you that for free for social sites, or you can use free Google Analytics to view time of day and day of week engagement stats on your blog or website.

You can make a good argument for the individual account that time of day may not matter. What matters is what works for your schedule, and that time may not fit in a specific time of day. If you still want to use time-of-day engagement, you can use tools like HootSuite or TweetDeck to schedule your tweets (and, in the case of HootSuite, your Facebook and LinkedIn posts as well). It's more important that the way an individual interacts be vital, interesting, and real, and that happens less with scheduled updates than it does with you sitting in front of your computer or phone having a real conversation in real time.

Tracking casual connections online

After you master the art of the organic measurements, you need to track your casual connections online and work on conversion and lead generation. The best way to do so is to use your website or blog to its full potential.

You can easily slap up a blog and not put analytics behind it or forget to create great landing pages, but doing so doesn't help you make blog visitors into fans, leads, or customers.

The most basic thing you can do for your blog is make sure that you put Google Analytics, at a minimum, on your site.

WordPress is currently one of the more popular and easy-to-set-up site blog tools. Chances are, you already have your blog set up in WordPress or know someone who does who can help you if you get stuck.

First, make sure that you're hosting your blog yourself. You can go to a site like Bluehost (www.BlueHost.com) and sign up for one of its monthly hosting plans (in general, under $10 per month for unlimited domain name hosting) and also purchase your domain name (the yourwebsite.com portion of things).

If you sign up at a service like Bluehost, you can then have it help you install WordPress and get your blog set up. (How to set up WordPress blogs is a topic for *WordPress For Dummies* by Lisa Sabin-Wilson.) After you install WordPress, you're ready to get set up to take measurements of your site and get ongoing snapshots of how it's working (or not) for you.

Adding Google Analytics to a WordPress blog

You can put Google Analytics on your WordPress blog in two ways. I cover the old school way first: Copy some code into your blog's footer page.

1. **Head over to** `http://google.com/analytics` **and enter your Google user name to sign in.**

   Your username is always the Gmail account you use, just like the other Google toys.

2. **Add a new Analytics account.**

   This account will be *yourdomainname.com* — the site you want to track. This step brings you to a page with a bit of JavaScript code.

3. **Copy the entire code showing inside the Tracking Code box into your clipboard.**

4. **Open your WordPress dashboard in another browser tab.**

5. **In the left column, click Appearance.**

6. **Go to the Theme Editor.**

7. **Open the Footer file.**

8. **Carefully scroll down to view the Footer file code and insert the JavaScript you copied form Google Analytics before </body>.**

9. **Save your changes.**

As you can imagine, this method comes with a few risks for the beginning blogger — like accidentally deleting a snippet of code you need. Don't panic — there is another, simpler way that uses plug-ins to do the same thing with less risk.

To use plug-ins to install Google Analytics on your WordPress blog, you need to go back to the tab where you have Google Analytics open.

1. **In your Google Analytics Dashboard, simply click the word Edit next to the URL of the domain name you want to get the code for.**

2. **Copy the code beginning with UA into your clipboard or simply write it down (it's short); then go back to your blog.**

   The code that begins with UA in your Google Analytics ID.

3. **In your blog dashboard, click Plugins in the left column (see Figure 6-1).**

4. **Click Add New in the drop-down menu that appears.**

5. **Use the plug-in search to find the Google Analytics plug-in.**

6. **Click Install gin.**

7. **In the Plugin settings, add your Google Analytics ID.**

   This is the UA-#######-# that you copied or wrote down in Step 2.

8. **Save your changes.**

About 24 hours after doing either of these methods, your analytics will begin tracking. For the first day or so, it will look like nothing is happening — you're new! Give your analytics time (and feed it content), and you'll start to see some action.

Using advanced features of Google Analytics

As you see more action on your site, start exploring some of the unique features of Google Analytics to get the most out of your effort. For example, if you're testing two different site designs, you can quickly use Google's In-Page Analytics tool (see Figure 6-2) to see where people are clicking the most on each site version in a given time frame.

This feedback helps you choose which design is better at converting to sales or leads. When you're working with limited time, the In-Page Analytics tool can remove hours of guesswork from the equation.

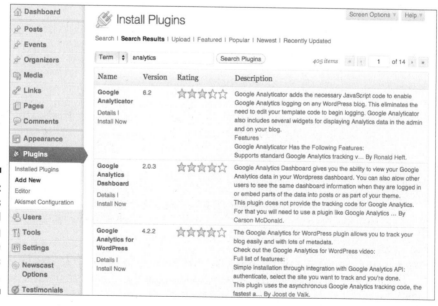

Figure 6-1: WordPress dashboard showing Google Analytics plug-ins.

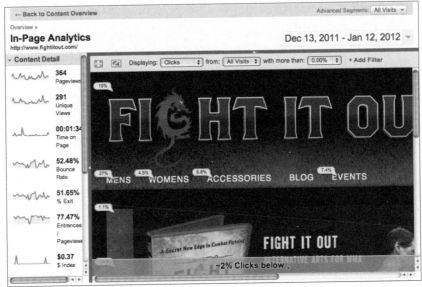

Figure 6-2:
Google
Analytics
In-Page
Analytics
view.

If you're more advanced, you can use Google's Website Optimizer tool for A/B testing instead. However, the ins and outs of that tool are a topic for a different book!

If you're running marketing campaigns or simply trying to raise awareness for a cause, you can use In-Page Analytics to see how well your social shares are performing during the time frame of the promotion, contest, or outreach.

Create your landing pages, share on your social networks using your preferred URL shortener, and then return to In-Page Analytics to see, in near real time, how your campaign is performing. Are people clicking the landing pages, or is the site showing business as usual? If visitors aren't clicking, you can use this knowledge to hone your message from the starting gate.

As you can see in Figure 6-3, which shows a new site design test for Magnitude Media (`http://magnitudemedia.net`), the top navigation bar is getting the most action on the left (Home, Services, and Blog). Because one of the goals was to funnel people to those three areas, I knew the site was getting a good start.

Looking at the other numbers, I could also see where I needed to tweak the design to make it *stickier* (keep people on the site longer). This is a quick-fire use of social media metrics to look at something in near real time and make quick adjustments that help your brand convert better.

Figure 6-3:
In-Page
Analytics
example.

You can see that the individual has the luxury of using some of the instant view features of analytics and more time for manual tracking (to a point).

The organization, however, needs to avoid getting sidetracked by instant metrics and focus on the long-haul tracking that will show them the bigger picture and allow drill down for fine-tuning.

Seeing How Organizations Use Metrics

The organization uses metrics in a different and more automated way than an individual or micro business. With many more branches, topics, staff, divisions, locations, profiles, pages, and sites to track, a manual approach is not time efficient for the larger company.

The command centers for social media monitoring, engagement, and management at companies, such as Dell, are well known. Many tools have enterprise-level solutions at enterprise-level pricing For example, Radian6 has a complex pricing model starting at roughly $600 per month — much more than most individuals want to spend, even on such a useful tool.

Although a business can see good metrics tracking results from manual tracking methods, scaling manual methods to the larger organization is incredibly time consuming. While your larger company is getting its feet wet, you might start off using mostly manual methodology for your listening and brand management information intake.

In addition to Radian6, other companies offering enterprise-level measurement either as their focus or as a part of their overall product or system include Crowd Factory, Alterian SM2, CustomScoop, Spiral16, Meltwater Buzz, MediaVantage (formerly DNA13), IBM Coremetrics, Webtrends, Sysomos, Lithium, Collective Intellect, Attensity360, Awareness, Crimson Hexagon,

Cymfony, and others (see Figure 6-4). Each of these solutions comes in at enterprise-level pricing as well. Expect to spend at least $250 per month on an enterprise solution, and often well into the five and six-figure range for the larger companies out there.

Though the price tag isn't for the faint of heart and may be out of reach of the typical *For Dummies* reader's pocket, as your company grows, you may want to consider budgeting in this type of solution so that you can maximize your time value to dollar spent ratio. An enterprise solution gives you a more ready-made approach than the typical free or manual analytics and metrics approach. Many (though not all) of the typical metrics you need to create campaigns and tracking for will already be a module or app inside these programs.

Shop wisely! All these products offer a demo, which is usually a guided tour given by a sales rep. If you ask, you can usually (but not always) be given 14 to 30 days access to all or part of the tool. Some of the live demo versions are limited, so you may need to combine the sales demo with a short period of access.

Try more than one service. Find the one that is more comfortable for you and your team to use with the features that give you the data you need. This big-ticket item can help your business immensely, so don't be afraid to take your time deciding.

Even after you choose an enterprise-level service keep Google Analytics running in the background so that you can compare data sets and see whether anything is being missed.

Figure 6-4:
Metrics
showing
climate
change
data.

Creating Your Own Listening Dashboard

It's important to craft a metrics dashboard for listening to your brand online. Google Analytics makes it easy for you. As I'm wrapping up this book in spring 2012, Google is rolling out a new version of its Analytics program (see Figure 6-5). As with all Google programs, you can choose which version you like better (old or new) for a long time before Google insists that you upgrade.

In previous chapters, I give instructions using the "old" interface settings. For this chapter, you use your Gmail account login and the new version of Analytics so that I can show you how to take advantage of some interesting new tools.

One thing you'll notice right away is that both Analytics and AdWords have become more socially focused. This is no accident! Social search and engagement have begun to have more and more weight in search results and the overall Internet experience for your customer base and for you. Search engines and metrics programs have added these features to stay competitive. Previously, you could get social data only by setting up your own goals and filters for it. Google Analytics now offers some pre-set social tracking you can take advantage of.

In the following sections, you create several dashboard versions in several services and even dashboards with different focuses within Google Analytics itself.

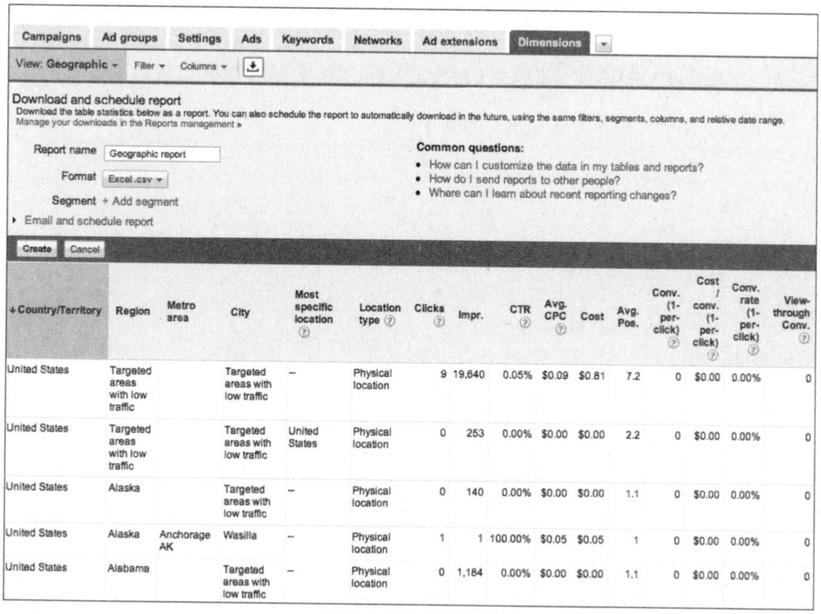

Country/Territory	Region	Metro area	City	Most specific location	Location type	Clicks	Impr.	CTR	Avg. CPC	Cost	Avg. Pos.	Conv. (1-per-click)	Cost / conv. (1-per-click)	Conv. rate (1-per-click)	View-through Conv.
United States	Targeted areas with low traffic		Targeted areas with low traffic	–	Physical location	9	19,640	0.05%	$0.09	$0.81	7.2	0	$0.00	0.00%	0
United States	Targeted areas with low traffic		Targeted areas with low traffic	United States	Physical location	0	253	0.00%	$0.00	$0.00	2.2	0	$0.00	0.00%	0
United States	Alaska		Targeted areas with low traffic	–	Physical location	0	140	0.00%	$0.00	$0.00	1.1	0	$0.00	0.00%	0
United States	Alaska	Anchorage AK	Wasilla	–	Physical location	1	1	100.00%	$0.05	$0.05	1	0	$0.00	0.00%	0
United States	Alabama		Targeted areas with low traffic	–	Physical location	0	1,184	0.00%	$0.00	$0.00	1.1	0	$0.00	0.00%	0

Figure 6-5: Google AdWords and Analytics reporting using Dimensions.

Adding widgets to the Dashboard

The first thing you need to do is make a list of possible goals for each dashboard to focus on. This list isn't be set in stone — it's just a starting point. You can then add widgets to each one that support your goals and give you the information you need to move forward on them and adjust them as needed.

You'll have a more generic dashboard as well, one that you (most likely) will check more often than the others. Google Analytics provides a pretty comprehensive one for you out of the box. You can choose to leave it as is or add widgets to include other data you think is important to follow daily, weekly, or monthly.

The first way to customize a Google Analytics Dashboard in the new layout is to add quick widgets to your main Analytics Home page, default titled My Dashboard:

1. **Log in to your Analytics account.**

2. **Click the URL (domain name) of the site you want to set up.**

3. **Next to the *domainname.com* [DEFAULT] marker in the upper left, click the Home link.**

4. **Review the contents in the Home window and remove anything not relevant to your needs**

   These windows of information are called *widgets.*

5. **To add more or different content, click the Add Widget button.**

   The Add a Widget dialog box, shown in Figure 6-6, appears.

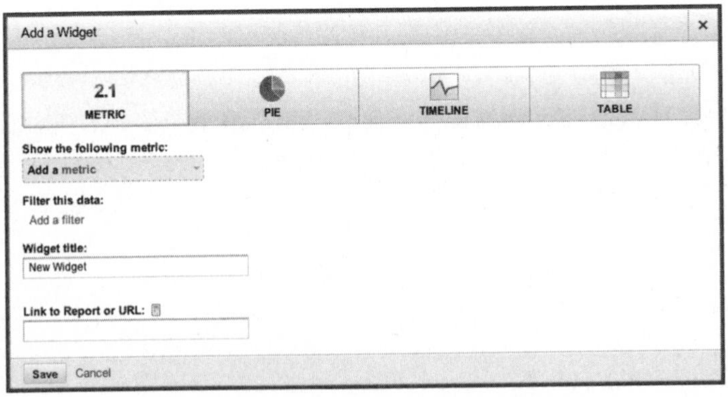

Figure 6-6:
You can choose which type of widget you'd like to add.

6. **Choose the type of widget you want to add.**

   Your choices include metric, pie, timeline, or table.

7. **Fill in the information requested.**

   You need to choose a metric type, a URL to track or a report to link to, and so on.

8. **Click Save to save your widget.**

9. **Repeat the preceding steps until you've added all the basic widgets to your dashboard.**

 You can make several dashboards for different goals, so you don't have to cram every metric that you want to track into one window. This window is meant to be your overview of daily or weekly metrics that you can glance at quickly.)

Creating additional dashboards

The second customization of your Google Analytics Dashboard in the new layout is to create additional dashboards. That way, My Dashboard continues to function as your main quick-look location, and you can refer to narrower dashboards for custom tasks and custom tracking.

To create additional dashboards:

1. **Log in to your Analytics account.**

2. **Click the URL (domain name) of the site you want to set up.**

3. **Next to the *domainname.com* [DEFAULT] marker in the upper left, click the Home link.**

4. **In the Home window, click the word Dashboard in the left sidebar.**

5. **In the drop-down menu that appears, click +New Dashboard.**

   The Create Dashboard dialog box, shown in Figure 6-7, appears. You can title your new dashboard and choose a blank canvas to start or a pre-set series of widgets.

6. **Choose the blank canvas option.**

   That way, you can add your own widgets and customize your new dashboard to your goal.

7. **Name your new dashboard something relevant to your goal and click Create Dashboard.**

In the next window, you get a chance to add your first metric, choosing from metric, pie, timeline, or table.

8. **Choose which type of metric you'd like to add and set your parameters.**

   Feel free to play around here until you see what you like — don't be afraid to toggle metrics on and off or delete a metric that doesn't work like you thought it would.

   If you're looking for metric ideas, you can try creating something like a Table metric for the most popular pages on your site. For this, open the new widget window and select Table. Choose Pages, Visit, % Exit as your columns. Make the table six rows and call it Top Content. Save it, and you're all set!

9. **Continue adding widgets until you have a complete metrics picture for your goal.**

10. **Repeat Steps 1 through 9 for each dashboard you'd like to create.**

Figure 6-7:
You can create a dashboard from scratch or use one that comes with a pre-set series of widgets.

Create dashboard	✕
Blank Canvas	Starter Dashboard
Untitled Dashboard	Create Dashboard Cancel

Creating a dashboard when you're using other systems

What if you have a system in place that isn't Google Analytics or adds on to Google Analytics using another tool or tools? You're still going to need a dashboard to collect your data for easy viewing.

The simplest solution is to create a spreadsheet to use as a home base for your data. You can set Google Analytics to export each report you create as a .csv. You can add that .csv file (and a .csv file from any other analytics program you're running) to your spreadsheet. You can sort your spreadsheet by site, program, goal, keyword, and more. You may find over time that you create more than one spreadsheet or data grouping, as your metrics get more and more complex and useful.

Knowing When to Listen and When to Talk

A calendar is going to be an essential part of your arsenal as well as your spreadsheet(s). You can find useful metrics tracking by date, time of day, holiday, and time of year. Date tracking helps you discover when your audience is engaging with you, when your goals and campaigns are having the most traction, when your conversions spike, and more.

In fact, applying your date metrics to a calendar of engagement and a calendar of listening is key. You won't find useful date metrics in the short term. Expect it to take anywhere from one month minimum to three months before you start seeing useful date metrics over time.

Look for patterns over time. Is your audience made up of early risers? Perhaps you get more attention for your content from folks surfing the net during the middle of the day at work. When do people talk most to or about your brand? Are there times of day where listening and collecting metrics data will deliver more information than others?

Incorporate your competition into the date metrics you're doing. Use that competitive intelligence to structure your next launch or campaign or simply to decide when to become more visible in any given day for the purpose of building your own business.

As you use spreadsheets and calendar layouts to build a mental picture of the best times to talk versus the best times to listen, you may find that visualizing these times even further using an infographic or GANTT chart is helpful.

After you've done your research and gathered metrics on date and time for optimum use, use these metrics to compile an engagement calendar. An *engagement calendar* is a plan that tells you (and anyone helping you communicate and listen in on your online presences) when to engage on each platform, including your blog and social media, and when to listen. It also serves as a reminder to keep your engagement consistent and useful because you can add topic suggestions based on content metrics as well.

Brands that plan ahead and include some scheduled interactions based on metrics along with their more organic posts and replies find greater success in the online market place. Search engine results are more and more heavily weighted by how well you perform in the social sphere. It's not just about how much attention you have (number of fans or followers) but about how well you get them involved, engaged, and enthusiastic about what you do.

Comparing DIY Metrics to Metrics Systems

There is a bit of debate still about whether or not a fully automated metrics system is the best way to go. There is still a lot of "hope" and "kumbaya" bandied about in social media and online marketing. Hope and kumbaya are great — you definitely want that emotional engagement with your brand — but hope is not a business model. You also have to have a plan.

DIY metrics are an essential part of measuring your success online, but they can't be your only metrics measurement. You'll have days (or sometimes weeks) where you are too busy to maintain DIY metrics systems. You may not have staff trained to pick up your system for you when you travel or are sick. Your computer may break and need to be out a week for repairs. You absolutely must have an automated metrics systems, even if it's just one of the free ones, in place.

By allowing automated metrics systems to run in the background, you're catching and sorting data so that you can be free to do the work and make the connections that will make your business grow. Then you can visit the data and use it to make your work better. It's that simple. DIY metrics come in handy for tracking things the automated metrics don't yet track.

Chapter 7

Creating Content for Conversion

In This Chapter

▶ Making content compelling

▶ Looking at hidden content metrics

▶ Remembering to track multimedia content

▶ Following your content as it's shared

*I*n this chapter, I talk about a variety of different ways to make amazing content without burning up your time and how you can track that content and the conversations and interactions that take shape around it. Tracking shared content can be a bit tricky now that conversations happen everywhere people are, not within the confines of your blog or site, but you can do it.

Recognizing Compelling, Shareable Content

I would argue that much of the battle for great metrics starts with great content. Even if you run an ecommerce site or a static site and not a blog, you still need to view everything on it as potentially shareable content and think of ways to use it for two-way metrics.

What are *two-way metrics?* Tracking content as it's shared from your site, including those off-site conversations that may lead to conversion, and tracking incoming metrics to see what parts of your site convert, compel, or repel your visitors.

If you've been around the Internet at all the last few years, you've heard people bandy about the terms SEO (search engine optimization), SMO (social media optimization), keywords, meta tags, and the like. All of these long-standing tactics for getting people to find your content are still valid, but the way they're used has changed dramatically with the rise of social tools like Twitter, Google+, and Facebook.

A solid rule used to be that using your keywords in your content would help your content rise to the top quickly (and in many cases, make it sound incredibly awkward upon reading). Stuffing your page with keywords is less important than creating good content people want to read, watch, or listen to now.

Finding your content comfort zone

To create compelling content, the first thing you need to do is find your *content comfort zone*. Because creating content takes time and time is at a premium for any business owner or freelancer, you need to find the medium you're most confident in that you can execute well and quickly.

Obviously, my chosen medium is the written word, but yours may be video, photographs, or perhaps an audio podcast. If you create content with video, photos, or audio elements, you still need a little of the written word to help people find you and see what your content is all about.

A good title and a short description are key for each piece of content you create, as are no more than ten tag words. These elements help with the old school search engine crawlers that look for you based on keyword criteria.

Here are a few more things to remember about creating compelling content:

- ✔ Keep it short.
- ✔ Keep it simple.
- ✔ Make it interesting, new, useful, or fun.
- ✔ Use keywords (but don't sound like a robot!).
- ✔ Track everything.
- ✔ Have one call to action in each piece of content.

Figuring out how to share your content

After you have good content and a few good words, how you share it becomes important. You can set your content to track by title and a variety of other criteria in your analytics program if you host it on your blog, but what if you want to create a lot of videos? Videos take a lot of bandwidth, and hosting them yourself may not be financially feasible.

If you need to host your multimedia content elsewhere and then embed it on your blog, where you host it becomes important.

YouTube is great for hosting videos for a variety of reasons:

- ✔ It's currently free.
- ✔ It has built in analytics.
- ✔ It's owned by Google so it works well with Google Analytics.
- ✔ It's very trackable by other analytics programs, such as Radian6.
- ✔ It has discovery options that allow you to somewhat restrict your links (private, unlisted, and public).

SlideShare (free) is great for hosting slides, presentations, PDFs, and other content you may want to store elsewhere due to size and then embed on your blog. SlideShare Pro (paid) also has analytics built in, as well as lead generation, which allows you to track real-time leads generated from content as well.

Following Your Content with URL Shorteners

Don't forget to follow your content because social is now a large part of search results for people. Search results from all major search engines give weight to content that is getting a high social score due to being talked about or shared on social sites like Twitter, YouTube, Google+, Delicious, Reddit, StumbleUpon, Tumblr, Pinterest, and others.

A great way to follow content is to use an URL shortener that includes metrics. A *URL shortener* is exactly what it sounds like — a service that makes the link to your content smaller and easier to share on social networks. Layered on top of your other analytics solutions, a URL shortener gives you a way to follow a link as it's carried off of your site through conversation. It helps you find and engage with your customers and potential customers no matter where they're talking about your content.

One example of a great URL shortener is Bit.ly. Bit.ly allows custom links, which makes each link easy to remember and share. It also tracks your link as it travels online and then delivers information to you about who is engaging with that link and sharing it further.

You can choose from many URL shorteners. (In fact, we covered quite a few in another Wiley book — *Twitter For Dummies,* which I wrote with Laura Fitton and Michael Gruen!) Bit.ly is just one example. Whichever one you like best, make sure that it has analytics and make sure that you remember to create campaigns to track the original URL and the shortened URL (a campaign group) in your site's analytics program.

As you can see, getting good metrics to study and use requires a many-layered approach. Your web site is your home base and the spot on the web that you own and control, so you should be directing all traffic there. However, it's a social web, so you have to be prepared to follow your content and grab those metrics wherever they go.

Seeking Out Hidden Content Metrics

Tracking content requires you do a bit of stealth thinking. If you make the tracking obvious, the content won't be good, and people won't come back for more — one hit wonders are fine, but you want those visitors and shares to convert into leads, sales, supporters, or enthusiastic fans, not just wander off.

Hidden content metrics may be a strange way to think about it, but you can get information back from anything you put out into the web, if you set it up correctly. For example, the comment system you use on your blog matters.

Some comment systems offer social sharing, a feature you want, but you also want them to either offer their own metrics tracking or integrate with your URL shortener of choice so that you can track those shares. A favorite in my office is Disqus for its social shares, mention tracking, and integration with Bit.ly.

Using your *permalinks* (the links that lead users to a specific post) matters as well. If you're a WordPress user, then you're familiar with its date and number-based default links. Having a link that is `http://yourdomain.com/?123` doesn't help you find and track your content. Going into your WordPress settings and changing the default post link to end with the title of your post is much smarter and makes your links more metrics-friendly.

Use trackable links for things you link to inside your content as well. If you're going to link to a source, tag it with a Bit.ly link so that you can see how many people were interested in that source and what happened with the sharing.

Use full titles, descriptions, alternate text, captions, and image tags for images and photos. (This not only helps your metrics tracking, it helps you come up in more image search results.) Make sure to have a featured image that shows up when the content is shared if it's a written post. (In fact, every written post should have a trackable image in it.) Be sure to include `alt` tags in the image (right-click the image and add the tags in the Advanced section of the image edit window that pops up).

If you use PDFs, you can do a lot of interesting things with the files to track their metrics. (Unfortunately, this functionality is often used by malcontents to spread malware or viruses via PDF, so you may find that choosing PDFs to enclose tracking data causes a drop in attention.) If you use them sparingly, you can use PDFs to not only track metrics and follow shares and open rates and more, but also for lead generation through embedded forms and other multimedia content.

Layering your content helps as well. For example, you can easily imitate a SlideShare Pro feature in a PDF or video file. You can insert a lead-qualifying screen that asks for contact info at the halfway point (or end point) of your slides. This technique converts well and is a fairly non-intrusive tactic for voluntary information gathering from self-identifying customers.

Audio content can be a bit tricky for metrics. In the case of audio files, it's fairly simple to track the page where the file is hosted, but if someone manages to download the file, it's easy to lose track of it. If you're strong in programming, you can embed some tracking in the audio file format (similar to what they do for DRM or for the track and album information that you see in iTunes when you select Get More Info on a file. You can also choose to use a service such as Blubrry (www.blubrry.com), libsyn (http://libsyn.com), or Podtrac (http://podtrac.com) for recording audio that tracks this information for you.

Trying to use hidden metrics is a great reason to learn some basic coding as well. You can create many hidden metrics that would make this a totally different book. You can find fantastic, free online resources for learning to code, including free online courses from Stanford (http://see.stanford.edu/default.aspx) and MIT (http://ocw.mit.edu/index.htm), but my current favorite is Codecademy (www.codecademy.com) — it makes learning code fun. Wherever you start, learning code will make doing advanced metrics work easier (and have other benefits for your business as well).

Tracking Video, Audio, and Photo Metrics

One of the big challenges of the social Internet is tracking video, audio, and photo content to see how they work for you.

One of the best ways to track metrics of your creative, multimedia content starts with your hosting choice. It's not often that people can afford to host their own multimedia content, especially video, because it can lead to expenses related to increased bandwidth and storage. It's important to host elsewhere and embed video in a site you own, but what other solutions are out there for someone who doesn't want to do that?

You want to track everything, but you need to be able to sort through what's important to know. What's important to know will change over time. Metrics help you keep up (and, in fact, stay ahead!).

Looking at hosting choices

If you don't need a branded website — or simply don't have the budget for hosting, even at the current reasonable hosting rates out there — then Tumblr is a great resource for photo blogs and audio content. Tumblr is also great for sharing the content of others and makes the blogging experience more social.

Tumblr has some great tools to give your blog style, but more importantly, it integrates with (you guessed it) Google Analytics. (You're probably beginning to see why Google Analytics is a favorite tool — hundreds of sites and tools integrate with it.) Tumblr also uses URL slugs, XML sitemaps (good for search crawlers), and other features to ensure that your content is analytics friendly.

If you're a photo blogger who uses Flickr to host your photos, Flickr finally introduced its own metrics for photographs (see Figure 7-1). These analytics not only track views but calculate "interestingness" and other values and also integrate the Creative Commons licensing guidelines right into the site so that you can more easily prohibit (or allow) distribution of your photos.

Figure 7-1: Sample of Flickr analytics on an image of a tattoo.

Google's Picasa has some interesting applications for photo bloggers as the service grows up, the most important of which being its integration into Google+ and (soon) more deeply into Google Analytics. Additionally, Flickr has a charge for exceeding a certain amount of bandwidth, but Picasa is currently free. Picasa is not as user-friendly as Flickr, however. If you're not an experienced user, you may experience a longer learning curve — this "getting started guide" may help:

```
http://support.google.com/picasa/bin/answer.
          py?hl=en&answer=157000
```

 Facebook is trying to place itself into a position to be your website replacement, offering Insights for pages and other features and making changes to its site that promote photo sharing, blogging, and other deep content. Definitely learn to read and use your Facebook analytics, but my advice is to host your content on your website and embed the link on Facebook. You'll still get the benefit of Insight tracking without the risk of hosting your content on Facebook (Facebook has rights to use your content if it's hosted there, even without your permission).

An interesting point regarding multimedia content is that bandwidth is a metric in its own right. It can tell you important information, such as popular times and days for viewing or listening to your content, and, in fact, track growth in popularity overall. Measuring bandwidth is also key for self-hosted content, as it will prevent you from exceeding your bandwidth allotment and thus getting your site shut down temporarily by your host.

Tracking downloads

Another set of multimedia metrics to track are downloads. How many PDFs, photos, videos, or audio files with a link to be downloaded were actually downloaded in a given time frame?

How many downloads were started and then stopped and how far people got in the process can tell you whether your site is slow, you need to address a problem, or your content isn't compelling enough for sharing.

Taking a Look at Shared Content Metrics

Shared content metrics are given a lot of importance right now in the social web space. On the social web, sharing is a given.

Gone are the days when people wanted to visit or promote a website with locked-down content. If they see something of value (or, judging by my RSS feed sometimes, anything cute and furry like a kitten), they immediately want to tell everyone they know to go look at it.

In fact, people want to be the first to tell people they know to go look at it and the source everyone else uses to share it as well. In the social web, being the source for something that goes viral holds a sort of mental cachet for people.

Google has capitalized on this trend in Google+ with its metrics for that sharing platform, Ripples. Ripples gives people sharing and interacting with content on Google+ an immediate, gorgeous visual of the strength of that content being shared in Google.

Figure 7-2 shows an example from a piece of content shared by actor Wil Wheaton that dramatically shows how far a post can go.

What's interesting about Ripples from a metrics standpoint is its obvious future implications for Google's other metrics tool, Analytics, and its potential future application to shared content on the web. However, at the time of this writing, you still need to share content on sites like Google+ with a trackable link as well so that you can bring it in to your metrics dashboard.

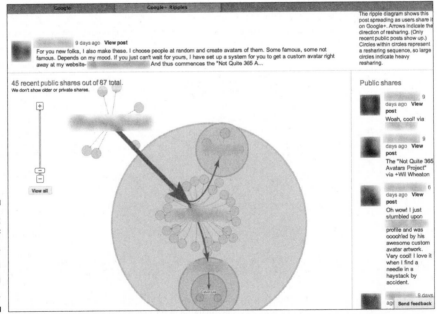

Figure 7-2:
Sample of
Google+
Ripples on a
Wil Wheaton
post.

The Social Metrics plug-in for WordPress users (see Figure 7-3) has been a standby way to get a quick per-post snapshot of how people are sharing your blog content. It helps you quickly see what kinds of content your visitors find most compelling so that you can deliver more of that type of content. It lays the content and share numbers out in an easy-to-read grid for you.

Interestingly, Google, in its continuing bid to be the number one source for pretty much everything online, has introduced social as a component of its new Google Analytics. The social analytics it tracks tell you deep data about who is coming to content from which social sites and how they're interacting with your content socially while there (see Figure 7-4). It's setting itself up to be much more than just a simple count of shares and will become a valuable deep metrics resource for you.

Other shared content numbers include how many times your content has been shared on sites like Reddit, StumbleUpon, Twitter (via RT button or Favorite clicks), Google+ (via the +1 button or Ripples), Facebook likes, LinkedIn shares, and more.

You can easily get distracted by those numbers, but they only measure the moment someone found your content shareable. They're great vanity numbers that fuel inconsequential things like Klout scores, but as a standalone metric, the number of shares doesn't tell you much without other information. In short: Number of shares is only a small part of your metrics dashboard.

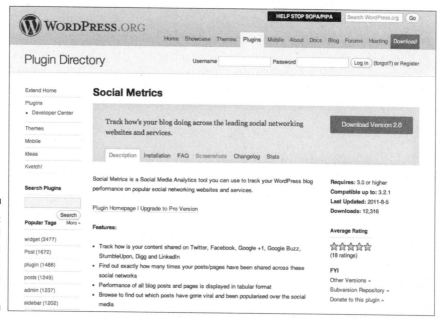

Figure 7-3: Social Metrics plug-in installation screen.

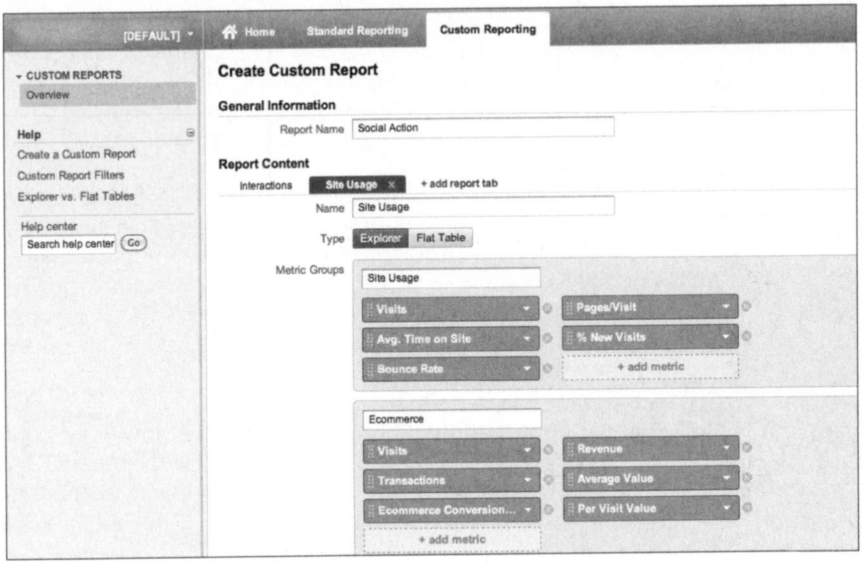

Figure 7-4:
Setting up
a Social
Action
report in
Google
Analytics.

Social sharing is also the easiest number to inflate. All it takes is using a set of services that encourage social sharing, such as Disqus comments, Tumblr blogs, or plug-ins like AddToAny, and you'll see your numbers climb simply because you made it easy to click a button. It's what folks do when they get to your site that matters, and that's where having deeper metrics will come in to play.

Social sharing numbers are important to note when you start tracking the advanced analytics like day splitting, phone call tracking (yes, you can track phone call analytics!), and more. The number of +1 shares, for example, may not mean anything by itself other than that someone found your content interesting enough to share, but combined with everything else you are track-ing, such as referral pages, time on site, exit pages, interactions and clicks on site, hot spots, date and time data, country and browser information and more — you can create some compelling informational stories around this simple click to share data.

Part III
Putting Your Metrics on Steroids

The 5th Wave   By Rich Tennant

"You know it dawned on me last night why we aren't getting any hits on our Facebook page."

In this part . . .

After your social media metrics dashboard is set up and you understand the tools available to you, you're ready to dive in to the nuts and bolts.

This part talks about the foundation of good metrics and offers tips and techniques used by metrics rock stars to lay their foundations for success.

This part helps you build a base for metrics that will allow you to grow exponentially and navigate any changes in metrics that may come up as social media changes over time.

Chapter 8

Becoming a Metrics Guru

*I*t's totally natural to want to jump ahead to the fun stuff and skip the hard work of setting up a great foundation. I can tell you that trying to come back and add the foundation later is more work than just starting off on the right foot in the first place, though!

In this chapter, I go over the features you need to have in place. I also talk about what you need to know to run a great metrics dashboard and get the deepest picture possible of your site and your content and how it's all working for you and for your brand.

I cover protocols and best practices along with the nitty-gritty of tracking, conversion, metrics language, and abbreviations. I also show you how to get a handle on how often to check your metrics for each campaign, how to use your metrics history to your advantage, and how to use metrics in unusual places, such as your RSS feed. I also discuss looking for metrics patterns.

If you read this chapter, you should leave with the ability to create and run an intermediate-level metrics dashboard.

Following Metrics Protocols

Best practices and protocols are always a touchy subject. Best practices, especially, can differ from individual to individual and medium to medium.

For example, clear rules govern e-mail campaigns to help prevent spam, and these rules include metrics.

After someone has opted in to your e-mail campaign, acceptable e-mail metrics include

✔ Acquisition (subscription)

✔ Behavior (open and click rate, bounce rate, unsubscribe rate)

✔ Outcomes (retaining subscribers, reaching goals, conversion rates)

You can find similar goals in social media metrics (and, in fact, I would argue that e-mail is a form of social media that should be included in your metrics dashboard). E-mail metric measurement has best practices as well — notice how the e-mail metrics rules don't allow invasive practices? You should apply that noninvasive policy everywhere — don't be invasive or predatory when gathering your metrics data.

The first part of your metrics protocol should be determining whether the metrics you're tracking are right for you and for what you and your brand need to know to effect positive results. While Parts I and II advocate "measure everything," the amount of data pouring in is enormous. You then need to use best practices and protocols to sort that data into what you really need to know to fine-tune your dashboard. The following sections walk you through some tests to help with that process.

Action testing

Over time, take each new metric and put it to the test of action. If you have a high exit rate on three pages, for example, first take a look at the pages and see whether you can tweak the content or improve the layout. Track the metric a while longer; if it doesn't improve, think about what it means. If everyone must exit your site at some point, does that metric matter? If it isn't important to you, relegate that metric to the "track once in a while to make sure that the site is working" pile and move your attention elsewhere.

Another example is a PPC (pay-per-click) campaign (see Figure 8-1). If you're doing segmented analytics, you'll be able to quickly see the metrics from organic search terms and the metrics from your PPC campaign and tell whether your campaign is working. If it isn't, you can save yourself money by ending that campaign. If it is, you know to funnel more money to that campaign. This metric can lead directly to conversion and sales on your site, so it's important to keep it in your dashboard.

Competitive Analysis Tools	Monthly	Kws	Bids	Share	Text Ads	Display Ads	Traffic
AdGooroo	$$$	X	X	X	X	X	X
Compete	$$$	X	X	X	X		X
iSpionage.com	$$	X	X	X	X		X
Keyword Competitor	$$	X	X	X	X		X
Keyword Spy	$$	X	X	X	X		X
SPYFU	$$	X	X	X	X		X
Comscore	$$,$$$	X	X	X			X
Hitwise	$$,$$$	X		X			X
Keyword Discovery Tools							
Wordtracker	$$	X	X	X			X
Google Adwords Keyword Tool		X	X	X			X
Microsoft Desktop Tool		X	X	X			X
Rapid Keyword	$	X					X
WordStream	$$$	X	X				X

Figure 8-1:
Pay-per-click
campaign
metrics.

Attention testing

By attention testing, I don't mean the attention of your site visitors or social media connections — though time on page and other similar metrics may be important to your brand. I mean testing *your* attention.

You should be able to monitor and analyze your metrics in about an hour a day for most brands. (If you're a large company like Ford, this won't be the case, but if you're Ford, you also have the awesome Scott Monty, enterprise tools, and a staff and are not this book's target market!) That amount of time may seem too short after you see how much data the social web willingly gives up for your analytical pleasure, but the first test — action — should help narrow down that data.

If you're spending too much time on analytics study, you aren't putting those analytics to work for you or your brand and you aren't spending enough time on converting those numbers to profit. Without profit, you don't stay in business, so it's important to reach balance.

Nonmetrics measurement (value) testing

The interesting thing about social media is that it offers a variety of metrics not related to click rates and online search results. Part of your protocol should be periodic tests to see whether you're delivering value or simply behaving like an advertisement.

Measure the number of comments your blog generates, the number of replies for your tweets, the comments (not the likes) under your Facebook posts, and the thread of discussion around Google+ shares. Measure the reach of these discussions. Are the posts and content items not only being discussed, but being reshared other places and discussed there also?

If your posts generate engagement, then you can begin to convert that to loyal customers, fans, and brand awareness by getting to know your customers on a much deeper level than by simply tracking what pages they visit on your site or which ad they clicked. It's a manual measurement still at the time of this writing, but I'm sure someone is working on an app for that.

Take a look at the social monetary value metric of your social sharing also. This one requires a combination of nonmetrics measurement of social shares and referrals and micro- and macro-tracking goals in your analytics program. I look at how to set these programs up in Part IV, but for now, it's possible to put a monetary value on this combination of metrics, which can help you budget your social media efforts.

Permission testing

People in the social web space give you plenty of information for free as a trade-off for using various social sites and performing actions on the web itself.

Run checks and balances on all your social media metrics and social media outreach and campaigns to constantly make sure that you're exercising permission-based marketing principals.

In short, track everything, but don't use black hat tactics to invade the privacy of others or perform other nefarious actions on your unsuspecting customer or potential customer.

Roadmap testing

Every metrics dashboard should also have a metrics and marketing roadmap behind it. Clearly define your business objectives and the steps needed to reach each one so that you know where your metrics fit along the way.

Constantly refer to this roadmap to see how your metrics are performing. How are the KPI (key performance indicators) you identified doing? Do they need adjusting to match the goals and overall objective? Did you determine how to tell whether you were successful? Every campaign needs milestones. Did you set up segmenting in your campaign and metrics so that you can get a clear vision of what went right or wrong?

Having these items in place is key to the success of your metrics (see Figure 8-2). It also assists you in involving your boss and coworkers in the process, which helps you budget in metrics and marketing and get better cooperation to the group's goals overall.

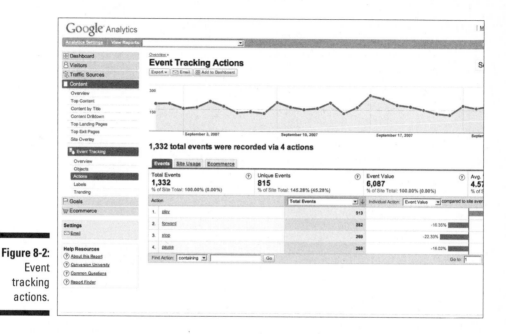

Figure 8-2:
Event
tracking
actions.

In the end, you determine your own best practices and protocols that work for you and your brand, but this short list should get you started. As you develop your best practices and protocols, I'd suggest making them into a manual or roadmap guide that everyone you work with can access. It helps clarify the role of metrics across the organization.

Getting Familiar with Metrics Language and Abbreviations

The world of social media, the social web, and metrics seems to come with its own language. Without turning the chapter into a glossary or full-fledged dictionary, I thought I'd quickly cover some terms you'll continue to hear and see the most while navigating social media metrics:

✓ **Analytics:** The catchall phrase for the data gathered from people viewing and interacting with your website or a piece of content that you have shared in social media, such as IP address, location, page views, conversions, and so on.

✓ **Bandwidth:** Can refer to the amount of data being served by your web host (for example, a regular video download uses bandwidth, but a high-quality video download uses more bandwidth) or to the amount of attention your customer has to give your content and engagement.

✔ **Bounce rate:** When a visitor to your website leaves after only viewing a single page, it's a *bounce.* Your bounce rate is a number reflecting the percentage of all visitors who leave after only viewing a single page in a given time frame.

✔ **Business objectives:** A list of goals and objectives set down in writing for a company to achieve, often going hand in hand with a written mission or brand statement.

✔ **Conversion:** A procedure web visitors complete on your website that leads to new business, sales leads, product sold, items downloaded, or other voluntary acts beyond simply viewing the site.

✔ **Dayparting:** Using analytics data to figure out what day(s) of the week and time of day your site (or ad) gets the most conversions and then optimizing accordingly (see Figure 8-3).

✔ **Goals:** A statement of business intent. For example "I want to make more money" is a hope, not a goal. "I want to seat 15 percent more people this month using online ads" is a goal.

✔ **Key Performance Indicator(s) (KPI):** Parameters intended to measure the business and marketing goals you set.

✔ **Macro conversion:** The measurement of an outcome from a site visit (for example, a purchase).

✔ **Micro conversion**: The measurement of the incremental steps that may lead to a macro conversion (for example, printing a product page, which may show intent to purchase in store; or printing directions, which can indicate the same thing).

✔ **Opt-in:** Often called permission marketing, requires your potential customer to opt in to how they want their data used (or not used).

✔ **Pay-per-click (PPC):** Internet advertising model in which advertisers only pay the ad host when the ad is clicked.

✔ **Search crawler:** Sometimes called a *spider,* is the search engine's automated program that surfs the web by leaping from one `href` link to another and tracking the links to provide search results.

✔ **Search Engine Optimization (SEO):** Using keywords, content, and other tactics to improve how well a site appears in natural, organic search results.

✔ **Segmentation:** Targeting your marketing efforts and analytics results by particular criteria, such as age, location, income, referring site, or browser.

✔ **Social Media Optimization (SMO):** Sometimes known as social SEO, uses targeted social media engagement to bring new visitors and attention to a website and its content.

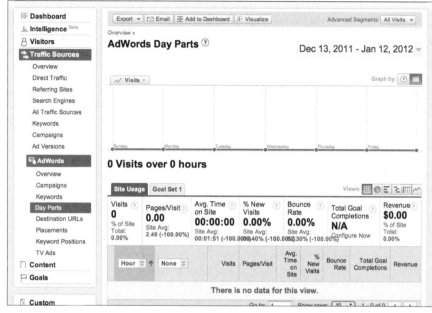

Figure 8-3:
Dayparting
looks like
this in your
Analytics.

Tracking and Converting

Sometimes folks get stymied by the data that pours in as their online efforts start to show results. You can easily get bogged down in the piles of information coming in — especially at first, before you've fine-tuned your dashboards.

One way to get a handle on things is to remember that you don't want to simply be tracking your metrics; you also want to be converting. Tracking and converting go hand in hand — one complements the other. Don't get me wrong; it's not as simple as throwing a switch, but you will have an easier time knowing what to track if your goal of conversion is always in the back of your mind.

Using In-Page Analytics

One of my favorite Google Analytics tools for changing your thinking to a track and convert model instead of a simple track-it-all model is In-Page Analytics. You find In-Page Analytics under the Content section of the Standard Reporting tab.

Clicking In-Page Analytics brings up your website and a snapshot of where people are clicking on each page. If you're tracking to convert, In-Page Analytics gives a nice, quick look into how well your site is designed. Better UI (user interface) leads to more click-throughs. More click-throughs (successful calls-to-action) lead to more conversions.

The first key to using metrics to convert is to identify which metrics are actionable. By putting your metrics to the test from Chapter 6, you can quickly determine the answer to this question.

Analyzing your sales funnel

After you've narrowed down the metrics, you can begin to analyze where your visitors leave your *sales funnel*. (An example of a sales funnel for an ecommerce site is category page view to product page view to shopping cart view to purchase.) You can see an example in Figure 8-4.

If you notice in your metrics that you have a lot of folks abandon their shopping cart, you know that you can adjust something about the shopping cart program to possibly keep them on site. If you notice people jump out of the funnel in the product page view, you can use metrics to fine-tune those pages to have better calls-to-action to get people to the shopping cart section of your funnel.

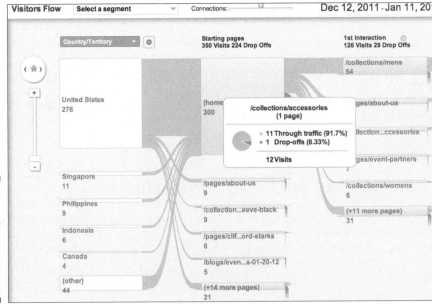

Figure 8-4:
Google
Visitor Flow
view lets
you envision
your sales
funnel traffic.

What if you have a lot of folks make it into the purchase portion of the funnel, but they're only one-time customers purchasing small-ticket items? In that case, you'd use your metrics data to help redesign your website UI to act more like a supermarket: designed to make things easy to find, but also to lead people to buy more than they came to the store for.

Better metrics tracking also allows you to use your social media engagement to find out why something isn't working. If you've developed a relationship with your customers, you can dig deeper into why they aren't doing as much with your site as you'd hoped. Your customers can give you valuable feedback on form length, UI, shopping experience, branding, and more, from their point of view.

When you're thinking of tracking data and conversion at the same time, your website, web content, and social media marketing becomes a powerful tool. Thinking of both allows you to cut through the noise of the other folks generating content out there. Use your metrics data to drive better customers your way through better web and social media efforts.

Listening Frequency

I talk about how much time to spend listening in Chapter 6, but it's important to reiterate here: It's tempting to spend vast amounts of time listening to and studying your metrics data, especially after you figure out how it can help you narrow your sales funnel quickly and make your content and site better overall.

Don't forget, however, that you still need to give your customers good service! One of the things you'll begin to track on social media metrics is sentiment. *Sentiment* is the emotional aftertaste left by your brand after a customer interacts with it. You want this feeling to be positive as often as possible!

You'll be able to tell whether you're spending too much time on the tweaking and not enough time on the service or product you offer if the sentiment surrounding your brand begins to decline. Google Analytics doesn't track sentiment, but many other programs, including Radian6, do.

You can also maximize your listening time by maximizing your metrics. Dayparting, segmentation, sentiment tracking, *eye tracking* (if you have the means, you can actually track what parts of your site visitors view most, and when, and then follow where their eyes go on the page), click tracking, comparison data — all these things lead to better understanding your customer. The company who knows their customer best and delivers what they need wins the war for the customer's attention.

Using Your Metrics History

One of the best tools in your arsenal is the ability to compare data across time with most analytics tools. If you read Chapter 1, you took a baseline of your metrics, and it comes in handy over time as you compare where you are to where you were.

As you're tracking your business metrics over time, you'll begin to get some interesting meta data (such as being able to see your performance over the Christmas holidays for the last four years, right down to the times of day and hours that folks came to your site).

You can also compare subsets of micro data, such as measuring the clicks on your call-to-action newsletter subscription button that came from Facebook fans that entered from your page this month versus two months ago when you introduced it.

The default comparison view of many metrics tools is month to month (so they may have a default that allows you to compare the 30 days that are current with the 30 days prior, for example). That comparison is useful, especially if you're trying to

✔ Fine-tune your blog posts to quickly become more sticky and need to see short bursts of recent data to do so.

✔ Grow a site out quickly so that you can rapidly move to engage and keep new segments of your market as they find you.

If you're building a business, however, you need to take the longer view. Instead of going for the quick data and quick fix, take a look at your real long tail data over time. Look at your dashboards over time and see what the data you've saved tells you about how your business and customers have changed, and use that knowledge to adjust so that you can attract more long-term customers that will help your business succeed.

Turn on comparison data by default. If you're seeing the comparison consistently, you'll be more likely to see data that will help you increase conversions.

Finding Metrics for Feeds

Great metrics tools for feeds (I'm specifically referring to RSS [Real Simple Syndication] feeds here) are hard to come by. Though feeds are widely used to keep up with news and content, even in the age of the tablet, getting the open data on a feed has been hit or miss. (I talk about how the tablet and mobile surfing is changing metrics in Chapter 9.)

FeedBurner, bought by Google, was one of the best ways to run a feed with analytics attached, and it integrated their AdSense program to help you make a bit of money off of your feed. Google recently announced that it wouldn't be developing for FeedBurner anymore, however. It doesn't sound like Google will kill FeedBurner, so it may still work for some time, but Google won't be developing for it, which means it might break, which is too bad. Use with caution for that reason. (*Note:* I am still a happy FeedBurner user at the time of this writing.)

Other feed metrics programs that have had some success besides FeedBurner include Pheedo (`http://site.pheedo.com`), FeedBlitz (`www.feedblitz.com`), and BBU's RSS Feed Campaign Tagger plug-in for WordPress. (A mouthful, this last one lets you tag your feed links so that you can catch them in analytics programs if you don't use FeedBurner.)

The two basic metrics for feeds that most services measure are number of subscribers and number of clicks. Using tags and other methods can get you even farther with other programs. Having a call-to-action in your feed also helps you convert, and you can definitely track conversions.

FeedBurner allows you to put AdSense ads as a call-to-action right in the feed, but even adding a call-to-action in the post excerpt helps convert feed readers using a feed reader service into active leads. You can also use the URL shortener technique when feeding your RSS feed to social media sites for better tracking there.

Tablets and increased phone use may be slowly edging out the RSS technology. However, it will be a while before everyone has access to the new tools, so you need to keep an RSS feed alive on your site.

Deciphering Metrics Codes and Patterns

As you track your metrics over time and begin to use some of the next layer tools, such as segmentation and dayparting, to analyze your online and social interaction, it's important to keep your eye peeled for patterns of use, interest, and engagement and the secret codes your visitors and fans/followers are sending you through their activity.

One helpful and interesting metric you can track is shifting attention patterns on your blog (see Figure 8-5). By sorting your metrics data by type of post, visitor segment, time on post, and bounce rate and doing a comparison over time, you will see a pattern of attention emerge. You can then fine-tune your content according to the data you gather about your most popular posts in your metrics history.

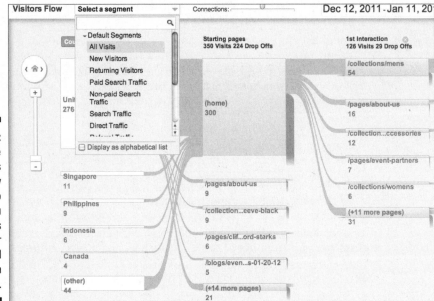

Figure 8-5:
Google
Analytics
Visitor Flow
view also
lets you
see patterns
in visitor
use and
attention on
your site.

What I mean by that is not to write the same post over and over in different ways to try to keep those visitors coming back, though keyword popularity should be factored in as well. I mean taking the posts that held people's attention the longest and looking at what made them special: Were they a list? Did they have more images than usual? Was it an interview? Did it inspire comments? Did you install a new plug-in that day?

Take the data you gather, apply it, and then tag and track that new piece of content you created (video, post, photo, or audio file). After you've had a chance to gather attention data on the new content, compare it to the popular content you used as your model. Keep adjusting over time to increase the engagement level of your visitors and turn them into true fans that want to take your content out into social media to their networks (micro conversion).

Chapter 9

Taking Metrics Off the Reservation

*W*hen you're tracking metrics, remember that not everyone finds your site or social content on a desktop or laptop. A massive uprising of mobile users and tablet owners now are looking for you on the go.

In fact, mobile phones put the Internet into the hands of a new economic demographic that couldn't be reached before — people who have the means to shop and who want to buy online, but who may not have access to a laptop or computer regularly.

Mobile and tablet use also catches that busy demographic of people on the go who need to shop for items, price check or comparison shop, or perhaps make a reservation at your restaurant or acquire tickets to a show.

With the many ways people use their mobile phones and tablets to find you, you should be tracking that as part of your social media metrics dashboard. You can track these metrics in a variety of ways, and this chapter helps you be prepared.

Tracking Mobile Metrics

As you may have guessed already, you can do some mobile tracking in Google Analytics. Google certainly seems to have its finger in every pie, doesn't it? Because of this, there is no time like the present to start laying plans for a mobile version of your site if you don't already have one. Talk to your web designer about the best way to make that happen.

You can track mobile activity using Google Analytics in four ways:

- ✔ On a regular website being accessed by mobile devices
- ✔ In a native application (app) built for iOS (Apple) or Android (Google)
- ✔ On a website built for a non-smartphone with a browser (low-end mobile devices)
- ✔ Mobile ad metrics inside Google Analytics for AdWords

For this book, I focus on the first and last items in the preceding list.

To take advantage of tracking activity in a native application built for iOS or Android, you need to find out more about coding an app and using Google's Analytics for Mobile Apps SDKs. You can find out more about the SDK for Apple at `http://code.google.com/apis/analytics/docs/mobile/ios.html` and for Android at `http://code.google.com/apis/analytics/docs/mobile/android.html`.

Tracking activity on a regular website being accessed by mobile devices

To access the data for activity from mobile devices (smartphones and tablets) on your regular website using Google Analytics:

1. **Log in to your Google Analytics account.**
2. **Select the website you want to track mobile metrics for.**
3. **Click the Standard Reporting tab.**
4. **In the left column, click Audience.**
5. **Click Mobile.**
6. **Select Overview or Devices to see metrics for the last month (see Figure 9-1).**

   Looking at your Mobile metrics overview in analytics tells you basic information about your visitors and breaks them out into web visitors and mobile visitors. Just looking at the overview tells you only how much of your traffic comes from folks using smartphones and tablets; it doesn't tell you which smartphones and tablets they are.

   Knowing your target market for your site and for your social media efforts, this big-picture number tells you whether you're falling short or reaching any goals to reach people on mobile devices. If you aren't planning this type of mobile site yet, I highly suggest you do. This will help keep you ahead of the game as the web moves to a more mobile user base.

To get a better picture of how your site reaches people in their pockets, so to speak, look at the Devices metric instead of Overview. This breaks the visitors out into the type of device folks are using to view your site. This information gives you an idea of which mobile browsers to design for.

7. (Optional) Drill the metrics down even further in this screen.

For example, you can choose different dimensions and secondary dimensions to sort by. You can simultaneously sort by device, site usage, location, and ecommerce use, for example. Or you can search by certain devices and exclude others.

8. Adjust the date to see metrics for specific time periods (see Figure 9-2).

The ecommerce figure is especially interesting for mobile shopping if you have a web-based store or sales process of any kind. This number gives you a look at how your site is converting for traffic from the mobile markets and on tablets. It lets you see, for example, that Android users turn into leads or sales less often than iPad users. You can then drill down on the site itself to see what may be happening in the Android browser to draw people away from taking action.

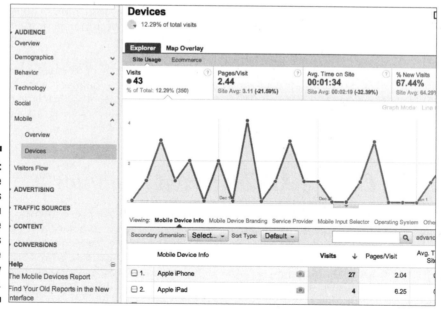

Figure 9-1: Google Analytics shows you the mobile devices folks use to view your site.

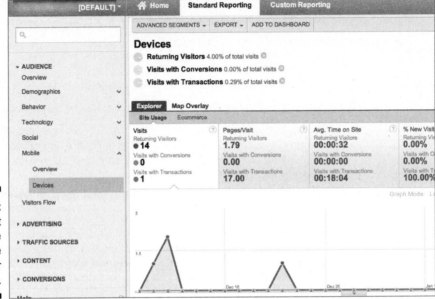

Figure 9-2:
Looking at
the device
usage
metrics over
four weeks.

If you're designing an app for your brand, don't leave metrics out. If you can make it Google Analytics-compatible, it will appeal to more people. If you can't, people still want to know how the app is performing for them, so make sure to give them a way to find out.

Google remains the best free option, but a variety of freemium, premium, and enterprise-level applications are out there to help you keep up with your mobile metrics. (See the sidebar "Looking at other tracking options.") However, if you're on a budget, Google Analytics and AdWords are still your best bets.

Linking AdWords and Analytics

I briefly mention tracking mobile ad metrics in the preceding section. Google is probably the easiest place to do this, using a combination of AdWords and Analytics. By first linking AdWords and Analytics (which helps your metrics overall anyway) and then splitting your campaign in AdWords and matching the split and campaign in Analytics, you can get a great look at mobile ad performance.

You can find most of the relevant metrics in Google Analytics under the Campaigns and Conversions tabs. You can also set goals and fine-tune the results even more if you're using your links wisely across your ads.

Looking at other tracking options

What if you don't want to use Google Analytics to track mobile metrics? Are there other mobile metrics sites out there? Absolutely! One popular program that combines mobile ads and mobile metrics (and a bunch of other social stuff) is JitterJam (see figure), recently acquired by Meltwater. If you have the means to use JitterJam, it's one of those solutions highly recommended for being useful and thorough in what it does for your mobile needs, as well as tracking social metrics across other platforms, similar to Radian6. One thing I've noticed is that JitterJam is one of the best for adding in Gist-like features and allowing you to import your contacts and include them into your metrics — not even the almighty Google does this (yet)!

Radian6 and Sysomos are also enterprise-level solutions that track social metrics, including mobile metrics.

AuriQ also has enterprise-level mobile metrics, as well as an IT-focused bandwidth metric service. It doesn't offer a free demo, however, so the medium-sized business may be priced out of this tool.

Kontagent mobile analytics (kSuite) is a new mobile-focused analytics tool from analytics company Kontagent. An interesting feature of this analytics package is the "virtual economy tuning" feature that helps you narrow your mobile sales funnel.

New startup Trendslide, in private beta at the time of writing, is one of the stronger looking new contenders in the mobile metrics arena. Its offering is intriguing, as it plans to put analytics and statistics in your pocket from just about every app, service, and web platform that gets used. Trendslide is definitely one to watch.

Individual mobile apps often have their own analytics as well. Sometimes these metrics are available on the app website and sometimes inside the app itself. If you have a choice between downloading two apps, the recommendation is always to go with the one that has not only better reviews, but better metrics for what you do with it.

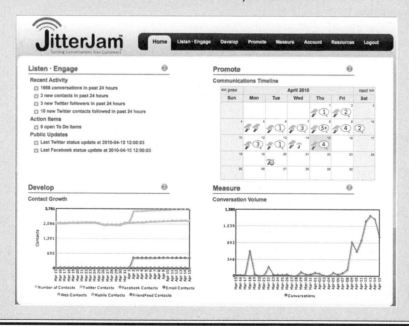

Venturing into E-Mail Metrics

E-mail marketing is a whole other ballgame entirely, with its own vocabulary. And, of course, you can track e-mail metrics in Google Analytics. You may be surprised to find out, though, that I recommend against relying solely on Google Analytics for this task.

Your first challenge with e-mail marketing is not violating e-mail marketing rules and being put in "e-mail jail" for being spammy (see Figure 9-3). Because e-mail marketing is permission-based marketing and faulty e-mail marketing can trigger the reflex for folks to list you as spam, it's best to use a program designed for the purpose of e-mail marketing from the beginning of each e-mail campaign or newsletter you send.

Figure 9-3: Mail Chimp is a great e-mail marketing platform for avoiding e-mail jail.

In fact, if you're a Gmail user who does DIY Internet marketing for your business and you've ever tried to send your newsletter out on your own, you may have received the "You have exceeded 100 e-mails per hour" message and had your account locked for 24 hours. Other web hosts like Bluehost or Go Daddy limit the number of e-mails you send an hour as well.

Not only are there volume limits on sending e-mail, there are limits on sending unsolicited e-mail, e-mail without an unsubscribe link, and more. In the case of e-mail marketing, it's important for your metrics to use a service because not using one may mark you as a spammer and prevent your e-mail from being read at all.

Checking out e-mail marketing services

What services are out there to help you avoid being labeled a spammer? A lot, as it turns out! An entire industry is built around e-mail marketing, giving you lots of options to choose from. I keep it simple and cover MailChimp, Constant Contact, and WhatCounts here, which are a few of the more reliable services.

 It isn't uncommon to have people leave MailChimp for Constant Contact, or vice versa. You'll notice as you check out both services that each one has its own personality and are tailored to reflect that. I have seen no differences in success rates of campaigns using either service, so you have to decide on your own.

MailChimp

MailChimp is a free program for e-mail marketing that works with most websites, blogs, and social sites to build your e-mail lists. MailChimp handles all of the possible issues with an e-mail campaign right from the start, making sure that your list is based on folks who have opted in to it, that you have a clear button to unsubscribe, and that e-mails are sent at intervals that don't interfere with regulations.

The integration MailChimp offers with services you probably already use, such as BatchBook, Eventbrite, Facebook, WordPress, Google Analytics, and others, means that you can grow your lists faster as well. With both an import and export list feature, you know you have control over your contacts.

After you create your first newsletter or other mailing, MailChimp sends it and tracks the key e-mail metrics for you. MailChimp also gives you access to a list dashboard where you can see list demographics and e-mail metrics graphed over time. MailChimp is my favorite free solution, though I suspect it may one day follow the trend and become freemium.

Constant Contact

Constant Contact, shown in Figure 9-4, is a popular freemium solution that works well. Chances are if you subscribe to e-mail newsletters, you've seen Constant Contact's name. It has been around for quite some time!

Like MailChimp, Constant Contact is designed to handle all the stress of creating and delivering an e-mail based newsletter or marketing campaign for you. Each service has strengths and weaknesses, but one of the things you get when you pay for Constant Contact is a set of slightly more complex metrics.

In Constant Contact, you can easily drill down for useful information from a list you've had going. You can quickly see who has never opened one of your e-mails, for example, allowing you to either reach out personally to that person or remove them from your list to avoid wasting effort.

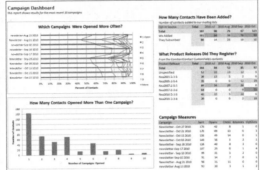

Figure 9-4:
Constant
Contact
e-mail
metrics view.

WhatCounts and others

Formerly known as Blue Sky Factory and purchased by WhatCounts in 2011, this popular enterprise-level e-mail marketing solution comes with some deep dive metrics and offers a variety of products.

If you're a large corporation, an enterprise-level solution like WhatCounts may be just the thing you need to scale out to thousands of customers. If you are a small to medium business, MailChimp or Constant Contact will do just fine for your price points.

Don't overlook other enterprise-level solutions like Omniture, Salesforce, and others either. I single out WhatCounts here because it's an up-and-comer in the space, but plenty of e-mail marketing solutions with metrics are available if you have the budget.

Knowing which e-mail metrics to measure

So what metrics do you need to measure in e-mail? It's a fairly short, but important, list:

- ✔ **The size of your e-mail list:** The number of e-mails in your list that are unique. Note: This number isn't necessarily the same as the total number of subscribers!

- ✔ **The number of new subscribers to your list:** In this case new subscribers are those that you added after the date of your most recent mailing, not over time.

- ✔ **The number of folks who opt out (unsubscribe):** Having people unsubscribe is normal. People weed out their inboxes all the time (especially when they're trying to increase their productivity or clean out their inbox).

If you notice that folks seem to opt out fairly quickly after opting in, you may want to make sure that your content is delivering what you promise in your signup form.

✔ **Bounce rate:** The bounce rate in e-mail marketing is different than the bounce rate on your website analytics. In e-mail, there are two types of bounces:

- A *hard bounce* means the e-mail will never be delivered — usually the person has left a company or changed e-mail providers, and that email is no longer valid. Treat those like unsubscriptions.

- A *soft bounce* may mean that the person's e-mail inbox is full or having a similar issue. This person may eventually see your e-mail, but it's not likely. If the e-mail gets a soft bounce several campaigns in a row, I recommend treating it as a hard bounce as well.

✔ **The open rate of your email campaign:** the open rate is fairly self-explanatory, as it tells you how many people opened your e-mail. Some e-mail programs calculate only if the e-mail is opened the first time. Some e-mail programs calculate if the person comes back and opens it a second or third time.

If you're running a campaign that needs to track all opens, one of the paid e-mail programs will be the solution you want to use.

✔ **The click rate of links in your e-mails:** You may find yourself reviewing this measurement the most often, as it tells you how many times links in your e-mail are clicked. This is important to know if you run classes or have other sales-converting links in your e-mail.

If links clicked is important to you, make sure that you set your e-mail campaign software to track not only whether someone clicks within the e-mail, but also if she clicks more than one link.

✔ **How fast or how much your newsletter or e-mail campaign lists are growing:** This just refers to how many new subscribers you have versus how many unsubscribers or hard bounces. My general rule is that if my click rate is steady or rising and my open rate is solid, I don't worry too much about this number. If I see a decline across those three factors, I know it's time to review my campaign and my list.

✔ **The number of folks who open e-mail compared to the number of clicks they make:** This open-to-click ratio is useful for deciding whether your calls-to-action and marketing language are effective within the e-mail.

✔ **How much each click costs:** This cost-per-click metric is useful in figuring out how much each e-mail campaign actually costs you when you send it. This metric takes a little finagling and needs to include not just the cost of the software solution you've chosen (easy to price because most charge by the message) but also the cost of your time, any design work, and so on.

✔ **What your conversion rate is:** I like to tell clients that the true measure of ROI is a combo of "Are your customers happy?" and "Are you making money?" — not a pile of metrics data about page views or a fan count — and this final metric speaks directly to that.

If your e-mail campaign is converting well, you'll be able to track the person through the entire sales funnel from your e-mail — from subscribe to open all the way to purchasing a product or service from you (see Figure 9-5).

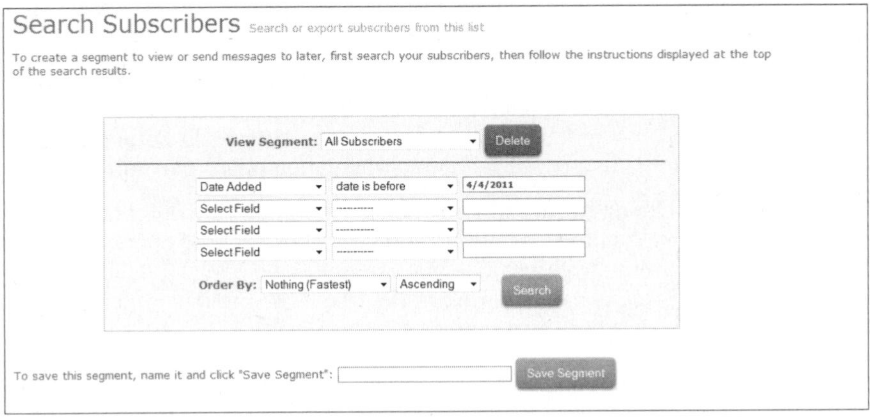

Figure 9-5:
Segmenting an e-mail list is as effective as segmenting metrics and gives you more control.

Search Subscribers Search or export subscribers from this list

To create a segment to view or send messages to later, first search your subscribers, then follow the instructions displayed at the top of the search results.

View Segment: All Subscribers   Delete

Date Added ▾   date is before ▾   4/4/2011
Select Field ▾   ---------- ▾
Select Field ▾   ---------- ▾
Select Field ▾   ---------- ▾
Order By: Nothing (Fastest) ▾   Ascending ▾   Search

To save this segment, name it and click "Save Segment":   Save Segment

Increasing your conversion rate

One way to increase the conversion rate from your overall email marketing is to create a combination social media and e-mail push and optimize your outgoing e-mails for shareability and click rate. Then use an analytics program, such as Google Analytics, in addition to the e-mail metrics program, to track success and reach.

Social media gets most of the attention lately as overtaking e-mail in popularity, but e-mail remains one of the best ways to get someone's undistracted attention. Unlike the more scattered and noisy world of social media, where you can hear everyone talking and sharing, when you're in someone's e-mail box, you're the only thing they see for at least a few seconds.

It's important to learn to optimize that undivided attention, and the best way to do so is with combined tracking. By porting data on e-mail metrics from Google Analytics or your other metrics tracker of choice and from e-mail metrics into your spreadsheet system, you can play with the data, massaging it to get the most information possible from each set of metrics.

Tracking reach

One metric you should be tracking is reach. What e-mail metrics make up this admittedly vague concept? That's easy: E-mail forwards, social shares, and subscription referrals.

You can track e-mail forwards in your e-mail metrics program. If you're inspiring someone to send your e-mail to a friend or friends in their e-mail contacts list, you're doing your job well as an e-mail marketer. If you see forwards leading to clicks from the new potential subscriber, that's even better!

Social shares occur from within the e-mail. Smart marketers encourage social shares by offering people a chance to be featured in a future e-mail for having the most shares of the e-mail or some other reward.

Shared e-mail campaigns are wonderful ways to increase your reach to more people who will give you their focused attention for a short while. You can convert those people into customers in future e-mails.

If you can offer a way for folks to suggest your e-mail subscription to others, it will increase your list number. Although not all e-mail campaigns offer this feature, you can often add it manually.

Be careful with this one! You don't want to auto-subscribe people — you simply want to give them a way to opt in if they choose. Remember — permission-based marketing!

As you send these three metrics out into the wild, make sure that you're tracking them in Google Analytics and in your e-mail metrics. As you see which is most successful for your brand, you can begin to target your e-mail campaigns to that action.

Tracking influence

If you're using your spreadsheets and metrics dashboards well, you will also be able to begin pinpointing your e-mail influencers through these metrics. This growing list of influencers will let you know who to target special promotions toward and who to give rewards to for their efforts to increase your reach. Never forget to show your gratitude.

After you find your influencers, you can make mini-campaigns to target them and use your metrics to track the success of these campaigns. Make sure that you use a combination of smart e-mails, metrics, and short URLs to get the metrics data for these. That way, you won't lose any nuance and can make your campaigns continually stronger and more effective.

Also make sure that in all e-mail campaigns, your Unsubscribe button is clear and easy to find. That way, people will unsubscribe instead of clicking the dreaded Mark as Spam button if they decide they no longer want to opt in to your e-mails.

Chapter 10

Making Your Investment Accountable and COUNTable

*O*ne of the best uses of metrics is making your social media efforts accountable and countable. No metrics system is perfect — and, in fact, you'll find it best to have more than one system — but metrics help prove the path to real ROI.

If you're on a tight monetary and time budget, knowing which efforts are working is going to be key to your success. This knowledge will prevent wasted time and make your social media efforts more focused with better results.

Metrics give you a way to track leads, sales, attention, influence, and interest. Every business needs to have their metrics dashboards ready before they do anything else (and if you already started your campaigns online without metrics in place, now is the time to get them going).

Making Your Metrics Business-Centric

One of the key things you can do to make your metrics pull better data is to make them business-centric. Focus the data you pull on your business and your competitors' businesses. Pay close attention to your customers' needs and to what they say about not only your brand, but also what they want and need.

How do you do all of that? Create a system of link, referral, and keyword tracking; set achievable goals; and run specific, targeted campaigns. Create optimized content for sharing and conversion.

Listen to your customers through your metrics so that you can deliver what they want — they may not be interacting with your brand to get content, for example, but to get help. Metrics allow you to discover that goal.

Keywords

Not all keywords are created equal. Different segments of keywords gather different types of information. Visual planning helps me create better keyword metrics, but visualizing the data you want to gather may not work for you.

Create a mind map. I use Mindjet, which isn't free, but you can use several free options, such as XMind. Use a business goal as the center of the map and branch out from there into keyword groupings.

As you create your map, notice that your keywords naturally begin to fall into related categories. Those categories in turn are relevant to different aspects of your business.

As you begin to dive into your analytics and adjust for these keyword groupings, patterns begin to take shape (see Figure 10-1). These patterns help you steer your metrics in the right direction. Use your spreadsheets and mind-mapping software to track patterns, or you can visualize them weekly on a white board.

Some keywords will be most relevant to generating new results (new clients, new attention, new subscriptions), some to enriching your current results (making your existing customers or subscribers happy), and some to finding out what your competition is up to. The best metrics program will have the whole combination — if you don't, you'll notice it in the gaps you see in your reporting.

What if you don't like mind mapping? That's fine; so many analytics programs export keyword reports to CSV files that it's easy to pull your keywords into a spreadsheet and run analysis and pattern mapping on them in Excel once or twice a month (or more often, if you have a heavily targeted campaign to watch). Simply import your keywords for the desired time frame, sort by segment and sentiment, and get a clear view of how you're doing.

Figure 10-1:
Look to your
search traffic
report and
other metrics
for patterns
emerging.

Sentiment

Sentiment is a bit harder to track, but brands looking to see how they are perceived online definitely need to keep an eye on it. Tools like Radian6 and JitterJam (recently acquired by the Meltwater Group) track it for you, but what if they're out of your price range?

If you're looking to track specific social sites, you can try specific apps like Twitrratr — a free sentiment-tracking tool for Twitter. You can even use the site's own search.

For example, at `http://search.twitter.com`, you can search for a key-word or keyphrase, or perhaps your brand name, plus a sentiment emoticon to find sentiment. It's rudimentary, but it does the job.

Putting the keyword, keyphrase, brand, or campaign into social search with the emoticon is the simplest way to track sentiment. Don't forget to utilize your Boolean search strings to narrow it all down.

If you start seeing strong sentiment toward your brand that isn't good, you can go back and use your referral and content page metrics to figure out the problem. If all your content is coming up daisies and roses and you still have negative sentiment, something may be happening offline that you need to address. Check those keyword metrics to help find out what and also interview your customers (or a selection of them) to see whether you can ferret out the cause of their unrest.

Goal setting

To make your metrics really soar for your company, you need to practice the fine art of goal setting. To get the full effect of a campaign, the campaign has to have a measurable goal. More than that, the campaign needs to have an incremental series of actionable items you can track.

Say, for example, that you want to book 5 percent more seats in your restaurant this month. You want to do this increase through your website because you just launched a new online reservation service. You have two goals here:

✔ Raise awareness of the new site feature

✔ Make 5 percent more bookings

You want to make your metrics comprehensive and be able to track the goal as far across the web as you can. Do the following steps:

1. **On your website, create a landing page designed to support both goals.**

   Make sure that the page has great copy and images that tell the story of the new feature and how it will help customers.

2. **Populate your landing page with two calls-to-action.**

   One call-to-action encourages folks to share this new website feature with their friends. The other one encourages them to try out the feature by booking a seat.

3. **Track the call-to-action for bookings.**

   This step is easy. If they book a table, you have solid real-world ROI in your wallet to show you it was successful.

   Tracking the shared call-to-actions will be trickier and is where things like Google Analytics and setting goals comes in. I recommend using an `http://bit.ly` (or other) shortened URL inside the Share button or widget for that call-to-action. This way, you can track it even as it leaves your control (at least until it gets pulled out of the shortener — at that point, you need keyword brand searches to keep up with it).

   Another option is to use referrer tags instead of shortened URLs. One example would be `http://magnitudemedia.net /?ref=New+ Reservation+System+Landing+Page+CTA`, which will track that `ref=` tag inside Google Analytics. This option may make dashboards for specific landing pages and testing easier to format.

4. **Inside your analytics program, set up goals using the shortened link as well as the landing page (see Figure 10-2).**

   It may take a few days before you start getting useful numbers.

5. **Name your goal.**

   Make the name something you'll remember. You'd be surprised how easy it is to name your goal something forgettable!

6. **Define a funnel.**

   Google Analytics gives you up to ten pages to define a funnel. This step helps you see where folks may drop out of the process.

7. **Assign the goal a monetary value.**

   For the booking goal, choose the revenue you expect to get from a typical reservation for two, such as $40. For the sharing goal, choose a percentage of that. In other words, if you expect 1 percent of shares to book a seat, choose $.40)

8. **Fill out the goal details.**

9. **Save your goal and start tracking your campaign.**

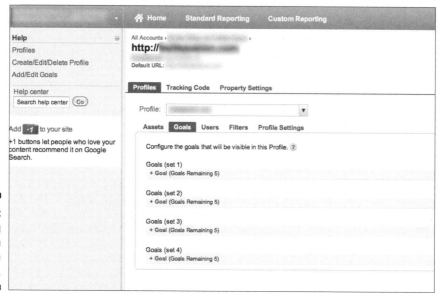

Figure 10-2:
Setting
goals in
Google
Analytics.

If you link your AdWords account and your Analytics account, you can see how any of the ads that relate to this goal and that use the short link or referrer tags are performing. This metric allows you to adjust the ads for optimum performance every couple of days.

Practicing Bulletproof Metrics for Companies

Making metrics bulletproof for your company is simple: Be detail oriented and think in paths. What I mean by *think in paths* is to always envision the path your customer would take to and through your site (or store). Then make sure that your content, design, and metrics follows that path. Use metrics to periodically analyze your vision of the path for conversion rate and usefulness.

As you look at actual customer paths and patterns, you'll find that in most, but not all, cases, your customer doesn't come to you for your content. Your content may compel them to stay, but more often, they come to you for something entirely different (help or customer service, directions to your store, a phone number, or your hours — things like that).

Metrics help you analyze what your customers and potential customers really want so that you can give it to them first, rather than giving them what you think they should want. Should is a dangerous word in business, and it can hamper your metrics.

Metrics also help bulletproof your site by finding the weak spots quickly, such as the points of your website where you lose the most customers or the forms that most frequently get abandoned. Take a look at why and make changes based on the data you gather in your metrics program, and you'll see your real ROI (new customers, sales, and so on) increase accordingly.

One thing that can make your metrics soar is incorporating the new social measurement features into them (see Figure 10-3). Use the referring sites and social metrics section of Analytics to figure out which social sites have the most traction for your brand.

 Follow the incoming traffic from social media using the Visitor Flow feature in the new Analytics. This feature gives you a stunning visual of the path your visitors take. You can narrow the path by location, date, referring site, content, and more, which gives you a clear picture of drop-offs and why they happen.

If you see in your visitor flow that you get 36 percent of your traffic from Twitter and 15 percent from Facebook, but more conversions to reservations come from Facebook link visitors, then you know to work harder on Facebook.

Figure 10-3:
Social
metrics
plug-in for
WordPress.

Perhaps your converting traffic comes from your YouTube site — in fact, from one particular video. You know to promote that video link harder and perhaps make another, similar video to attract that market.

However you use the right series of links, goals, and campaigns to make bullet-proof metrics, don't forget that you'll need to constantly adjust what you measure and how you measure it. The only constant on the Internet is change. Be ready to embrace that mantra for success.

Measuring Collateral

One thing the new social media universe can do is save you money. You'll need less collateral and traditional advertising than you have in years if you utilize social media well and measure it well for success. However, because not everyone is online, you will need traditional media for some things.

Did you know that you can measure traditional media collateral? You can use several methods to gather metrics in regular marketing collateral:

- Always include your landing page link on all print material.
- Include a hashtag like the one in Figure 10-4. #SMM4D is the hashtag for this book, for example.

Figure 10-4:
An unusual use of a hashtag offline!

✔ Use a QR Code if you have printed signs in your store or posters out and about in the wild. Generate this code with a service like YouScan.me so that you can get metrics on it. Also ensure that the link is your shortened URL to your landing page for triple the metrics (or use referrer tagged links, if you prefer).

✔ Include your call-to-action for your web campaign somewhere in your printed material to encourage people to share with their friends using the link you can measure.

✔ Make the ask. If you ask people to interact with your collateral or reward them for it, they will.

Measuring Foot Traffic

With the help of your staff, you can measure foot traffic resulting from web efforts and use web tools to increase foot traffic. Everyone who has customer contact will need to understand what tools you're using and know when you're running a special or other deal to encourage interaction and new customers.

In addition to ensuring that your staff knows what's going on, make sure that your customers also are aware by using these techniques:

✔ Use signage in your stores or other brick-and-mortar venue to encourage check-ins on services like Yelp and foursquare (see Figure 10-5). These services have metrics you can track, and they encourage return visits for specials and other offerings.

Figure 10-5:
An example of a foursquare check-in sign encouraging your customers to participate.

- ✔ Use signage in your stores and conversations with your staff to tell people about your web presence (Facebook page, website, and so on) and how it can be useful to them (menu items, special items, new merchandise listings, and more).

- ✔ Don't be afraid to ask your customers to like your pages or share them. Likes and shares increase the web traffic you can measure, which helps you make better campaigns and reach more people.

- ✔ If you see people using phones in your store, use QR Codes or other mobile push efforts to help them shop and convert them to loyal customers. Many of these tools also offer analytics. Wouldn't it be nice to get analytics on the real shopping habits of your customers?

- ✔ Get creative! Keep an eye out for someone tweeting about your business while they are in your store or about going to your business later that day. Then do something nice when they arrive.

  One airline, KLM, did this, meeting people at the gate who tweeted that they were flying with them with in-flight swag based on the interests they'd expressed in their Twitter bio and tweet stream. It was a huge hit.

In the end, remember that even though I'm talking about metrics and measurement, I'm talking about metrics for social media. Social media is an engaged and involved platform where you can easily convert people to happy customers simply by using metrics to pay attention.

If you can become a destination point for the social media savvy consumer, you'll find that measuring foot traffic becomes key to that success. For example, the Roger Smith Hotel in New York has become known as the "social media hotel" where those in social media go to see art and films, have meet-ups, eat, drink, and stay.

Every time the hotel gets foot traffic from social media, those people tell their connections, and their foot traffic grows. By measuring this continually, the hotel is constantly fine-tuning their efforts and offering more interesting things to their visitors to turn them into loyal, repeat customers.

Kicking ROI to the Curb for Real Metrics

ROI, ROI, ROI — it's a common buzzword bandied about a lot, but so often misused. ROI is not page views and other "surface" metrics. These metrics contribute, sure, but ROI is more about how well your company is doing.

The first measure of real ROI is always "Am I making money?" It's easy to get sucked into the kumbaya of social media, the "join the conversation" mantra, but in reality, you're in business to make money so that you can support yourself, your business, your employees, and your dependents and hopefully have a rich and full life as well.

If social media isn't helping you do all those things, your metrics will help you figure out why and correct it, all for a fraction of the cost of throwing yellow pages and newspaper ads out into the wild untagged.

The second measure of real ROI is repeat business. If your social media is engaging and your metrics are strong, any business that offers its customers value will see repeat business. If you don't see repeat business and positive customer sentiment about your brand, metrics, again, will help you see how to fix it.

The third measure of real ROI is positive word-of-mouth marketing. Do your metrics show that people are talking about your business? Do those conversations lead to conversions on your site? If you can answer yes to both questions, then this ROI metric is strong.

The last measure of real ROI is a healthy business. Are you running yourself ragged trying to update every social media site and do it all for your company? Stop it! Stop it right now!

If you're spending more than an hour a day on social media, website maintenance (unless you're making a major overhaul), engagement, and the basics of metrics, then you aren't managing your time well, and your business will suffer. Burnt out is bad for business.

Get your time under control. Your metrics are there to help you fine-tune what you're doing where online so that you can build your business, not run yourself ragged trying to out-social the Joneses.

Pay attention to what metrics tell you about where your customers are. If you're spending hours a week making YouTube videos because someone told you video is the thing to do right now but your customers never click the links or come to you from your videos, reassess.

These folks may be coming to you from Twitter, or Facebook, or, heck, even LinkedIn. Pay attention and put your best efforts in the strongest places for your business. It will save your time and sanity.

Using Nonmainstream Metrics Tools

You can use a few tools to measure some of those out-of-the-box metrics I talking about. These tools include

- ✔ **Foursquare:** This simple location tool allows you to see analytics for real-time visits to your brick-and-mortar location. It also allows you to offer deals and specials and see tips about your business.

- ✔ **Yelp:** Yelp for Business, shown in Figure 10-6, also tracks metrics for both real-time visits and planned visits. You can see reviews of your business and offer limited deals.

Figure 10-6: Yelp for Business metrics page.

✔ **TripAdvisor:** This one offers insights for certain kinds of business in the travel and tourism industry, as well as customer reviews and recommendations.

✔ **Facebook:** Facebook's Insights on its business pages are a fairly comprehensive look at the demographics of who is coming to your site, placed into easy-to-read graphs and charts.

It's actually a bit creepy, how much they know about your page's fans. Combined with Facebook's check-in feature and events app, you can do quite a bit with Facebook to track your company's success there.

✔ **PeerIndex:** Similar to Klout but offering some deeper metrics, this one is more about brand than customer loyalty information.

✔ **Kickstarter:** This one is for the brand that has a product to get to market and needs funding. It offers analytics on each of its campaigns.

✔ **PayPal:** If you have a PayPal button on your site, you can track the conversion rate (if someone abandons their purchase) using the links you're allowed in the button-creation form for confirmation of purchase or abandonment. Put these as goals in your analytics program.

✔ **SlideShare:** If you put content out to your customers on SlideShare, it offers analytics to its pro users (see Figure 10-7).

Figure 10-7: SlideShare metrics page.

- ✔ **YouTube:** The granddaddy of video now offers on-page analytics as well as the ability to have goals set in your analytics program.

- ✔ **YouScan.me:** This QR Code generator is one of many out there to choose form. It offers metrics on users who scan the code. It's up to you to use links, like Bit.ly links, that can be tracked.

Part IV
Keeping Your Finger on the Pulse of Living, Breathing Metrics

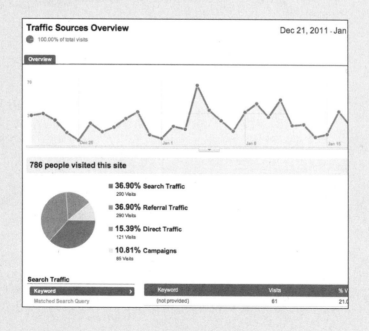

In this part . . .

In this part, I give you a hard look at metrics pitfalls, talk about avoiding common metrics mistakes, and show you how to spot charlatans and spammers.

You also discover how to spot and avoid fake metrics and shallow metrics and the different ways people try to game the system.

You want results from your AdWords, not to be blocked or avoided, and this part tells you how to keep on people's radar.

Chapter 11

Avoiding Metrics Bankruptcy: Simple Steps to Avoid Common Metrics Mistakes

*Y*ou may wonder how in the world you can make mistakes with data that is being delivered to you in neat reports and graphs. Metrics services do a great job of gathering any and all data you tell them to find, after all.

That's just it: If you put garbage in, you get garbage out. Your metrics will only ever be as good as the directions you give your metrics programs and team.

What good is a huge pile of unsorted data? It can make your conversion goal a needle in a haystack. The key is to find out how to tell what's real and what's fake in metrics.

Recognizing the Signs of False Metrics

Looking for the signs of a false or bad metric is actually pretty easy. A false metric is any number that doesn't support or give you insight into achieving actual goals.

If my goal is to get ten more Facebook fans by the end of the week, then the Likes count on my Facebook page would be relevant to that goal. If, however, my goal is to get five more people booked into my restaurant by the end of the week, how many fans I have on Facebook doesn't directly support that number.

To get the right metric, you need to dig deeper. Assume, for this example, that you're running this campaign only on Facebook. How many fans on Facebook went to the website and looked at the hours and contact information?

How many fans on Facebook clicked an Open Table link? How many abandoned their reservation part way through? Why? How many actual bookings did the restaurant have this week, and how many were directly influenced by Facebook?

How many of the bookings interacted with the page during their visit? What did they post? Pictures of food? Comments? How many checked in? What is the after visit sentiment on Facebook? Those would be examples of some of the metrics you'd seek out here.

Digging Deeper than Surface Metrics

Klout scores, Twitter followers, and other metrics are what I call *surface metrics*. Useful to the point of simply seeing that your account is gaining interest and being discovered, these numbers don't tell you much about the quality or potential of the engagement.

You can actually get a better idea of how your Twitter followers, for example, are working for you by using real metrics. If you've been in social media for a while, you've probably heard of Gary Vaynerchuk, owner of Wine Library in New Jersey and VaynerMedia, among other things.

This December, Gary, who had over 900,000 followers at the time of the tweet, tweeted out a video he made titled "There is no such thing as social media" — a very catchy title tweeted out by someone who has a highly engaged following.

As Mack Collier pointed after studying the tweet's effectiveness, that tweet garnered him 5,539 views and 47 retweets. That's a return of .5 percent. That demonstrates that even for the most followed people in social media, follower count is a largely irrelevant number.

How would you make this irrelevant number into a useful metric? By tracking how many of those video views converted to leads and sales on the VaynerMedia or Wine Library sites using goals and advanced segmentation data from within our analytics.

One reason I tell folks to give little credence to Klout scores or Empire Avenue trade prices or other social media surface numbers also comes from the fact that they are noise metrics.

Klout and Empire Avenue (see Figure 11-1) both (at the time of this writing) reward noisy users more heavily than users who generate fewer interactions of higher quality or value. They give more weight to folks who tweet or Facebook ten times in two days about the new Kia than they do the person who tweets or Facebooks one time in a month with more comprehensive and helpful information on cars in general.

These services reward brand advocacy, it's true, but that doesn't tell you much about true influence. If you tweet ten times in two days about Kia, I'm going to either filter you or the keyword Kia out, just to turn down the noise level.

If you tweet one helpful article about choosing between similar models of car that happens to mention Kia, I'll be more likely to read it, engage with the data or content, and pass it on.

Noise-to-signal ratio is always a leading indicator of bad data. Trends can also be part of fake, or bad, metrics. Trends are useful for business predictions, but it's best to be careful how you measure them.

If you're using a trending topic on Twitter as a form of measurement, just the fact that it's trending is cool (if it wasn't promoted by a brand) but not really a great measurement. Measure instead how that topic is driving people through your funnel — to the profile, to the website, to the conversion. Use those metrics as part of your advanced segmentation and follow the flow to and through your site.

Figure 11-1: Empire Avenue.

If you still aren't sure how to tell good metrics from bad ones, the simplest way to look at it is "What has this data done for me lately?" Fine-tune your metrics until they perform for you. Don't be afraid to change your data sets until you get it right. The nice thing about the Internet is the ability to make adjustments in real time for better results.

Preventing Fake Metrics

"They" say 78 percent of statistics are made up on the spot. Metrics can be faked as well. Metrics can also gather data on the wrong thing, giving you poor results that are as good as (or, rather, as *bad* as) fake.

One way to prevent getting fake metrics from a consultant or your team (or just from bad use of analytics) is to make sure that everyone on the team has at least read-only level access to the analytics program of your choice.

Adding a user to Google Analytics

Having everyone able to access the metrics allows everyone on the team to offer feedback on how the metrics are doing and what they're measuring. It also gives you a chance to open up talking points about different kinds of metrics and what makes each one valuable to team members who might normally gravitate toward surface metrics instead of meat-and-potatoes measurement.

If Google Analytics is your weapon of choice for metrics, adding a user is fairly easy:

1. **Log in to Google Analytics.**
2. **Choose the URL of the site you want people to have access to.**
3. **In the window that appears, click the gear in the upper right corner of the orange toolbar.**
4. **On the next page, click the Users tab.**
5. **Click the New User button.**

   The Add User to Profile window, shown in Figure 11-2, appears.
6. **Add a completely new user by e-mail address.**
7. **Give them User level access, not Administrative access.**
8. **Save your settings.**
9. **Repeat this process until you've added the whole project team.**

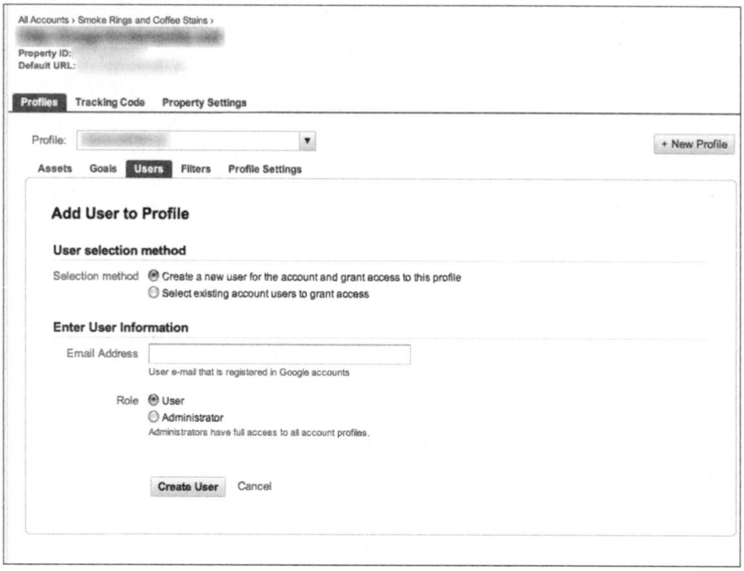

All Accounts › Smoke Rings and Coffee Stains ›

Property ID:
Default URL:

Profiles   Tracking Code   Property Settings

Profile: ▼   + New Profile

Assets   Goals   **Users**   Filters   Profile Settings

Add User to Profile

User selection method

Selection method ⦿ Create a new user for the account and grant access to this profile
                  ○ Select existing account users to grant access

Enter User Information

Email Address [   ]
               User e-mail that is registered in Google accounts

Role ⦿ User
      ○ Administrator
      Administrators have full access to all account profiles.

[Create User] Cancel

Figure 11-2:
Adding a
user to your
Google
Analytics
account.

Creating a custom report in Google Analytics

When you're adding users, sometimes you may run into a snag, such as the CEO not wanting user access because he doesn't have time to log in. In that case, you can create a custom report and e-mail it to the entire team (recommended) or to the person who wants an easier way to participate in metrics discussions.

To create a custom report in Google Analytics:

1. **Log in to Google Analytics.**

2. **Choose the URL of the site you want people to have access to.**

3. **In the next window that opens up, click the Custom Reporting tab in the orange toolbar.**

4. **On the next page, click the New Custom Report button.**

5. **Fill in the metrics you want to track using the drop-down fields and tabbed areas.**

   You can make this report comprehensive, or you can set up more than one report for different goals and segments. Use your best judgment on what will work for your team here.

6. **Download the reports as CSV files to e-mail to the team.**

Creating a custom alert

You can also create a custom alert that gets e-mailed to the team by going to the Users tab and selecting Create Custom Alert. You then follow the on-screen instructions and choose an e-mail to send the report to (see Figure 11-3). These custom alerts are less comprehensive than the custom reports, however.

If you use the old version of analytics, a handy e-mail button right on the front page of your dashboard lets you send the complete analytics overview in a weekly report via e-mail.

Avoiding Metrics Pitfalls

There are many metrics pitfalls out there. You can easily avoid most of them with a little planning and a different outlook on what you want your metrics to do for you.

Don't overstate your numbers

Metrics excite some people, but for many, they're math. Math has this stigma of being boring (even when the information it gives us is useful), so sometimes you see metrics that are inflated or otherwise altered to be more exciting.

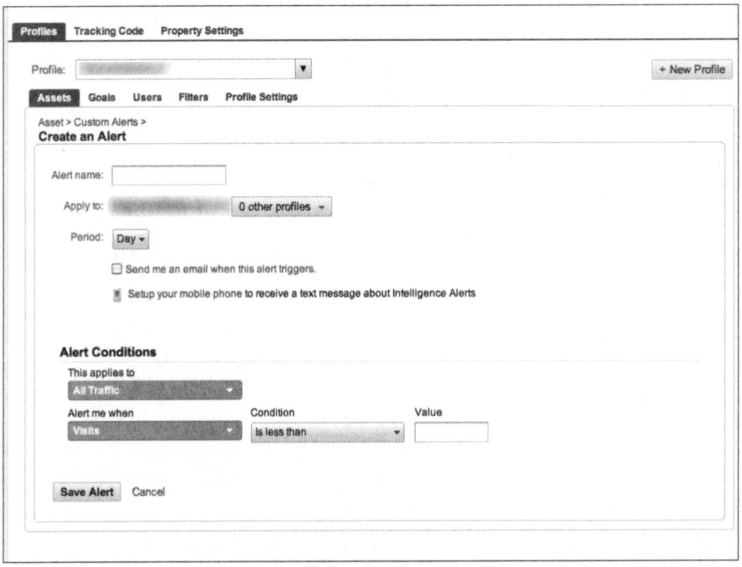

Figure 11-3: Creating a custom alert.

Avoid this mistake. One problem is that it makes people stop listening to you if your numbers always come in overstated. Another is that is calls all your data into question and helps no one.

There is no shame in a low metric, if it's true. A low metric is simply an opportunity to improve your efforts or improve your data collection. It's a way to open up discussion on the underlying issue that is causing the low number. Low metrics may not look valuable on the surface, but they are often the most valuable number you can receive — a chance for improvement.

Don't get obsessive

Checking your metrics daily is often a bad idea. Unless you're running a well-targeted, well-planned, multichannel 24- or 48-hour campaign, most daily metrics don't give you the whole picture.

It's tempting to obsess about daily numbers, especially when you first start out and feel like you're all alone on the Internet. You click the day's metrics hoping to see that first ripple of interest. Then the obsession begins, and you feel the need to check every day. Don't!

You see, data takes time to become useful. The better (and more sanity-inducing) way to handle metrics is to check them by campaign date, weekly, or monthly. This timeframe also gives you more useful ways to compare metrics across time, as you'll have a more substantial data set to work with.

Segment, segment, segment

Segmenting metrics is often overlooked by folks that are new to analytics, but it's an essential skill. Take the time to find out how to segment metrics for your campaigns. It will give you better data.

In the old version of Google Analytics, segmenting was a little harder. In the new version, Google has made it easier for you. Google Analytics now has a tab called Advanced Segments under the Standard Reporting tab inside your Analytics Dashboard.

The Advanced Segments tab lets you set up a variety of default segments, such as new visitors, bounced visitors, non-paid search traffic, and similar items. Begin there and track a selection of segments. (You can choose up to four.)

Track these segments over a week or two to find out how the data is structured. After that time, you can go back in and add custom segments. As you layer your data by segment in addition to visitor flow, you get a more realistic picture of how your customers are engaging with your brand and what kind of work you need to do to improve.

Don't track yourself

Google Analytics gives you a way to exclude certain IP addresses, including your own (see Figure 11-4). This exclusion is useful if you know you have staff members who interact with your site for testing, your mom clicks your page every day, or other visitors come by that are loyal fans, but not necessarily relevant data.

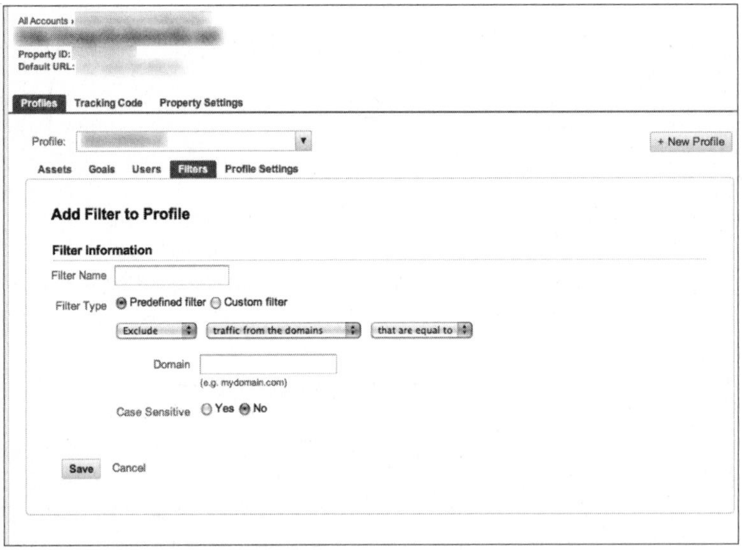

Figure 11-4:
Filtering out an IP address in Google Analytics.

To exclude certain IP addresses:

1. **Log in to Google Analytics.**

2. **Choose the domain URL you want to work with.**

3. **From the page that pops up, click the gear symbol on the right side of the orange toolbar.**

4. **Choose the Filters tab.**

5. **Click the Add a New Filter button.**

6. **Add the IP that you want to filter out.**

If you want to get advanced, you can also filter them *in* to track repeat customers flow.

7. **Save the filter.**

8. **Repeat Steps 1 through 7 as many times as you need to fine-tune your metrics.**

Meeting Metrics Gurus, not Charlatans

You can easily tell the metrics charlatans out there. They're the ones working so hard to convince brands that "there is no way to measure ROI of social media." That's a bunch of hooey — of course, there is.

In fact, if you tune out the charlatans and incompetents, you find that you can not only measure social media and online metrics in a wide variety of ways, but you can find plenty of smart people that will tell you their biggest secrets of metrics measurement every day!

If you wonder who I consider metrics gurus and recommend following for your continued education in metrics after you've mastered what I cover in this book and get hooked on data, at the top of my list is Christopher Penn, author of the *Awaken Your Superhero* blog, and K.D. Paine from K.D. Paine & Partners. Avinash Kaushik of Occam's Razor is another great resource for analytics and SEO help.

What do all of the metrics gurus have in common? A focus on deep metrics, an ability to follow the long tail and see extended results, advocacy on comparing data sets and advanced segmentation, and a willingness to share many of the great new discoveries they make and the tricks of their trade every day.

Gaming the System — Not!

Give Google credit that the major changes it's been making to its search algorithm over the last year or so and to its Analytics and AdWords tools in the last part of the year have started making it just that much harder to game the system when it comes to metrics and search results.

If you wonder what I mean by *game the system,* I'm referring to using black-hat SEO tactics, such as link farming, irrelevant landing pages that live outside of your site structure, duplicate content, baiting, link stuffing on social media, and comment and forum spambots to improve your page results in search.

You don't need to game the system to get good metrics and use that data to organically appear higher in search results. You simply need to know how to read your data and listen to your customers and potential customers.

Use your metrics instead to gather data on the content your visitors view the most and create touch points within that content to help your ROI. Use advanced segmentation to create converting calls-to-action on your page, including a welcome message designed to make visitors from certain sites feel welcome in a manner fitting the site that sent them your way.

You still need to do your basic SEO, too. Even though search is skewing toward the three R's — *recent, related to you (your social graph), and relevant* — having the SEO basics in place will only help you. Keywords (used well), meta tags, appropriate links, solid content, and more will still help you.

Social media sites and engagement are being given more and more weight in search results and discovery. Having accounts on the main sites, such as Twitter, Facebook, and Google+, will only help you, especially if you're active on these sites and keep your brand relevant.

Using Layered Metrics to Avoid False ROI

Layered metrics is something I use as a kind of shorthand to refer to metrics that track multidimensional data. For example, tracking site visits or unique page views doesn't give you a lot of deep information, but using advanced segments and other analytics features does.

Connecting accounts like AdWords to your analytics also has a domino effect on data gathering, creating a more complete picture.

Gathering better data

How can you take a standard metric and make it more complex, in turn gathering not necessarily *more* data, but *better* data? In short, how do you avoid false ROI?

1. **Start with any surface metric that you think will become useful.**

2. **Decide which goal the metric is going to support.**

   This step gives you an idea what information you need to layer on top of it.

3. **If you use Google Analytics, you're going to want to create a dashboard for the metric and create custom reports tracking advanced segments for the metric.**

   The dashboard you create will house some of your layers for this metric.

4. **Inside the dashboard, create custom widgets by clicking the New Widget button.**

5. **Set up your spreadsheet outside of Google Analytics to gather data from other sources and to import CSV data from Google Analytics.**

6. **In Google Analytics, go to the Custom Reports section and create more detailed reports using advanced segmentation to track aspects of the metric.**

   You can track metrics like demographic data, time of day of engagement with the brand, and other information.

7. **After you create your dashboard(s) and reports, do a weekly review to ensure that you're collecting data that supports your goal.**

   If you aren't getting useful information, go back in and make adjustments.

8. **Use the data that you're collecting to make projections about your goal.**

   These data-driven projections will help you create better goals and reach success faster.

9. **As you get better and faster at sifting through the data, make micro campaigns using social media tools.**

   These micro campaigns will help drive traffic where you want it to go on your website (or drive interaction and engagement with specific calls-to-action).

10. **Use the data to project business goals into the next year.**

    You can even project five years ahead as you get better and better at understanding the data you're receiving.

Reaching your goals

Building a layered metric structure sounds complex, but it really isn't. The hardest part is setting it up. As long as you follow through with good content, customer responsiveness, and calls-to-action that convert, a great layered metric will help you reach your goals.

After you start reaching your simpler goals, you can add in offline data (as you get better at collecting it) to truly see how layers can improve the information you gather.

If you have to generate reports on a regular basis, putting this data into visual form will help you. Use the spreadsheet to create charts and graphs over time that show a variety of data points intersecting with the goal and then tie these in to brand sentiment data to show where you need outward facing improvements.

Chapter 12

Making Metrics Work for Your Brand

In This Chapter

▶ Using metrics to expand your brand

▶ Converting sales

▶ Sharing information and other benefits of metrics

*Y*ou can use metrics for more than just data accumulation and tracking. You can also apply them in a very conscious way to grow a brand.

Applying metrics to growing a brand requires you to be part studious observer, part mad scientist. By keeping a vigilant eye on your data and applying both tried-and-true formulas and formulas you create to analyze that data, you can mold metrics into something useful.

By using metrics as the cornerstone of your arsenal for brand growth, brand awareness, and competition in a tough economy, you can succeed where others who have their business blinders on may fail. Metrics are your secret ingredient.

Growing a Brand with Metrics

Metrics are excellent tools to build awareness of your brand and grow your business, working hard to give you the data you need to expand your reach. Not only are metrics good for growing the business profile, you can use them for other growth aspects, such as hiring new help.

One of the first places you should check in your analytics program is the overview of where your traffic is coming from. You can find this overview in Google Analytics as follows:

1. **Log in to Google Analytics.**

2. **Select the domain you want to track.**

3. **Click the Standard Reporting tab.**

4. **In the left sidebar, click Traffic Sources.**

5. **Click Overview under Traffic Sources.**

    The Traffic Sources Overview, shown in Figure 12-1, appears.

6. **Look for the pie chart and pay attention to the segments Search, Referral, Direct, and Campaigns.**

Breaking down the pie

You can use this referral source data to see how well your various online marketing efforts are working. If most of your pie is Search, then you know your SEO is strong, and any AdWords campaigns and keyword pushes you're running are strong. If more of your pie is Referral, then you know your social media and landing page campaigns are doing well.

Figure 12-1:
Traffic
Sources
Overview
in Google
Analytics.

If your pie is off kilter, you can see which areas you need to work on and know where to put your resources. This helps you make spending and time allotment decisions for your business. It also helps you assess your existing efforts.

If you have a strong e-mail campaign (yes, e-mail is social), then you'll see good results in the Campaigns segment of the pie (formerly called Other). If this segment is weak, it's one of the first things I'd recommend you work on — e-mail is often overlooked, and your e-mail list is one of the best ways to get and hold people's attention through direct value-add campaigns and information sharing.

Getting into advanced segmentation

What quick analysis can you get from your metrics to help you make business decisions? You can get great intelligence on how well you're reaching your target market.

Say that you need to run a campaign to sell widgets in Kansas. You can use advanced segmentation to create user-defined metrics reports on your campaigns and goals. Advanced segmentation can narrow your metrics down to location, technology used, landing page data, mobile versus web browsing, conversion rate, and more.

To get into the Advanced Segmentation menu and start customizing your metrics reporting, simply do these steps:

1. **Log in to Google Analytics and click the domain you want to track.**

2. **In the Custom Reporting tab, click New Custom Report and then click Edit.**

3. **Define your metrics parameters to create your new, segmented metrics report.**

To ensure that you're getting the most complete data, make sure that your landing pages and campaign keywords are in place before you set up advanced segmentation. Without these tracking mechanisms, you'll get only surface level data that doesn't help you make the deepest decisions possible. You can also select the Advanced Segments tab instead of (or after) you set your parameters in the Edit tab.

Creating a social media traffic report

You can create as many reports as you like, so instead of trying to cram all your data into one report, think of how you want to use the data and create reports that help you funnel what you learn into something useful.

Say that you want to set up an example of a useful advanced segmentation report in Google Analytics that focuses on social media traffic. This report would tell you how effective your social media efforts are. To set up an advanced segmentation report:

1. **Inside Google Analytics, click the New Custom Segment button under Advanced Segments.**

2. **Name your new segment.**

   Something like Social Media Traffic is good because it helps you remember what you'll be gathering data on.

3. **In the drop-down menus, create Includes for each network by selecting Include.**

4. **Next to Include, select Source from the drop-down menu in green.**

5. **Add your source URL without the** `http://`.

   For example, add `plus.google.com`.

6. **Add an** OR **statement so that your report catches all traffic from all sites.**

   If you were to add an AND statement between each site include line, you'd only get results that came from all sites simultaneously — not likely to happen!

7. **Repeat Steps 3, 4, and 5 for as many social network sites as you want to track (see Figure 12-2).**

   I recommended tracking Twitter, Facebook, Delicious, Plus, StumbleUpon, and Reddit.

8. **Save your changes.**

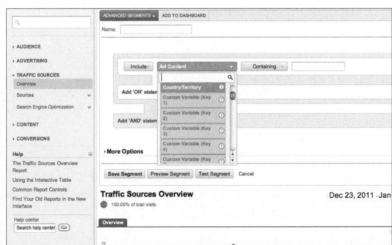

Figure 12-2:
Adding your Includes to the advanced segmentation report.

What about other criteria? Location segments can be useful if you are looking to break into a new market or to test how you're doing in your existing market.

To set up a location segment:

1. **Inside Google Analytics, click the New Custom Segment button under Advanced Segments.**

2. **Name your new segment.**

   In the same section of your analytics dashboard, start a New Custom Segment.

3. **In the drop-down menus, create Includes for each network by selecting Include.**

   Your first Include should be your country or territory if you want to track location.

   You can also add additional conditions to the report.

   Some conditions you may want to include are connection speed (if you're looking for broadband saturation) and time on site (if you' re judging stickiness in a new territory).

4. **Test your segment.**

5. **Save your segment.**

In the new Google Analytics, if you want to build layered reports, you need to add New Custom Segments each time and then come back to the Advanced Segments dashboard and apply them to the overall report. So, for example, to add to the Geolocation Report, you'd go back in and create the "time on site" condition, save it, and then apply it from the dashboard.

Looking at the Unique Visitors number

One of the more confusing numbers in the Analytics dashboard is the Unique Visitors number. It seems vague and mismatched, often reading as a different number on the front Dashboard page and under the Advanced Segmentation area. This number actually tells you quite a bit more than you'd think about your visitor patterns, however, and you can use the info to create even more detailed advanced segmentation reports. Say that your Unique Visitors count is 100 on the Dashboard page and 117 on the Advanced Segmentation pages (85 new and 32 returning).

The 85 Unique Visitors are folks who came to see your site and did not come back during the timeframe you're searching. The other 32 came back to see your site again. (This is a good thing!) The difference in numbers is 32. (These are the folks who came back at least twice, so 85 + 32 = 117.)

If your numbers were still off, say 120 instead of 117 with 85 new and 32 returning, you could continue to drill down using simple math to find out which of those visitors came back still a third time. If your site is getting that many return visits and you've filtered your own IP out of the results, then you know your site is sticky.

If you're only getting visitors that bounce away from your site never to return, you can use advanced segmentation to figure out where you might need to improve using time on site, entry pages, and other parameters. Over time, you can pinpoint and fix any trouble spots and even figure out where the next best place for you to grow your market is.

Tracking social sharing

Another metric to track while trying to grow a brand is social sharing. This data also circles back around through your Social Media Traffic report, giving you a snapshot of your site's reach coming and going, so to speak.

The easiest way to track social sharing is via tools you place on your site and track the use of. An oldie but goodie example is the Tweet This button provided by the Twitter API, which tracks the reach of an article via tweets and trending data.

Things have come a long way since the Tweet This button first came out, though. Now there are plug-ins for WordPress like Social Metrics that take snapshots of where you're being shared and how often. Used in tandem with Bit.ly or Awe.sm (link shorteners with analytics), these tools can do extensive tracking of where your content is shared. In fact, Social Metrics has some export to CSV features in its Pro version that you can add to those spreadsheets you've been using to track, sort, and learn from your data.

Combining KISSmetrics with Google Analytics

I talk a lot about Google Analytics because it's both ubiquitous and free. KISSmetrics, shown in Figure 12-3, is one paid metrics solution that's been out for a while and that is receiving high praise from icons in the online world. KISSmetrics is a paid solution, but an intriguing one with fairly reasonable price points.

When you sign up for KISSmetrics, you notice several things:

- ✔ The setup time is less than 10 minutes if you know a little bit about how to work with your website.

- ✔ KISSmetrics makes some sweeping claims about what you'll learn about your business from their metrics in one week (and the claims aren't far off).

- ✔ KISSmetrics provide all the code you need to implement each vertical and condition you want to track.

- ✔ Its metrics are people-centric; KISSmetrics remembers details about your visitors beyond page clicks and location.

Some of the many things KISSmetrics is designed to track include how people come to your site, which of your channels work the best to bring people that convert to your doorstep, what that conversion rate actually is, when people slip out of the sales funnel during signup or checkout, whether customers are being successful at learning and using your site (on-ramping or onboarding), which customers take advantage of your trial without buying, and which features of your site actually get used.

If you have the budget (starting at $29 per month after a 30-day free trial), KISSmetrics is one tool I'd recommend you experiment with in addition to Google Analytics to add that layer of people-tracking that Analytics lacks. In fact, Google Analytics is one of many services that KISSmetrics works well with via API integration, and the setup is simple.

When I say people tracking, I mean that you can tie in properties in KISSmetrics to a single visitor. For example, a new customer is a writer and used a 10 percent off coupon, found you on LinkedIn via your company page services link, and works for a Fortune 100. If you "tell" all of that information to KISSmetrics by associating properties with this customer, KISSmetrics will remember it. You can then use it to create advanced segments and data slices on your data.

Finding and Getting New Business

Finding and acquiring new business is where people-centered metrics like KISSmetrics being integrated via API into data-centered metrics like Google Analytics is the most valuable. Combining these data sets creates a one-two punch of useful data that can help you target new business.

The Google Analytics Keyword Report is a great place to start your push for more customers. (It will help you with your content also, among other things, because it's a multipurpose tool.) First, expand the Keyword report to include the most you can view at one time — currently 500 keywords.

As you take a good hard look at all the various ways real people interact with your site and your brand, you can see the treasure trove of leads and new customers that are out there waiting for you to find them, anticipate their needs, and make sure they can easily interact with your brand. The metrics behind the machine are as much about quality and innovation as they are about quantity. A lot of data doesn't mean much if you aren't using it to its full potential.

Discovering how easily people find you

One thing your Keyword Report can tell you is how hard people are working to find information that is leading them to you. You can see what I mean by that statement in those keywords that list you as showing up on page 2 or 3 of the results for that word or phrase.

To get a page 2 or 3 click means that person was really working hard to find an answer or solution. If the keyword relates to a problem your brand can solve, use your content and social graph to work harder to be on page 1 of the results, thereby reaching more customers. Don't forget to create this goal in your Analytics so that you can track your success over time.

Combine the Keyword Report analysis with new calls-to-action. If you have the resources — either via plug-in for WordPress or web designer at your disposal (even if that's you) — do some A/B testing here. Put up a subscription form on the page being optimized with the keyword you want to become a page 1 result for.

Design two buttons. Put them in different places on each version of the test. Track them over time in analytics as part of your goal and get real feedback on which one will work better with your new visitors.

Meeting your customers' content needs

Another way the Keyword Report can help you, aside from SEO, is to tell you how to change your content to reflect how your potential customers think. For example, if people search for a keyphrase or keyword about your brand's services that isn't referenced in your page, you may be missing out. Those people are going to put the same keyphrase or keyword into your on-site search box to locate more information, so be prepared.

Did you know that your Keyword Report has a bounce rate just like your website does? They do. High bounce rates on pages optimized for particular keywords is a cry for help. Definitely do A/B content testing on those pages to find out why people search for, and find, the content they need for their keyword search at your brand page, but the page doesn't hold them there.

Where the people aspect comes in through tools like KISSmetrics is in monitoring how people are using the site. As you grow that keyphrase or keyword goal, you can use action metrics as a layer to filter down past the data and into the why of a person's visit.

If you can find out how to anticipate your customers' needs before they can articulate them on their own, your sales will go up through positive word-of-mouth from customers who feel well taken care of or who simply got an answer quickly and easily from you and your brand.

Also pay attention to your Top Content Report. These are the highest performing pages on your site. Each of these pages should have calls-to-action that turn visitors into leads and sales. Each call-to-action should become part of a related goal that you track in Analytics so that you can optimize the lead generation and conversion over time.

Tracking other important data

Track your Thank You pages as well. You do have these, right? It's not enough these days just to have a form submitted or have an e-mail sent through your website and then simply return folks to the page they were on or your home page. Now people expect the validation of the confirmation page telling them they did the task correctly and their work wasn't in vain.

Make your Thank You page trackable and actionable with good content and a human touch. Set it up as a goal as well. You want to see where people go next on your site, or if they choose to leave in spite of your fun message.

Speaking of other unexpected pages to use for better lead generation and conversion, what have you done with your 404 Page Not Found page lately? Is it funny or smart? Does it have calls-to-action on it to route people through your site if they land there on accident? Is it being used to convert? You can share a funny 404 page on sites like Pinterest, Google+, Twitter, and more to brighten someone's day (see Figure 12-4).

Tallying Up the Advantages of Real-Time Metrics

Whether or not real-time metrics are useful depends entirely on your brand and what kind of service or product you offer your customers.

If your brand would benefit from watching people interact with your page in real time, you have a variety of solutions available to you; Woopra, KISSmetrics, Clicky, Google Analytics, and more all offer real-time metrics for a view of your site in action.

Figure 12-4:
Amusing 404
Not Found
page from
Mint.com.

Why would you want to use real-time metrics? You're

- ✔ Running a contest
- ✔ Running a time-sensitive rewards campaign
- ✔ Running a timed vote drive
- ✔ Monitoring a poll for a prize
- ✔ Testing a new site design in action
- ✔ Analyzing time-on-site issues
- ✔ Requiring a real-time look at time on site to conversion data
- ✔ Checking on broken site features while site still live
- ✔ Looking for broken links in real time
- ✔ Providing customer support
- ✔ Troubleshooting
- ✔ Reaching out to customers
- ✔ Finding out the visitor path from referral source to exit

Some tools offer an enhanced experience in real-time analytics. Woopra, for example, is no longer entirely free to get this feature, but if you move to a paid plan, you can chat with visitors on your site while they are there (if they also run Woopra).

Whether or not you want to surprise your visitors by suddenly popping up a chat window, real-time metrics have many uses for the brand that is trying to offer better customer service or a better site or just trying to see what its customers really want out of its site so that it can provide better service.

One thing I've noticed is that in the case of real-time metrics, at the time of this writing, Google Analytics had a long way to go to be as useful as some of the other solutions. You're going to have to work a little harder to get useful data out of Google's real-time metrics.

If you've used Google Analytics for a while, this observation won't surprise you. Many of the stats in that tool default to a month view that ends the day before the day you sign in to check your stats. Certain reports won't even run correctly if you try to force Google Analytics to see what happened on your site today!

It's best if you stick to another real-time solution while Google works the kinks out of this one (and it will). Meanwhile, don't forget to integrate your real-time solution with Analytics. Tools like KISSmetrics work with the Google Analytics API, making your life much easier.

Chapter 13

Using Branded Metrics for Business Success

*H*undreds of options for white labeling metrics are on the market. In this chapter, I walk you through a few outsourcing options, in no particular order. (If you don't see your favorite here, we probably ran out of room!)

What White Label Really Means

White label means taking someone else's platform or solution and branding it with your logo, either to indicate to customers that they're interacting with your brand or to resell as your own service.

White label also applies to the ability to brand a product as one's own. Even though it's much better to perform analytics on your own and then deliver them to clients, team members, or partners in reports you create yourself, some companies prefer not to do this data tracking. For those companies, paid products (never free) take the data they collect and rebrand it for remarketing, internal reports, or client deliverables.

These solutions are often not quite as customizable as the solutions you can do yourself.

Knowing What to Look for in a Service

When shopping for a service to white label and resell, look for the following:

- **Website design:** It doesn't have to be Picasso, but it needs to be maintained, current, error-free, and ad-free, with clear contact information and an About page.

- **Testimonials:** Customer testimonials from people and brands you have heard of are a good indicator of credibility.

- **Customer list:** Not all services need to list their customers, but in this case, I recommend looking for those that do. A customer list allows you to contact customers and find out real satisfaction rates. It also allows you to see the product you're considering in action.

- **Free trial period:** Reputable software should offer some kind of demo or free trial period so that you can try out what they offer and make sure that it works for you.

- **Support:** How do they support the product? Is it an impersonal FAQ or something more accessible, such as live chat, e-mail, or phone support? Bonus points if supporting your clients also via white label support is an option.

- **Clear cancelation instructions:** Hopefully, it won't come to this point, but it always pays to make sure that you have a clear, easy way to cancel the service if it isn't working out for you.

- **Data use and privacy policy:** Make sure they clearly indicate how they will use your and your client's data, especially if they are hosting the solution for you. Make sure their privacy policy is easily accessible. Bonus points if they let you export your data to take with you upon leaving the service, or at regular intervals during your time with them.

- **Length of time in business:** This one can be harder to find, and may require a little digging. In general, it's best to use a company that has been in business for a while and has had time to test the product out and to build up a roster of happy clients.

Watching Out for the Pitfalls

The white label option for analytics (or any other service) comes with some hazards. Many say that outsourcing analytics undermines a brand's credibility. Customers want to work with a company that knows their stuff, not one that outsources. Customers expect you to be able to answer questions about analytics. To that end white label services that include help desk support may be your best bet if you must go this route. A better route, of course, is to use this book to master analytics and social media metrics and then move on to the many other excellent publications out there designed to help you learn.

If you do go the white label route, make sure that you have a plan in place for scale. A successful package solution can scale up very quickly, which can catch companies unaware. You don't want to hurt your business by growing faster than your infrastructure can handle.

If your white label solution is hosted on your server and not theirs, look into cloud server services that can scale up with traffic in real time. This way, you don't have a server crash when you get popular or when your site gets linked to on Reddit or StumbleUpon. In fact, make sure that the hosted solution has a plan in place on their server for this scenario also.

Looking at Your Options

You can find many white label options, and I describe several in the following sections. This mention isn't to be construed as an endorsement. Rather, I'd like to see you and your brand handle your own metrics. However, that's just not feasible for everyone, so you may need to consider other options.

Clicky

In addition to do-it-yourself capabilities, Clicky (see Figure 13-1) also offers a white label version of its product, hosted on its servers.

Figure 13-1:
Getting to know Clicky.

In this white label version of Clicky, you can have your own company, your own product or company logo, a custom style sheet (CSS) to match your brand, and your own domain (URL). For $49 per month, Clicky allows you to offer branded metrics as a solution to your clients and bill your clients at a rate you determine.

Under its service umbrella, your white label metrics brand can provide people with the metrics they want at no hassle, including Clicky's real-time metrics. Clicky has an API you can use to create an automated registration process as well.

Don't worry, users must be registered by you; the white label metrics solution is closed to the public. You hold the keys.

Google Analytics Premium

That's right, the free analytics kingpin has a premium version, for the low, low price of $150,000 per year. Google doesn't offer a traditional white label metrics solution, however.

Instead of creating a white label API for the money, Google offers you the chance to be a certified Google Analytics Premium Authorized Reseller and a Google Analytics Certified Partner (see Figure 13-2). These designations allow you to claim expertise in their product, place Google badges stating your certification on your website, and offer people analytics solutions for a price you set.

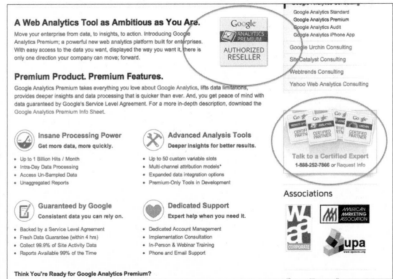

Figure 13-2:
Google
Analytics
Premium
offers
certification
badges.

The big draw for Google Analytics Premium is for the larger brands out there: It lifts all the data limits faced by sites using the free version. (Don't worry; the average website isn't likely to hit this data limit.) Unlimited use is important for a brands like Hewlett-Packard, Jet Blue, or Dell where you're getting vast amounts of web and social media traffic that you must track and convert.

Another feature big brands love is the ability to download reports with high data volumes. This means you can plug these numbers into your GANTT charts and future project projections and make more accurate predictions about the resources you'll need to grow your brands and reach new markets.

Other benefits include having your own account manager and a 24/7 emergency support line. Considering it's incredibly difficult to get a human to help at Google outside of Google+, where the company is unusually active, this access to help is a great selling point for a brand doing high volume tracking where you may run into website-killing snags.

Agency Platform

Agency Platform (see Figure 13-3) offers a combination of social dashboard and analytics to agencies for white label resale to its customers. This solution offers you access to a local or national plan ($189 per month and $254 per month respectively).

Figure 13-3: Agency Platform, another white label option.

The client login is hosted on your site with this solution, and it offers pre-sales help that it claims will help you close more leads. As an added benefit, you don't just get to use Agency Platform's hard work on analytics and SEO, you also get a variety of canned marketing reports you can brand as yours to share with clients.

This one also includes a team of content farm writers to generate content for your site as well. Frankly, I think you shouldn't offer analytics, SEO, social media, and marketing solutions if you need to use something like Agency Platform to get it done, but in the interest of being thorough, these types of canned solutions are out there if you want to go that route.

Truviso

Offering white label analytics for brands needing real-time metrics, Truviso focuses on a variety of conditions and goals. It also has segments for online video and other options.

Truviso (see Figure 13-4) claims to track real-time campaigns, cost per unique visit, geolocation data, social reach and share frequency, structured goal progress, demographics, time and dayparting, conversion costs, and more.

Truviso positions white label analytics as something that allows the brand to differentiate itself from its competitors strategically as much as something that will help with marketing the brand. This value-added approach is a little more low key than some of the other white label solutions out there.

Figure 13-4: Truviso's Lifetime Totals and other metrics.

Truviso also has a mobile metrics component, offering mobile data to clients. For some reason, Truviso doesn't include the mobile data in the white label metrics. That's unfortunate — mobile is fast becoming the larger share of the attention pie, and companies that don't track it can be seen as remiss.

Wildfire

Wildfire (see Figure 13-5) offers social marketing metrics with varying branding and white label options at a variety of price points. The lowest price point offers the least amount of branding and white label options, and enterprise-level pricing offers the most comprehensive white label options.

In fact, only the enterprise level offers analytics for multiple social properties, audience targeting, advanced analytics, and complete brand control. Wildfire is really a full planning and campaign management application as well, with metrics being only a part of the pie.

Figure 13-5:
Wildfire
offers things
like Map
View metrics.

Ventipix VPX QR

VPX QR Advanced Analytics & Campaign Management (see Figure 13-6) is an interesting bit of software you install on your own site. It does white label QR Code management and metrics.

Figure 13-6:
Ventipix is
a QR Code
metrics
solution.

QR Codes can sometimes be overrated. For example, Best Buy uses QR Codes in their stores to encourage checking out products and product reviews before you buy, but I usually find that logging in easily with product information makes me price shop while I'm online. Regardless, QR Codes have many useful applications, and this software lets you track that for you and for your clients.

One neat feature is that it creates QR Codes with your logo (or your client's logo) in the image. Another is that it works for traditional QR Codes, QR Codes with Extras, Data Matrix, Aztec, and Microsoft tags.

VPX-QR also allows you to edit the QR Codes after they're generated. As a result, a changed campaign doesn't have to cause panic; the QR Code updates when the information is changed. It also sports other features, such as subscription payment compatibility, calendar generation, shortened URLs, vanity URLs, Facebook Page compatibility, smartphone apps, and the influx of mobile data you'll receive about people actually taking action with the QR Codes.

Snoobi

Snoobi (see Figure 13-7) offers both cobranded and white label solutions for the client who needs to brand its client reports. The white label option includes both web analytics and Facebook analytics that the brand can then turn around and resell to its clients as a service.

Figure 13-7:
Snoobi's
Partner
Program
page.

Snoobi vows to never have royalty fees attached to your data, making it clear that your data is exactly that — yours. In fact, Snoobi makes it clear that your customer data is yours as well, right down to the invoices.

Snoobi also touts its support. If you want help, you can add a Snoobi expert to your package. That expert can either do all the analytics work or simply help you do it.

Whatever package you choose, Snoobi makes sure that you know you can take your data with you at any time. It also has extensive continuing education, meaning that you can get a crash course in web analytics from the pros.

Campaign Monitor

Campaign Monitor (see Figure 13-8) claims it was created "from the ground up for designers to resell as their own product." It does much more than brand metrics reports and analytics on e-mail campaigns, though. Campaign Monitor also allows you to white label e-mail, e-mail lists, and other engagement.

Campaign Monitor has a complex credit card billing system to manage the billing for you and your clients as well as using PayPal for those more comfortable with the PayPal interface. This system allows you to offer different levels of access to clients as well.

Figure 13-8:
Campaign
Monitor
wants to
be your
"dirty little
secret."

Billing is handled in the client's local currency: U.S. dollars, British pounds, the euro, Canadian dollars, Australian dollars, and New Zealand dollars. Toss in its templating system and WYSIWYG (what you see is what you get) e-mail builder interface, and Campaign Monitor makes it easy to upsell e-mail and e-mail analytics to your clients.

Some popular e-mail services companies are using this product. It's a point in its favor that it has been tried and tested and seems successful and easy to use.

Part V

Taking the Deep Dive into Advanced Metrics

In this part . . .

In this part, you discover the tricks of the metrics pros. You find out how to make metrics do your bidding and convert faster for better leads and stronger clients.

You also find out how to improve your calls-to-action and set better, more definitive business goals that you can better track and reach.

You use advanced techniques to master your metrics dashboards and climb to the top on the strength of your data.

Chapter 14

Mastering Metrics Moves

. . . .

In This Chapter

▶ Seeing how long it takes your page to load

▶ Getting the metrics scoop on videos and phone calls

▶ Taking your metrics offline

. . . .

You may be wondering what comes next after you master the basics of metrics? The answer is quite a bit!

You can command Google Analytics to bring back as much and as varied data as you can conceive of asking for and tracking. Half the battle is discovering how to optimize the data and not drown in the sheer volume of it.

After you discover more advanced techniques, you'll start seeing metrics as fun and useful and less like a chore. In this chapter, I show you how to make friends with certain types of URLs and codes so that you can enjoy even better metrics.

Did you know that you can measure phone calls? Did you know that on some platforms you can pinpoint the exact moment your content gained traction — down to the second and the influencer?

I cover those topics and more in this chapter so that you, too, know some of the tricks the metrics masters use.

Tracking Page Load Times

Few things annoy website visitors more than a page that loads slowly. In general, you have only a few seconds to keep someone's attention — do you really want to waste that precious time with slow page loads and lose your visitor altogether?

You can track page load times in a variety of ways:

✔ You can now configure the Google Analytics plug-ins to track page load times. You just have to add the line of code to your theme (if you're using WordPress or Drupal) or website.

✔ Extensions and add-ons for Firefox and Chrome track page load times for you. Page Speed Test is one of many extensions for Chrome, and Firebug is a popular add-on with plenty of options for Firefox. You can find many more add-ons just by browsing the Chrome and Firefox archives for the one that's right for you.

✔ By far the most effective way to track page load times is to use Google's page speed API:

1. **Add this line of code to the pages you want to track for load times:**

```
_gaq.push (['trackPageLoadtime']);
```

2. **Go into the new Google Analytics and flip the Site Speed Report to On (see Figure 14-1).**

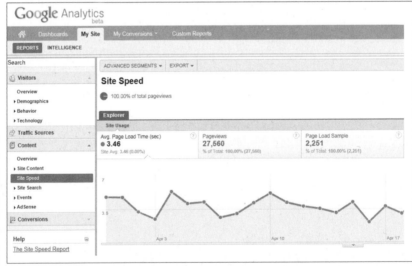

Figure 14-1:
You can check out your site speed in Google Analytics.

3. **By default, adding the code to your analytics measures site speed for pages across your entire site.**

You can go in and fine-tune where you put the code to track only your most critical pages, or you can leave it site-wide.

When measuring site speed, you want to pay particular attention to certain metrics:

- ✔ **Content:** Seek out which landing pages for your marketing campaigns are slow to load, losing conversions.

- ✔ **Traffic source:** Pinpoint which marketing campaigns have the fastest page load times and look at their conversion rates.

- ✔ **Visitor:** Does the location of a visitor affect the page load time experience? This metric helps you discover whether the problem is your website, your web host, or the Internet service in a particular region or country.

- ✔ **Technology type:** How does each browser or mobile platform experience load times on your site? Can you do anything to optimize for trouble spots?

Create a Site Speed Custom Report (see Figure 14-2) to help troubleshoot these issues. For example, if your target demographic is in a certain region and demographic that seems to be experiencing slow load times, you can run your report to get the data you need to fix the issue.

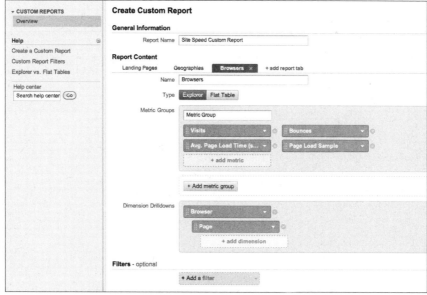

Figure 14-2: A Site Speed Custom Report helps you troubleshoot.

Watching Video Metrics

You've heard it from at least one client (if you're an agency) or perhaps from your boss, if you are a company just getting into social: "We need a viral video!" You've all had to break the sad news that you can't force a video to go viral, and that it has to hit that elusive sweet spot that compels viewers to share it. It has to become a *meme* (a piece of content online or a content theme that gets shared, reshared, added to, remixed and shared again by people online, such as lolcats).

You've probably then shared the good news that even nonviral videos that get good page views have direct, measureable benefits for marketing and brand education and outreach. Then comes the tough question: How do you measure video to make sure that you're optimizing the videos you create?

Looking at the Video ID Code

The first component to tracking a YouTube video is the *Video ID Code.* That's the row of mish-mashed letters, numbers, and symbols in the video URL. It comes right after /watch?v= and ends before the &feature in the longer URLs, as in

```
http://www.youtube.com/watch?v=ji5_MqicxSo&feature=youtu.
           be
```

The bold part of the preceding URL is the Video ID Code.

Now you have to put the code on your page or in a blog post in such a way that it gets tracked by Google Analytics. You do this by adding states, like this:

```
Var STATE_UNSTARTED = '-1';
Var STATE_PLAYING = '1';
Var STATE_PAUSED = '2';
Var STATE_BUFFERING = '3';
Var STATE_VIDEOCUED = '5';
Var STATES = {
'-1' : 'unstarted',
'1' : 'playing',
'2' : 'paused',
'3' : 'buffering',
'5' : 'videocued'
};
```

After you add states, you need to make sure that the title and video ID match your YouTube video and your div container, by adding something like this:

```
Var VIDEOS = {
'videoplayer' : {
id:'videoplayer', title:'TITLE', ytID:' ji5_MqicxSo',
        container:'videoid'
},
```

To then also make your `div` tags match, add the following code before the video embed code:

```
<div id="video1-container">
```

And don't forget your closing `</div>` tag!

Enjoying YouTube bonus tools

YouTube is owned by Google, which means that YouTube offers Google Analytics users a few little bonus tools to make life a bit easier.

You can grab your Google Analytics user ID (that number that begins with UA-) and add it right into your YouTube videos on your Premium YouTube channel, if you have one. This means that your videos are getting tracked in Google Analytics not only when embedded on your site, but also when played on YouTube, giving you more accurate reporting.

Add in the YouTube basic metrics now offered for a quick glance at number of views and other interactions below each video, and you can see how you can closely track videos.

Getting Data on Phone Calls

Everyone wants to get data on phone calls. Try as you might to get folks to fill out a web form, scan a QR Code with their smartphone, or send you an e-mail you can track, some people are just old school. They want to hear a human voice, and they're going to call you.

Until recently, you had no idea how to measure this metric, but now you can do so in a variety of ways, which I describe in the following sections.

Taking advantage of mobile metrics

You can use your mobile metrics to track phone calls. By putting a clickable phone number into your mobile landing page, your mobile visitors can click it directly to call your locations. This click is trackable in Google Analytics.

You need to give the phone number a bit of code so that Google Analytics can recognize which number is being called (if you have more than one location) or so that you can easily find the metric in your reports. That code is a simple modified `href` code you're most likely familiar with from blogging:

```
<a href="tel:800-xxx-xxxx" onClick="_gaq.push(['_trackEvent', 'Phone',
             'Clicked', 'Boston Office']);">Call 800-xxx-xxxx</a>
```

Using Google AdWords and Google Voice

The second method of tracking phone calls involves using Google AdWords and Google Voice. Google introduced the AdWords Call Metrics program to help solve this ROI dilemma for everyone.

How it works is simple. Inside your Google AdWords ad campaign, use the extension that adds your Google Voice phone number to ads as a metric (see Figure 14-3). Then when you create each ad, make sure to include the phone number. The phone number is clickable, and AdWords includes clicks on the number in its ad reporting now. If you did link AdWords and Analytics, you can take this metric even further.

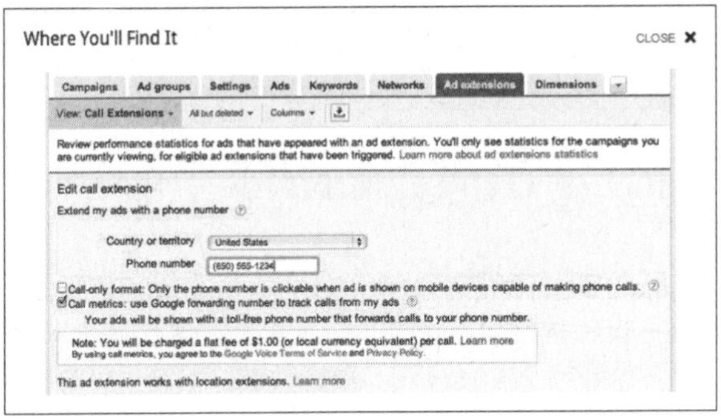

Figure 14-3:
You add your Google Voice phone number to ads as a metric.

Using a third-party solution

Third-party companies can route your calls through your analytics and landing pages to help generate reports. If you have the budget for this solution, it is certainly one option.

Google is adding new phone call tracking metrics over time, and you soon won't need to spend the extra money.

Some companies who have been offering this service include Mongoose Metrics, Blue Corona, ifbyphone, Marchex, and more. Mongoose Metrics has definitely been doing it the longest, even receiving a nod of approval from Google before Google introduced its own call tracking metrics.

Pushing Social Buttons

You've put the Share buttons on your site or installed a basic sharing plug-in. So now what? How do you know if people are using them?

You can install another plug-in, like Social Metrics or Google Analytics, to get another snapshot of how folks may be using them. Social Metrics doesn't really give you in-depth information, though, and the true metrics master wants as much information as possible.

The Google+ +1 button already has metrics in it for Google Analytics. Every other Share button needs some tweaking.

As you install each button, adding one simple line of code allows you to track it inside of Google Analytics as well:

```
_gaq.push ({'_trackSocial ', network, socialAction, opt_target, opt_pagePath ]);
```

For example, to track a Facebook Like button, that code would read

```
FB.Event.subscribe('edge.create', function(targetURL) { _gaq.push(['_
            trackSocial', 'facebook', 'like', targetURL]);
```

After you install this code in all your social Share buttons, you can track the activity through the Social Engagement Report in the new Google Analytics (see Figure 14-4). This report allows you to see at a glance not only which social platforms your visitors are most engaged in, allowing you to focus on them more in your social marketing, but also helps you find any weak spots.

As you track content across social buttons, you can determine which content topics and type of content are most compelling to your visitors and make your site content more engaging and sticky overall.

Keeping an Eye on Offline Marketing

Offline marketing can be as elusive to track as a phone call. How do you know if your billboard, poster, flyer, or mailer is bringing traffic to your site? It can be frustrating not knowing how the hard-earned money you spend on advertising is working to generate leads. (Actual sales have their own ROI — income — which is much easier to follow).

Figure 14-4:
The Social
Engagement
Report in
the New
Google
Analytics.

Using QR Codes

One popular method right now is the use of QR Codes. Keep in mind that QR Codes work only if the customer

✔ Has a smartphone handy and is willing to click

✔ Knows what a QR Code is and how to scan it

Fortunately, QR Codes have become fairly ubiquitous, so there is a good chance the customer knows how to use them.

Google has embraced the QR Code technology over Microsoft's version of the clickable code and other methods, unsurprisingly. This works in your favor because Google now generates a trackable QR Code for you that you can then layer on a trackable short URL and get double traction on metrics. When building your QR Code through Google's QR Code builder (see Figure 14-5), you add your analytics segments right into it during the build.

One more layer is needed in addition to something clickable like a QR Code on your offline marketing, and that is tracking code for each campaign. This tracking code helps you set goals for these codes inside analytics to give more depth to the metrics you get from successful click traction. A tracking code can be anything, but is usually a short series of letters or abbreviations similar to a hashtag (Hint: Some people use their hashtags to generate these tracking codes as well for cross-marketing purposes).

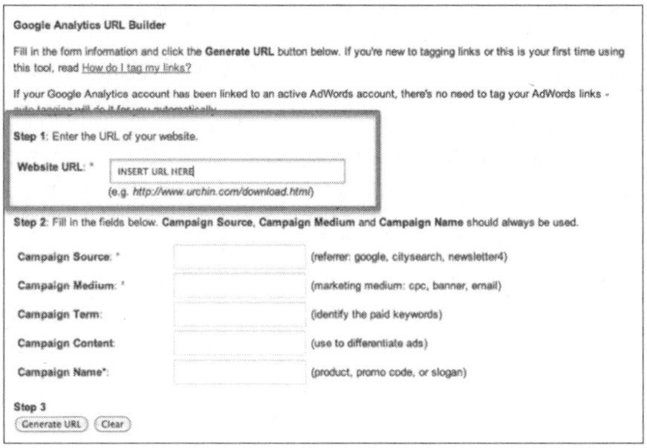

Figure 14-5:
Google's
QR Code
builder.

Another key component for offline campaign tracking is to make the referral URL you send folks unique to that campaign. By giving the campaign a landing page (preferably one with an URL built using the Google Analytics URL Builder) and tagging visitors with variables unique to the campaign, you make your metrics more useful. For example:

```
<head>
        <link rel="canonical" href="http://www.URL.com/valentine" />
        <meta http-equiv="refresh" content="1;URL=http://www.URL.com/?utm_
        source=NYTimes&utm_medium=newspaper&utm_campaign=VALENTINE2012 >
        </head>
```

Tracking television ads

A subset of offline marketing, and a large market, is television. Much like call tracking, Google has introduced a way to track AdWords TV ad campaigns in Analytics if your AdWords account is linked in to Analytics.

If you're wondering how on earth you get AdWords television ads in the first place, simply visit this link to get started with AdWords TV ads in national markets:

```
http://google.com/TVAds
```

To get to the TV analytics for your TV ads, follow these steps:

1. **Sign in to your AdWords account and go to the Reporting tab.**

   You should see your Analytics page.

2. **Click TV Campaigns under AdWords inside the Traffic Sources section.**

   This section automatically appears if your Analytics and AdWords accounts are linked. If you don't see it, you need to link your accounts.

3. **Sign in to your Analytics account and choose the URL/domain where the TV ads landing page is located.**

4. **Click Traffic Sources, click AdWords, and then click TV Campaigns.**

   From here, you can look at your metrics.

5. **Fine-tune the URLs and landing pages you're using in your television ads.**

6. **Set up any advanced segmentation and goals necessary to track metrics of TV ads.**

   In this Reporting area, you can set up specific reports to track performance metrics (how many times TV ads played, for example), visit quality (time on site from each TV ad, for example), Conversions (Goal Conversion Rates from each ad), and ecommerce (track revenue transactions on TV ad landing pages and more).

Keep in mind that call tracking and TV tracking both have a cost in AdWords! They usually fall under the PPC (pay per click) ad budget, so you need to consider cost when you set up these campaigns.

Integrating Metrics and CRM

Customer Relationship Management (CRM) and metrics — how can you integrate your analytics and your CRM effectively?

You can do so in two ways:

- ✔ If you have a CRM program that is analytics friendly, you can use the fact that Google Analytics tracks data at the profile level to your advantage. Set up one user profile that will be added as a user to all client analytics accounts. This profile then has access to everyone's analytics, and you can use Google Management API to drill down to the profile ID of each client and pull their data in to your CRM. You can find the Management API at this link:

```
http://code.google.com/apis/analytics/docs/mgmt/
           home.html
```

- ✔ You can use the _utmz cookie to extract your visitor's source data and include it in hidden form fields in your web forms. Using hidden form fields allows you to attach source data to the visible form fields that the user fills out, making your CRM data more complete. The _utmz cookie lets you attach hidden values like referral information (where the visitor came from), custom segment values, and number of visits to the standard form fields, such as user name and address.

You can use this code in your site in many ways (so many, in fact, that you could write an entire *For Dummies* book about utilizing cookies in various methods). The easiest way for most people is to use JavaScript at the site level, but you can also do it at the server level using ColdFusion, .NET, PHP, or the language of your choice.

Pinpointing Moment of Traction with Google+

The moment of traction could also be called the "best time to share on Google+ or other social sites," but I think it's better to avoid that. The best time for you may not be the best time for your fellow content generators, and this section is intended to help you find the best time for you.

I wish I could take credit for noticing this metrics master tip, but in this case credit (and gratitude for letting me paraphrase his observation in this sub-section) goes to eagle-eyed Christopher Penn who first shared his observation on search signals in Google+ and on his blog *Awaken Your Superhero.*

If you look at Google+ shares, you'll notice a rather unique URL. This URL was interesting when it was first spotted by Chris in mid-2011, but it has become a bit more important now that Google has begun to force Google+ and profile integration between all Google products, including search, onto users. By the time this book is published, everyone will have the personal search option to contend with, which is one way to track your analytics more accurately in the face of that added layer of complexity.

Here's an example of a typical Google+ URL:

```
http://plus.url.google.com/url?sa=z&n=132908154
       6445&url=http%3A%2F%2Fmagnitudemedia.
       net%2F2012%2F02%2Fearly-riser-with-a-social-
       tech-question%2F&usg=vnTdqmgsWQtHTrNDz928mYWbqMI
```

The stand out part of this URL outside of the normal variables is the 13-digit number within the URL that appears to be a UNIX time stamp. It's a UNIX timestamp with an extra three digits: Those extra digits are what Chris dubbed microtimes.

These time stamps are unique and change every time the URL is clicked. That's huge news for analytics tracking. If you're a Google+ user, you may have already experienced its analytics tool Ripples, which seems to visualize this data flow — you can track the velocity of the link itself and watch it become popular (or not) in real time.

If you've been following my advice to collect your metrics data in spreadsheets, you can see how having data this accurate will create *traction arcs* (a kind of visual of how well your content is gaining traction) you can graph inside your spreadsheets for your own content. These arcs, in turn, tell you not the best time to share in general, but the best time to share for you, which is much more useful. If you pay closer attention, you can also tell what kind of content works best for your audience and discover other useful data.

Chapter 15

Making Your Calls-to-Action Work for You

*Y*ou've probably heard the term call-to-action even before you picked up this book. When done well, calls-to-action can be quite effective.

This chapter goes into more detail on how to structure great calls-to-action, how to leverage them, and how to measure the results. Being able to track what people do with your calls-to-action is just as important as being able to create a good call-to-action item.

After you start gathering data on your calls-to-action, you need to use the other tools to turn that data into useful information. Then that information needs to become part of your business plan of action.

Building Great Calls-to-Action

One of the first hurdles you face when trying to engage visitors to your site or social streams is deciding what you'll ask them to do after you get their attention. Most people who are new to developing calls-to-action get overwhelmed and default to a simple Email Us — or just list their e-mail without even making it a link.

A good call-to-action won't ask your visitors or social media followers to think too much about how to do what you're asking. In fact, they won't have to wonder too deeply about what it is you really want them to do, either. Clarity is key.

Going beyond clarity, you have to make your calls-to-action easy to see as well. You won't have anything to measure at all if people can't figure out where to do what you want them to do.

Color

Calls-to-action often appear in the form of buttons or icons. Color is impor-tant (see Figure 15-1). Did you know that there have been psychological stud-ies on what colors motivate people to do or feel different things? You can apply this information to your marketing and measurement efforts.

Figure 15-1: Sample color wheel, a great way to visualize colors for your site.

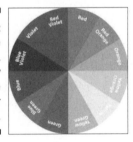

Here's a quick color reference guide:

- ✔ **Blue** creates a feeling of safety, security, and calm and is often used when the goal is to get people to trust you. (It's no accident that one of the Internet world's biggest privacy violators, Facebook, is blue.)

- ✔ **Green** creates a feeling of confidence, wealth, and, in certain shades, calm and is often used when you want people to shell out cold, hard cash. Sometimes the calming effect can backfire. (For example, hospitals are often green, but rarely calming.)

- ✔ **Red** creates a feeling of power, a sense of vibrancy, energy, and vigor and is often used when you want to show that you're an authority in a subject matter area. Caution: Overuse of red can trigger agitation and anger (and can also be hard to read).

- ✔ **Yellow** creates a sunny sense of optimism and cheer and is often used to imply that a company or product is fun and energetic. Like red, over-use of yellow can agitate people and push them away. Use sparingly.

- ✔ **Pinks** and **purples** create a soft sense of romance or indicate a dreamy, comforting feel. They're often (over)used if the target customer is a female in the age 18 to 24 bracket. The color pink has been somewhat co-opted by cancer causes, as well.

- ✔ **Orange** creates a feeling of youth and a general sense of action. A popular color in social media, orange is often used to indicate that a company is fresh and hip and that the customer should act quickly to book its services. Like yellow and red, orange can be hard to read if overused in design.

- ✔ **Black** creates a sense of wealth or aggression. Often used to entice people to spend money on more expensive items or to demonstrate power, black can be off-putting to some people or, if done poorly, make a site look outdated.

So out of all of those colors, which ones are the best colors for your calls-to-action?

If you look at Google+, Facebook, and other sites with notification indicators when you have new messages and so on, you'll notice that the predominant color for these chiclet indicators is red. You'll probably notice that you feel compelled to click, as well. If you guessed red as a great choice for a call-to-action button, you'd be right.

Something to consider, though, is the sense of immediate reward you get from clicking the Google+, Gmail, Facebook Message, or Direct Message indicator chiclets. If your call-to-action isn't going to give that same immediate feeling of instant gratification, then you may want to choose a different color.

If you can't — or don't want to — default to red, you'll want to choose a color that is contrasting to your site theme. If you've worked with a color wheel, you remember that contrasting colors are the ones directly across from each other on the wheel. So, on a predominantly blue site, an orange button would stand out.

Placement

So where do you put the button(s) after you know what you want them to look like? This burning question faces everyone with a website and a need for customers.

In this case, it's important to use metrics to help with placement. Do A/B testing on page placement. Run versions of your landing page that have the button(s) in different places. I recommend running two versions at a time, but I've had clients who ran as many as five test placements at once, delivering randomly.

Your metrics can help you determine which versions get the most clicks overall, which parts of the page get the most clicks, and which button colors and placements get the most conversions from clicks (for example, filling out a form or other further action).

If you're using some of the new page insights, you can even look at click percentages on the pages you're testing. This number not only gives you a visual of the data for your button placement, it puts it in context with the other clickable elements on the page: navigation bar, logos, creative content, and other calls-to-action. Having that perspective will help you make a more educated decision on which version of your page to use.

Some people find that running different versions of the landing page with calls-to-action for each incoming link source is effective. Just as you design a landing page for, say, a Twitter audience, you can tailor the buttons on that page as well. There is nothing wrong with keeping that A/B rotation up permanently, triggered by referral source.

What to say

What should your calls-to-action say? As a general rule, ambiguity is never going to be in your best interests. People respond well to clarity. Go ahead: Tell them what to do (see Figure 15-2).

There is a reason so many brand pages on Facebook have a landing tab that has a huge graphic pointing to a Like button and directly tell folks to Like This Page! for *[insert reward here]*. It works!

Your calls-to-action should have short, direct language that tell your customer or potential customer what you want them to do. The copy surrounding the call-to-action is important also. It should get people excited for the reward or result they'll get from clicking and converting.

Humor sells, but bad humor pushes people away. If you're going to use humor in your calls-to-action, make sure that you give it the human test before launching. In this case, use your metrics to A/B test a serious versus funny version of the call-to-action or two different versions of the funny idea.

In addition, here are a few more do's and don'ts of button text:

- ✔ **Don't be vague.** Submit and Click Here are vague.
- ✔ **Do create task or result-oriented text.** Register Free!, Subscribe Now, Create Account, Send E-Mail, and Get Event Notices are all specific, good call-to-action text options (see Figure 15-3).

Figure 15-2:
Daily Mile offers a call-to-action with clear instruction for the visitor.

Figure 15-3:
Human Design has a clear call-to-action for its e-mail list.

Calls-to-Action: Best Practices

I've watched folks agonize over best practices for calls-to-action and other website elements. While the following general rules will help you, in the end, it's key to remember that your mileage may vary.

✔ **Test, test, test.** Metrics are just as important when you're building your site as they are when you're tracking engagement. Track your call-to-action versions using your metrics program so that you can determine through testing which of these best practices translates well to your specific business.

That is the thing with industry general advice: Specific industries often have specific needs. Make sure that you test your versions for what works for you!

✔ **Size matters.** Size matters three ways, actually:

- Is the button proportional to your page and design? Does it grab attention without making your page look wrong to the eye?

- Does the size grab the attention of the viewer at all? Too small is hard to find. Think of 20 percent larger than surrounding page elements as a good place to start in sizing your buttons and then adjust up or down accordingly (see Figure 15-4).

- Does the size differentiate between two different calls-to-action on a page? Continue Reading at the end of a post and Subscribe For eNews are two calls-to-action that may appear on the same page. In that case, the eNews subscription should be larger than the Continue Reading button because that call-to-action is more important.

✔ **Position above the fold.** I talk about the need to A/B test a variety of positioning on your site to see what works best for you. That said, a few things tend to work well for everyone. Placement *above the fold* is key for the more important calls-to-action. Above the fold means that you put the button where folks can see it without having to scroll down the page.

Experiment with nontraditional button types and positioning. For example, a flyout button that appears on the side of a scrolling page above the fold works very well for certain kinds of sites and also stands out as unique.

Standard calls-to-action that people have come to expect on any site can go below the fold, but still need to be designed in a visible manner. This would include something like Email Us.

Figure 15-4:
gonna-
sphere's
variety of
sizes and
placements
make its
calls-to-
action
stand out.

✔ **Remember the value of whitespace.** A page that is too crowded is a page that isn't going to convert well over all. People who arrive there will find the page confusing, which will reflect in your bounce rate and other metrics. Use your *white space* (the space around an object) to draw the eye to your calls-to-action (and to your content). Use whitespace to help the eye flow where you want it to go on the page (see Figure 15-5).

✔ **Use contrasting color.** Make your calls-to-action the color of conversion — whatever color that works for your website, be it red or another contrasting color.

✔ **Offer secondary actions.** This one will take a while to master, but offering people a choice of action can help convert them to take action on the page. For example, you can have two buttons side by side: Sign Up Now next to Take Our Tour with an *or* in between can give people a sense of choice and encourage them to interact with the page and commit to one of the calls-to-action. Either way, your metrics are tracking them to see which they chose, how long the choice took, and where they navigated after. You can then use this data to refine your product, marketing, and design.

Figure 15-5:
Using white
space to
draw
the eye
to a call-
to-action.

✔ **Create a sense of urgency.** This won't apply in all situations, but creating a sense of urgency often encourages conversion. You can create a sense of urgency by making a countdown part of your call-to-action. You can also do it by making a time-sensitive action, a limited offer, or other incentive.

✔ **Make action easy.** Eliminate folks' fear that clicking will take up their time, cost them too much money, or be difficult to complete. For example, adding One-Click Sign Up to your button indicates that the process is easy and fast, eliminating that mental hurdle people throw out there.

✔ **Set expectations clearly.** If your users are going to get a trial offer that lasts 15 days from signing up and then move to autosubscription, make that clear on the button. Under Try WidgetX Out, add 14-Day Free Trial Included.

Applying Metrics to Calls-to-Action

Metrics plus calls-to-action pack a one-two punch needed to create a website or landing page that generates conversions for leads or sales. You can pump up your call-to-action buttons with metrics in a variety of ways. Some of the metrics that apply to calls-to-action are

✔ **Click-through:** Means how many who *saw* the call-to-action *clicked* the call-to-action. Click-through is generally measured as a percentage in most metrics/analytics programs. Comparing your percentages is a great way to compare your A/B campaign testing. It's also a great way to compare the same call-to-action across delivery types (e-mail, landing page, on-site page, and so on).

✔ **Click to Submission:** Means how many people fill out your form. Generally these forms are designed to capture leads, even if those leads are signing up to get a newsletter or other reward from you. Click to Submission is also measured in percentages. You can use the percentage to track which type of marketing, such as e-mail or a social share leading to the submission request page, gets the most response.

✔ **View to Submission:** Measures how many people fill out a static form on your site, like the one on your Contact Us page. This form is a call-to-action, but not a call-to-action button. It lives on a specific page on your site. This measurement usually lets you know whether you need to make the form simpler to use or faster to fill out. Where a user stops using your forms can be important as well.

Search engine Bing has made some interesting moves onto Google turf by adding calls-to-action next to its SERPs (Search Engine Results Page), which you can see in Figure 15-6. Its algorithm now uses metrics to figure out the most frequent actions taken on a site. It then puts three calls-to-action next to the site description when that site pops up in search results. This is huge news, currently only being rolled out for big brands, but if Bing trickles it down to everyone in the next few months, it may take a major slice of the search and metrics pie from Google.

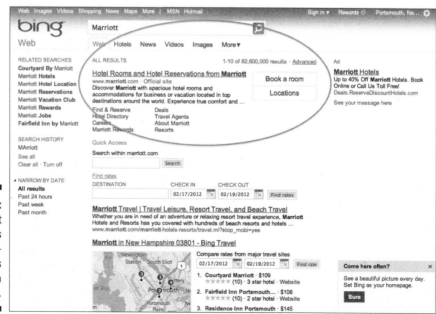

Figure 15-6:
Marriott Hotels gets calls-to-action in its Bing search results spot.

Traffic won't become leads or sales without a great funnel

So much social media focus is on pumping up your traffic, getting those eye-balls, finding your audience — and all of that is great. However, the one-two punch of metrics plus calls-to-action will help you turn that attention into something useful to your bottom line and growth.

Thinking of your calls-to-action as part of a sales funnel— and, in fact, considering it a conversion funnel instead — will only help you succeed. What components need to be in place for this? The key components include

- Calls-to-action
- Chances to provide examples of trust in your products or services
- Examples of authority and knowledge
- Brand confidence
- Metrics
- Trigger words
- Pushes to sale

The biggest part of this funnel will be metrics — the measurement of how people are traveling through the whole site conversion funnel will help you direct placements, buttons, and content to maximize keeping their attention.

Event tracking

So how do you see what's working to convert for you on your site? Two words: event tracking.

To set up event tracking using Google Analytics and your website (see Figure 15-7):

1. **Place a piece of code on your site.**

```
onclick="_gaq.push(['_trackEvent', 'category', 'action', 'opt_label', 'opt_
        value']);"
```

Using a form as an example, this code would go next to the input button code. (For a call-to-action button, it would go within the button link.) *Category* is the type of thing you're tracking (e-book, newsletter sub-scription, registration). *Action* defines the interaction of your visitor (click, button). *Label* helps you figure out what the event you're tracking is later and should be easy to remember. *Value* allows you to give your event a value, if you need to.

2. **Log in to your Google Analytics account and navigate to the domain where the event will take place.**

3. **Click Conversions in the left sidebar of the new Google Analytics dashboard.**

4. **Click Goals and then click Overview.**

5. **Choose Set Up Goals.**

6. **Configure your new goal to match the criteria and URL specified in the event tracking code you just implemented on your site.**

7. **Repeat these steps for each new event or call-to-action button you want to track.**

Make sure to create separate goals with related names for any A/B testing you're doing!

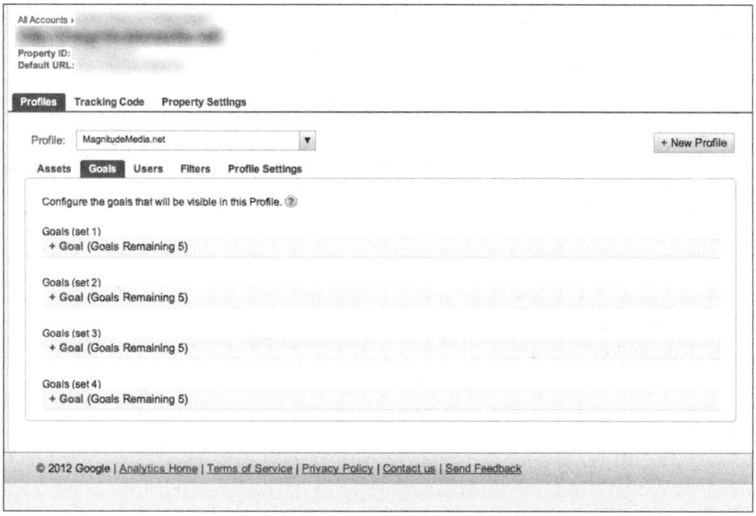

Figure 15-7:
Google
Analytics
Event
Tracking.

Creating Powerful Landing Pages

A powerful landing page incorporates every aspect of the conversion funnel idea into a cohesive (and hopefully, attractive) whole. Not only that, this landing page is appropriate for the audience it was designed for.

This means that you may have the same call-to-action across two or three landing pages, but the pages themselves are designed to appeal to the referring site audience: Facebook visitors want a completely different experience than Twitter visitors, and organic search traffic needs entirely different information as well.

All landing pages should allow visitors to navigate out to all points of the website, but the whole site doesn't have to lead folks back to the landing pages. They can remain active but hidden from the main navigation while still leading people to the rest of the site. Their purpose is strictly to convert.

A great landing page will tell people a few things:

- ✔ Why they are there
- ✔ What you want them to do
- ✔ How long it will take
- ✔ How to do what you ask
- ✔ What they get in return
- ✔ What any restrictions, time limits, or limitations are

How many calls-to-action per page is a matter of some debate. I find that two is plenty. People are distracted and scattered, so it's better to focus more and convert more than give too many choices and lose out.

The two calls-to-action on each landing page should be of varied importance. For example, a link to e-mail you is of less importance than a large button selling a trial subscription to your service and should be smaller. The conversion that matters more should be larger and live above the fold.

Keep in mind that landing pages are different animals than the rest of your site. On the rest of your site, you may have several calls-to-action in your sidebar or as part of your design. They should still be designed to reveal importance, but multiple is fine here.

You still want those to convert and be seen, but the focus of the rest of your site is generally your content, whatever that may be. Meanwhile, landing pages serve only one purpose — convert, convert, convert — and should be designed to do so quickly and effectively.

On each landing page, you want your event tracking and goals set up. You also want the URL of the landing page set up with its own tracking as well. You'll use a combination of the detailed event metrics and the overall page pattern metrics in your spreadsheets you've been keeping to track customer behavior on each page.

That customer behavior data will allow you to fine-tune the landing pages to convert better over time and to change them wisely when it's time for a fresh look and feel. Rather than reinvent the wheel each time you launch a new call-to-action, practice intelligent redesign.

Chapter 16

Setting Goals for Winning the Metrics Game

. . . .

In This Chapter

▶ Getting in the mindset of great metrics

▶ Defining better, clearer goals for measurement

▶ Changing the way you think about actionable items in analytics

. . . .

Defining good goals in metrics means learning to define great goals in business. Most people think they're setting goals, but they are really setting dreams and hopes. Dreams and hopes are great, but they don't act as a great foundation for measurable successes or give you incremental items to strive for in your day-to-day business.

If you've never written a business plan for your business, you'll likely be able to formulate a great one after reading this chapter. You'll have a more concrete plan for your marketing and for setting goals over time.

If you still haven't tried setting goals in Google Analytics or if the goals you've set haven't yielded great data, this chapter can help you fix that problem also.

Understanding Who Can Set Goals

In business and in analytics, the goal setter is the administrator. In the real world, this person is the manager, owner, or other person or people in charge. On the Internet, it's the online equivalent of the folks in charge of the account.

The person who sets up the Google Analytics account is the administrator, much like the person who sets up the business in the real world. You may argue that your marketing team makes a better administrator for analytics. I agree that they should be involved and perhaps drive the analytics car — but in the end, the buck stops with the owner when it comes to all aspects of the business. That means the owner deserve a seat at the analytics table as well.

The goals of the business should drive the need for business analytics. This statement seems very obvious to many, but to some folks, it's a real "aha!" realization.

The marketing department and the business ownership need to be in constant communication about the goals and needs of the business. The marketing department can't define reasonable metrics goals unless it knows where the business owner is headed. The business owner can't get where he's going with the business if the closest thing to a goal he has is the vague hope to make some more money. (Translation: Wouldn't everyone — define *how*.)

If your business has a good business plan, writing your analytics and marketing goals won't be a stretch. The keys to a good goal include being

- ✔ Specific
- ✔ Attainable
- ✔ Measurable
- ✔ Something you can build on for future goals
- ✔ Something the people helping you achieve them can understand how to accomplish

Fine-Tuning Your Goals

You can use sales funnel data to fine-tune your goals (see Figure 16-1). Part of fine-tuning your goals involves honing them down until they transition from hopes to milestones. Here are a few examples of things people mistake for goals:

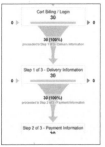

Figure 16-1:
Using sales
funnel data
to fine-tune
goals.

✔ **Want to make more money.** This is a hope and a dream and a great aspiration, but it isn't a goal. It isn't specific enough to be a goal.

✔ **Want more customers.** This one still isn't specific enough, though it's a better idea than "make more money." It's on its way to being more concrete and measurable.

✔ **Want more brand awareness.** This one could be measured if it were only more specific.

✔ **Want to become a thought leader.** Another good idea, but it's not quite specific enough in the long run.

How can you make these hopes and dreams into real goals? The first step is to make them specific — laser-point specific.

Here are some examples of specific goals that you can then turn into marketing campaigns and measurable metrics:

✔ Increase restaurant bookings by ten people per night in a three-month period. This goal is solid because it allows you to take a baseline measurement of how many bookings you have each night now and build from there.

✔ Obtain eight more sales leads per week through your website.

✔ Convert 5 percent of new website visitors to leads or sales per month in the first three months.

✔ Have 50 more people sign up for your newsletter or mailing list each month through your AdWords campaign.

✔ Design a display ad campaign in AdWords for a class with a goal to sell out the available seats or webinar slots.

✔ Create three new blog posts a week and have a goal of getting all new posts spontaneously shared on Google+ and Facebook within minutes of posting them. Track their reach. Have a secondary goal of broadening the reach from 10 views per post to 500 views per post within the first month.

✔ Get interviewed by two national publications within six months based on your demonstrated authority on a topic through your blog posts and other content-like videos.

As you can see, even from the few examples, it's not that you don't want to make money, get more customers, or have more brand awareness. It's that you need specific, incremental, measurable goals to achieve these things.

Making Your Goals Achievable

So what makes the difference between having more customers or making more money and a good actionable goal you can build a landing page and ad campaign and analytics measurement around? Definition and accessibility.

By forcing yourself to define your goals more clearly, it makes them easier to track. Goals you can track are goals you can continue to improve. As your business grows, your goals will continue to change.

One metrics tool you need, your spreadsheet, helps you gather your metrics over time, sort them by various variables, and see how achievable your goals are.

Definition and measurement

The following spreadsheet exercise helps you get more comfortable manipulating data inside a spreadsheet from Google Analytics.

First, you need to get a bit familiar with the Google Analytics Data Feed API. It sounds a little daunting, I know, but it's nothing to be scared of.

1. **Log in to your Google Analytics account and choose the domain name of the domain you want to track.**

   If your Analytics installation is new, make sure that it has begun gathering data! If it has been installed a while on your website, move on to Step 2.

2. **Place the following code into your Google Spreadsheet.**

   If you don't want to type this entire code block (although I recommend that you do for practice), go to www.dummies.com/go/socialmedia metricsfd to get a copy of the code.

   You can use the Script Editor found inside the Tools⇨Scripts menu.

   Note: The code I wrote to do the same thing is long and messy because I'm a marketer and author by trade. Many, many thanks to coder Mikael Thuneberg from www.automateanalytics.com for allowing me to use his (much prettier and shorter) code, with attribution:

```
function getGAauthenticationToken(email, password) {
//Fetches GA authentication token, which can then be used to fetch data
          with the getGAdata function
//Created by Mikael Thuneberg
 try {
```

```
if (typeof email == "undefined") {
return "Email address missing";
}
if (typeof password == "undefined") {
return "Password missing";
}
if (email.length == 0) {
return "Email address missing";
}
if (password.length == 0) {
return "Password missing";
}
password = encodeURIComponent(password);
var responseStr
var response = UrlFetchApp.fetch("https://www.google.com/accounts/
        ClientLogin", {
method: "post",
payload: "accountType=GOOGLE&Email=" + email + "&Passwd=" + password +
        "&service=analytics&Source=Mikael Thuneberg-GA Google Docs
        functions-1.0"
});
responseStr = response.getContentText();
responseStr = responseStr.slice(responseStr.search("Auth=") + 5,
        responseStr.length);
return responseStr;
} catch (e) {
if (e.message.indexOf("CaptchaRequired") != -1) {
return "Complete CAPTCHA at http://www.google.com/accounts/" + e.message.
        slice(e.message.indexOf("CaptchaUrl=") + 11, e.message.length);
} else {
return "Authentication failed (" + e.message + ")";
}
}
}
function getGAaccountData(authToken, dataType, includeHeaders, maxRows,
        startFromRow) {
//Fetches account data for the authenticated user
//Input authentication token produced by the getGAauthenticationToken
        function
//If dataType parameter is omitted, the functions fetches a list of
        profiles to which the user has access
//By specifying the dataType parameters as "goals", the functions will
        fetch a list of goals by profile
//By specifying the dataType parameters as "segments", the functions will
        fetch a list of advanced segments
//Created by Mikael Thuneberg
if (typeof authToken == "undefined") {
return "Authentication token missing";
}
dataType = (typeof dataType == "undefined") ? "profiles" : dataType;
```

```
maxRows = (typeof maxRows == "undefined") ? 200 : maxRows;
maxRows = (typeof maxRows == "string") ? 200 : maxRows;
startFromRow = (typeof startFromRow == "undefined") ? 1 : startFromRow;
startFromRow = (typeof startFromRow == "string") ? 1 : startFromRow;
if (authToken.length == 0) {
return "Authentication token missing";
}
if (dataType.length == 0) {
dataType = "profiles";
}
if (authToken.indexOf("Authentication failed") != -1) {
return "Authentication failed";
}
try {
authToken = authToken.replace(/\n/g, "");
dataType = dataType.toLowerCase();
var URL = "https://www.google.com/analytics/feeds/accounts/default?max-
         results=" + maxRows + "&start-index=" + startFromRow
var responseStr;
try {
var response = UrlFetchApp.fetch(URL, {
method: "get",
headers: {
"Authorization": "GoogleLogin auth=" + authToken,
"GData-Version": "2"
}
});
} catch (e) {
try {
randnumber = Math.random()*5000;
Utilities.sleep(randnumber);
var response = UrlFetchApp.fetch(URL, {
method: "get",
headers: {
"Authorization": "GoogleLogin auth=" + authToken,
"GData-Version": "2"
}
});
} catch (e) {
try {
Utilities.sleep(5000);
var response = UrlFetchApp.fetch(URL, {
method: "get",
headers: {
"Authorization": "GoogleLogin auth=" + authToken,
"GData-Version": "2"
}
});
} catch (e) {
return "Failed to fetch data from Google Analytics (" + e.message + ")";
```

```
}
}
}
responseStr = response.getContentText();
var XMLdoc = Xml.parse(responseStr);
var lapset2;
var TempArray = [];
var RowArray = [];
var HeaderArray = [];
if (includeHeaders == true) {
var rivi = 1;
if (dataType == "segments") {
HeaderArray[0] = "Segment ID";
HeaderArray[1] = "Segment Name";
HeaderArray[2] = "Segment Definition";
} else {
HeaderArray[0] = "Account Name";
HeaderArray[1] = "Profile Title";
HeaderArray[2] = "Profile Number";
}
TempArray[0] = HeaderArray;
} else {
var rivi = 0;
}
var sar = 0;
var lapset;
var dataFound = false;
if (dataType == "segments") {
lapset = XMLdoc.getElement().getElements();
for (i = 0; i < lapset.length; i++) {
if (lapset[i].getName().getLocalName() == "segment") {
sar = 0;
RowArray[0] = lapset[i].getAttribute("id").getValue();
RowArray[1] = lapset[i].getAttribute("name").getValue();
lapset2 = lapset[i].getElements();
for (j = 0; j < lapset2.length; j++) {
if (lapset2[j].getName().getLocalName() == "definition") {
RowArray[2] = lapset2[j].getText();
}
}
TempArray[rivi] = RowArray;
RowArray = [];
dataFound = true;
rivi++;
if (rivi == maxRows) {
return TempArray;
}
} else {
if (lapset[i].getName().getLocalName() == "entry") {
break;
```

```
}
}
}
} else { // datatype = profiles
lapset = XMLdoc.getElement().getElements("entry");
for (i = 0; i < lapset.length; i++) {
sar = 0;
lapset2 = lapset[i].getElements();
for (j = 0; j < lapset2.length; j++) {
if (lapset2[j].getName().getLocalName() == "title") {
RowArray[1] = " " + lapset2[j].getText();
dataFound = true;
} else {
if (lapset2[j].getName().getLocalName() == "property") {
if (lapset2[j].getAttribute("name").getValue() == "ga:accountName") {
RowArray[0] = lapset2[j].getAttribute("value").getValue();
}
if (lapset2[j].getAttribute("name").getValue() == "ga:profileId") {
RowArray[2] = lapset2[j].getAttribute("value").getValue();
break;
}
}
}
}
TempArray[rivi] = RowArray;
RowArray = [];
dataFound = true;
rivi++;
if (rivi == maxRows) {
return TempArray;
}
}
}
if (dataFound == false) {
return "No data found";
}
return TempArray;
} catch (e) {
return "Fetching account data failed (" + e.message + ")";
}
}
function getGAdata(authToken, profileNumber, metrics, startDate, endDate,
          filters, dimensions, segment, sort, includeHeaders, maxRows,
          startFromRow) {
//Fetches data from the GA profile specified, using the authentication
          token generated by the getGAauthenticationToken function
//For instructions on the parameters, see http://bit.ly/bUYMDs
//Created by Mikael Thuneberg: used with permission
try {
startDate.getYear();
```

```
} catch (e) {
return "Invalid start date";
}
try {
endDate.getYear();
} catch (e) {
return "Invalid end date";
}
try {
if (typeof authToken == "undefined") {
return "Authentication token missing";
}
if (typeof profileNumber == "undefined") {
return "Profile number missing";
}
if (typeof metrics == "undefined") {
return "Specify at least one metric";
}
if (profileNumber != parseInt(profileNumber)) {
return "Invalid profile number";
}
filters = (typeof filters == "undefined") ? "" : filters;
dimensions = (typeof dimensions == "undefined") ? "" : dimensions;
segment = (typeof segment == "undefined") ? "" : segment;
maxRows = (typeof maxRows == "undefined") ? 100 : maxRows;
maxRows = (typeof maxRows == "string") ? 100 : maxRows;
startFromRow = (typeof startFromRow == "undefined") ? 1 : startFromRow;
startFromRow = (typeof startFromRow == "string") ? 1 : startFromRow;
if (authToken.length == 0) {
return "Authentication token missing";
}
if (profileNumber.length == 0) {
return "Profile number missing";
}
if (metrics.length == 0) {
return "Specify at least one metric";
}
if (authToken.indexOf("Authentication failed") != -1) {
return "Authentication failed";
}
authToken = authToken.replace(/\n/g, "");
var startDateString
var endDateString
var dMonth
var dDay
dMonth = Right(("0" + (startDate.getMonth()+1)).toString(),2);
dDay = Right(("0" + (startDate.getDate())).toString(),2);
startDateString = startDate.getYear() + "-" + dMonth + "-" + dDay;
dMonth = Right(("0" + (endDate.getMonth()+1)).toString(),2);
dDay = Right(("0" + (endDate.getDate())).toString(),2);
```

```
endDateString = endDate.getYear() + "-" + dMonth + "-" + dDay
if (startDateString > endDateString) {
return "Start date should be before end date";
}
var URL = "https://www.google.com/analytics/feeds/data?ids=ga:" +
          profileNumber + "&start-date=" + startDateString + "&end-date="
          + endDateString + "&max-results=" + maxRows + "&start-index=" +
          startFromRow;
if (metrics.slice(0, 3) != "ga:") {
metrics = "ga:" + metrics;
}
metrics = metrics.replace(/&/g, "&ga:");
metrics = metrics.replace(/ga:ga:/g, "ga:");
metrics = metrics.replace(/&/g, "%2C");
URL = URL + "&metrics=" + metrics
if (dimensions.length > 0) {
if (dimensions.slice(0, 3) != "ga:") {
dimensions = "ga:" + dimensions;
}
dimensions = dimensions.replace(/&/g, "&ga:");
dimensions = dimensions.replace(/ga:ga:/g, "ga:");
dimensions = dimensions.replace(/&/g, "%2C");
URL = URL + "&dimensions=" + dimensions;
}
if (filters.length > 0) {
if (filters.slice(0, 3) != "ga:") {
filters = "ga:" + filters;
}
filters = filters.replace(/,/g, ",ga:");
filters = filters.replace(/;/g, ";ga:");
filters = filters.replace(/ga:ga:/g, "ga:");
filters = encodeURIComponent(filters);
URL = URL + "&filters=" + filters;
}
if (typeof(segment) == "number") {
segment = "gaid::" + segment;
}
if (segment.length > 0) {
if (segment.indexOf("gaid::") == -1 && segment.indexOf("dynamic::") == -1)
        {
if (segment.slice(0, 3) != "ga:") {
segment = "ga:" + segment;
}
segment = "dynamic::" + segment;
}
segment = encodeURIComponent(segment);
URL = URL + "&segment=" + segment;
}
if (sort == true) {
URL = URL + "&sort=-" + metrics;
```

```
      }
    }
    catch (e) {
    return "Fetching data failed (" + e.message + ")";
    }
randnumber = Math.random()*5000;
Utilities.sleep(randnumber);
 try {
 var response = UrlFetchApp.fetch(URL, {
 method: "get",
 headers: {
 "Authorization": "GoogleLogin auth=" + authToken,
 "GData-Version": "2"
 }
 });
 } catch (e) {
 try {
randnumber = Math.random()*5000;
Utilities.sleep(randnumber);
 var response = UrlFetchApp.fetch(URL, {
 method: "get",
 headers: {
 "Authorization": "GoogleLogin auth=" + authToken,
 "GData-Version": "2"
 }
 });
 } catch (e) {
 try {
 Utilities.sleep(5000);
 var response = UrlFetchApp.fetch(URL, {
 method: "get",
 headers: {
 "Authorization": "GoogleLogin auth=" + authToken,
 "GData-Version": "2"
 }
 });
 } catch (e) {
 return "Failed to fetch data from Google Analytics (" + e.message + ")";
 }
 }
 }


 try {
 var responseStr = response.getContentText();
 var XMLdoc = Xml.parse(responseStr);
 var lapset = XMLdoc.getElement().getElements("entry");
 var lapset2;
 var TempArray = [];
 var RowArray = [];
 var HeaderArray = [];
```

```
if (includeHeaders == true) {
var rivi = 1;
} else {
var rivi = 0;
}
var sar = 0;
var dataFound = false;
for (i = 0; i < lapset.length; i++) {
sar = 0;
lapset2 = lapset[i].getElements();
for (j = 0; j < lapset2.length; j++) {
if (lapset2[j].getName().getLocalName() == "dimension") {
RowArray[sar] = lapset2[j].getAttribute("value").getValue();
if (rivi == 1) {
HeaderArray[sar] = lapset2[j].getAttribute("name").getValue();
}
sar++;
}
if (lapset2[j].getName().getLocalName() == "metric") {
RowArray[sar] = Number(lapset2[j].getAttribute("value").getValue());
if (rivi == 1) {
HeaderArray[sar] = lapset2[j].getAttribute("name").getValue();
}
sar++;
}
}
TempArray[rivi] = RowArray;
RowArray = [];
dataFound = true;
rivi++;
}
if (dataFound == false) {
return "No data found";
}
if (includeHeaders == true) {
TempArray[0] = HeaderArray;
}
return TempArray;
} catch (e) {
return "Fetching data failed (" + e.message + ")";
}
}
function Left(str, n){
if (n <= 0)
return "";
else if (n > String(str).length)
return str;
else
return String(str).substring(0,n);
}
```

```
function Right(str, n){
 if (n <= 0)
 return "";
 else if (n > String(str).length)
 return str;
 else {
 var iLen = String(str).length;
 return String(str).substring(iLen, iLen - n);
 }
}
```

3. **After you save your code, authenticate your account using your Analytics e-mail and password.**

   For most folks, the Analytics e-mail is a Gmail address.

4. **After you have authenticated, fetch your authentication token with** `=getGAauthenticationToken(C2,C3)`.

5. **Send out your first query for data.**

   To do this step, you need the authentication token you grabbed using the line of code, the Google Analytics ID from the account you want to grab data from (the number starting with UA-xxxxxx-xx), and the parameters you want to measure (visits, date range, and so on) on each line.

   Then use a simple spreadsheet function line to get the information from the rows where the data is specified, such as `=getGAdata(C5,C8,C9, C10,C11)`.

   If you run into timeouts, you've asked to fetch too many rows of data and need to try again. (This problem doesn't usually happen unless you're fetching hundreds of rows at a time, so you should be okay.)

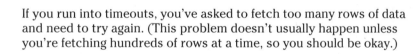 If this much code is daunting to you or you simply don't think you have the time to learn to automate metrics and you have the budget for a paid solution, the same person who let me share his code with you also has a fantastic automated solution that works with Excel for Windows and Mac, which you can find at www.gadatagrabbertool.com.

Accessibility

As part of making your goals accessible, you need to break them into appropriate chunks. While the spreadsheet technique described in the preceding section can net you a flood of data, choosing your goals to track wisely will net you better results in marketing and sales as well as customer service.

After you've broken down your goals, you also want to think of the other aspects of *accessibility* — making the data available to everyone who will have a part in reaching the goals.

Leaving your plan in the hands of one person or one department won't get you nearly as far as creating the type of organization and brand that shares data for a common goal. The insights that others in your company can bring to the path to success will be invaluable and make you a more well-rounded company overall.

In addition, other departments will have new ideas on what data is important to growth. They'll also have department-specific data needs of their own that you may have overlooked if you'd tried to wing it. Make sure that every department sees what's going on with the brand and understands how to use the data.

Building Goals for the Future

You may see "Building Goals for the Future" and think "Future!? I'm barely keeping up with this now." That may be true, but technology changes so fast these days, and people with it, that ignoring what the metrics tell you about how people will discover, engage with your brand, or use your product in the future is something you do at great risk.

Already since beginning the book, there has been a significant change in Google Analytics that required an update on several chapters for you:

- ✔ Facebook went public.
- ✔ A site that started in 2008 called Pinterest that allows people to band together based on interest started a meteoric rise to the top.
- ✔ Google+ got integrated with search.
- ✔ Studies show that kids who make only $15,000 per year prioritize buying a smartphone to have access to their apps and data.

And that is just the tip of the iceberg from one short four-month period of time!

The interesting thing is that metrics can indicate that these changes are coming long before they become a reality. It's all about learning to read the data. Think of it in relation to the stock market — the data fire hose coming from Twitter's millions of users has been determined, after much study, to predict the stock market. That's a pretty heady thought about a service where people chatter on about everything from their lunch to the latest political coup in 140 characters or less.

If you can predict things like stocks from innocuous interactions between relative strangers online, what else can data do to help you see into the future? Does a person's mouse movements and eye tracking tell you her gender, age, and psychological makeup? Yes, it does. Does game theory have a growing place in business? Yes, it does. Does an increasing number of the population access the web via a phone or tablet? Yes, they do. These things and more are either here now, or coming soon, and you can track all of it, use it to make ongoing goals, track those goals, and predict what's next for your brand.

Part VI
Predicting Future Metrics

"I've been in hardware all of my life, and all of a sudden it's software that'll make me rich."

In this part . . .

You've got your foundation set and your metrics dashboards are humming right along slurping up data like a sponge for you to sift and use to your advantage.

You've been experimenting with the tools and techniques used by the metrics masters and are starting to feel like a real metrics ninja as you watch your conversion rates (and profit margins) climb.

Now, in this part, you see where metrics is heading in the next few months and years so that you know how to stay ahead of the game.

Chapter 17

Measuring Mobile App Metrics

*M*obile tracking is getting better and better in recent months, but up until recently, it was mostly a manual process. As smartphones and mobile apps have grown in capacity, mobile metrics have steadily improved.

Tracking an application's metrics (an app) has gotten more and more simple, but apps are inherently isolated still. You can track each app, but solutions are still being created to track all apps.

Tracking mobile use is now part and parcel of good web analytics, provided people use the mobile browser to reach your landing pages and surf your site. Some programs for tracking metrics make this process more intuitive than others.

There are also new apps that bring all your metrics offline to you. If you're a busy business owner, getting your analytics delivered right to your pocket may be just the ticket.

Getting to Know Google Analytics SDK

If you make mobile apps or if you plan to have an app made for your business, you need to incorporate metrics. Google's Analytics SDK gives you ways to do that for iOS (Apple's iPhone and iPad) and Google's Android platforms (see Figure 17-1) right from the beginning of your app process.

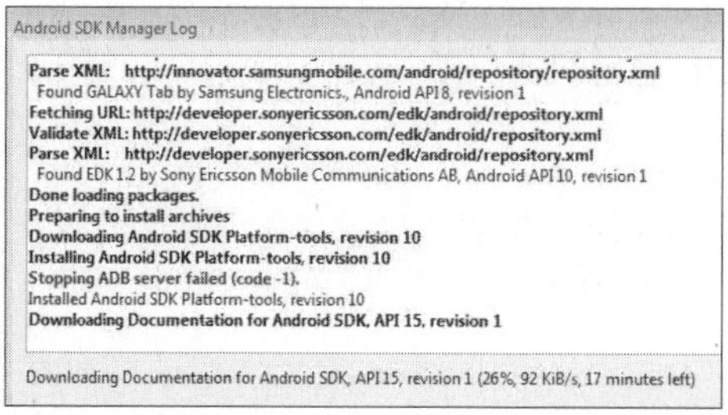

Android SDK Manager Log

Parse XML: http://innovator.samsungmobile.com/android/repository/repository.xml
    Found GALAXY Tab by Samsung Electronics., Android API 8, revision 1
Fetching URL: http://developer.sonyericsson.com/edk/android/repository.xml
Validate XML: http://developer.sonyericsson.com/edk/android/repository.xml
Parse XML: http://developer.sonyericsson.com/edk/android/repository.xml
    Found EDK 1.2 by Sony Ericsson Mobile Communications AB, Android API 10, revision 1
Done loading packages.
Preparing to install archives
Downloading Android SDK Platform-tools, revision 10
Installing Android SDK Platform-tools, revision 10
Stopping ADB server failed (code -1).
Installed Android SDK Platform-tools, revision 10
Downloading Documentation for Android SDK, API 15, revision 1

Downloading Documentation for Android SDK, API 15, revision 1 (26%, 92 KiB/s, 17 minutes left)

Figure 17-1:
Android
SDK
Manager
Log.

Some features you may find useful in Google Analytics SDK:

✔ **Easy Tracker Library:** This is where activity tracking comes in. I mention needing several lines of code to track activity of your users, but Google understands how difficult that can be and is working to make this feature easier to implement.

By using Google's new libraries, you should be able to easily add the code snippets to your application to track activity, manage sessions, and push all calls to the Google Analytics tracker to the main UI Thread. This makes the SDK more responsive inside your app.

✔ **Mobile Playground:** This is more of an open-source tool than a feature. It accesses all the APIs for Google Analytics available for Mobile Application developers in one place. You can find it here:

```
http://code.google.com/p/analytics-api-samples/source/
          browse/#svn%2Ftrunk%2Fsrc%2Ftracking%2Fmobile
```

✔ **Better bug reporting and feature requesting:** Google's SDK team has created a whole website to help you address issues implementing SDK and its features. Find it here:

```
http://code.google.com/p/analytics-issues/issues/list
```

✔ **Mobile tracking documentation:** This is now easier to find as part of the overall Google Analytics documentation. You can find it here:

```
http://code.google.com/apis/analytics/docs/mobile/overview.html
```

✔ **A whole new SDK version for both android and iOS:** The new version of SDK for both mobile operating systems takes care of several issues, such as crashes and memory leaks.

Using Analytics SDK with Android

To get going with Google's Analytics SDK for your Android app, simply follow these steps:

1. **Download the Google Analytics SDK for Android from the following website:**

   ```
   http://code.google.com/mobile/analytics/download.html#Google_Analytics_SDK_
           for_Android
   ```

2. **Add the library `libGoogleanalytics.jar` to your app project.**

   If this step leaves you scratching your head, don't worry. Your app developer will know what this means.

3. **Add these permissions to the Android manifest of your app:**

   ```
   <uses-permission android:name="android.permission.INTERNET" />
   <uses-permission android:name="android.permission.ACCESS_NETWORK_STATE" />
   ```

4. **Create a distinctive website profile inside your Google Analytics account.**

   Most app developers simply create a false/fake website profile for this purpose.

   Note: You'll need the Web Property ID from this profile to track users anonymously. You'll also need to disclose that you're doing this to the users who sign up for and download your app.

5. **Track your referring installs by making your links look like this:**

   ```
   http://market.android.com/search?q=pname:<package>&referrer=<referral>
   ```

   You want to do this kind of tracking, especially if you have more than one way to download your app — for example, the market, an advertisement, or a website.

6. **Go back into your app manifest and add this code as part of tracking referring installs:**

   ```
   <application>
   <! -- Used for install referrer tracking (analytics) -- >
   <receiver android:name="com.google.android.apps.analytics.
             AnalyticsReceiver" android:exported="true">
   <intent filter>
   <action android:name="com.android.vending.INSTALL_REFERRER" />
   </intent-filter>
   </receiver>
   </application>
   ```

These steps should bring metrics into your Android app. You can also get more detailed and track user activities within your app, but that requires quite a few more lines of code and some advanced knowledge of the SDK — something your app developer will likely already know how to do.

Go to this link to grab the downloads you need to work with the Android SDK and to see some advanced tutorials:

```
http://code.google.com/apis/analytics/docs/mobile/android.html
```

Using Analytics SDK with iPhone

To get going with Google's Analytics SDK for your iPhone app, simply follow these steps:

1. **Download the iOS Developer SDK from this link:**

   ```
   http://developer.apple.com/iphone
   ```

   You must have Xcode 3.1 or greater and run Mac OS X 10.5.3 or greater.

2. **Download Google Analytics for Mobile Apps iOS SDK from this link:**

   ```
   http://code.google.com/apis/analytics/docs/mobile/ios.html
   ```

3. **Create a new iPhone OS project inside Xcode**

4. **Move (drag) `GANTracker.h` and `libGoogleAnalytics.a` out of the SDK Library directory and into your new project.**

5. **Make sure that you include CFNetwork framework in your new project.**

6. **Link against `libsqlite3.0.dylib` by scrolling through the list of Frameworks using Add Existing Framework feature and then clicking that library to add to your project.**

7. **After you add the code using the preceding steps, initialize the tracker with the UA-xxxxxx-xx Google Analytics ID for the account.**

Go to this link to grab the downloads you need to work with Google Analytics SDK for iOS and for instruction on some of the more advanced features:

```
http://code.google.com/apis/analytics/docs/mobile/ios.html
```

Looking at Other Mobile Metrics Tracking Methods

Google Analytics SDK is one of the most ubiquitous tracking methods for mobile app metrics, but it certainly isn't the only option. Some mobile application companies choose to develop their own in-house metrics tools.

If you have the budget, developing your own tools is fine, but why reinvent the wheel when you have so many options that you can purchase and that will work as well or better? One solution you can purchase is Kontagent (see Figure 17-2), a useful SaaS (Software as a Service) product that offers many metrics options for the mobile app makers out there.

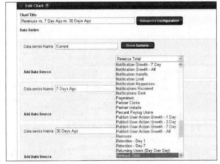

Figure 17-2:
Custom formulas in Kontagent.

Kontagent mobile metrics started as metrics for Facebook games and has since branched out into mobile social applications. Its out-of-the-box solution offers many of the same metrics as Google Analytics SDK.

Another SaaS option is TapMetrics, shown in Figure 17-3. This solution touts a five-minute install. For the iOS app makers, it also handles your iTunes Connect downloads for you, meaning that you don't have to go through the convoluted login process for iTunes Connect anymore.

Flurry is another option for folks that want to purchase a solution instead of building their own or doing the programming required to get SDK up and running. Flurry focuses heavily on the Android platform much as TapMetrics focuses on iOS.

You can choose from many more SaaS programs to get an out-of-the-box solution for tracking your app metrics. The ones I list in this section are just a few of the more well known that have been around longer than most. This is a new frontier, however — do your research and find the program that works for you.

Figure 17-3:
TapMetrics
analytics.

Practicing Good Mobile Metrics Habits

Inside your app are certain metrics you need to focus on tracking. You'd think that web analytics would translate to the mobile world and that you'd use many of the same metrics from your web analytics in your mobile apps, but that just isn't the case.

How people use mobile websites and apps on their phones and tablets is quite different than how they use a website, and your metrics should take that into account. You want your mobile analytics to focus on several metrics that are different than the typical platform type, platform version, screen size, use frequency, or other typical metrics:

- ✔ **Your funnel:** Your primary metric to track is your funnel. By performing a funnel analysis, you can ferret out the points in your app that act as a roadblock to your users. For example, if you want to convert users from mobile to web by getting them to sign up for a weekly e-mail from you, analyzing your funnel can find how many users you lose at each stage of the in-app subscribe process. This data allows you to improve future versions of your mobile app to convert better.

✔ **Demographic data:** More specifically, you want to capture demographic data points that may seem different and find the correlation between them. How does in-app user behavior correlate with different demographic data sets?

✔ **Location, location, location (and time and date!):** Where people use your mobile app is important. More important than simple geography, however, is the inclusion of time and date to the location metric. In addition to where your app gets the most use, time and date metrics will tell you if you get the most use for your football app when you expect it — during Monday night football — or if people are using your app a few days before the game during their commute to prep for the game ahead of time, for example. This data will help you design your next app version to fit your user habits.

✔ **App promotion:** If you want to have more people use your app, you need to promote it. This seems like a no-brainer, but in order to promote your app well, you need a social metric to help you discover who is sharing your app and when, where, and how. Not only that, by giving the user the sharing tool in-app and putting metrics behind the share mechanism, you'll get richer data that helps you identify the influencers who love your app.

✔ **How people navigate your app:** By nature, mobile apps work by doling out smaller amounts of information screen by screen. Unlike a website, you can't put everything on one page and call it good. How you path your app design is essential to happy users who enjoy interacting with it. Don't make it hard for your users to find what you want them to do. Metrics can help you identify the frustration points in your screen hierarchy before they turn users away.

✔ **How users use your app differently than intended.** No matter how carefully you design any app or program, for web or mobile, your users are going to use it how they want to use it — not how you intended. Users brought the RT feature to Twitter by developing their own convention for sharing. Google+ added searchable hashtags recently because users had been using them on other services as a user-created feature and simply ported their preferred use over to the next social site (see Figure 17-4). Measure the cool things your users do with your app and figure out which behaviors to incorporate into the next version — don't stifle user innovation.

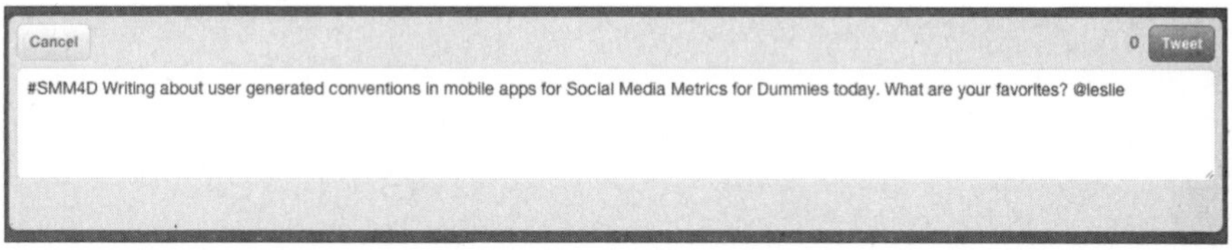

Figure 17-4:
Hashtag use
out in the
wild.

Cancel | 0 | Tweet

#SMM4D Writing about user generated conventions in mobile apps for Social Media Metrics for Dummies today. What are your favorites? @leslie

Don't forget to choose a solution that all parts of your organization can access. The engineers may need different data than the business development department, but they both need to see the whole picture of how the app is being used and where any problem points are. That broader knowledge will help them do their part much more efficiently than if everyone was operating solo.

Tracking Mobile Use of Your Website

Tracking mobile use of their websites is what most businesses are thinking of, still, when I say mobile metrics. Many folks just haven't gotten to the "make an app" stage yet. That's okay; building great mobile metrics habits even on your own site tracking will help you down the road when you're ready to make your first app.

What can analytics tell you about mobile traffic to your site? Mobile metrics can tell you volume, what your visitor buying patterns or lead generation patterns are, and what the demographic of your mobile site visitors are.

After you have a handle on these things, you can make your site stickier for the mobile visitors. This, in turn, will translate to a better mobile app experience down the road.

Knowing which mobile operating systems and devices draw the most visitors to your site can help you optimize for those users' experiences. As you get familiar with how each platform works, you can make simple changes to improve the whole experience of visiting your site for the mobile user. You can also insert metrics into the buttons these users click the most and the forms they fill out the most in order to generate more leads and create more conversions.

Tracking these metrics may reveal user habits you'd otherwise miss. For example, do your visitors from mobile devices feel comfortable buying on their phones, or do they come back to your site later to make a purchase? Is your form too long — does it lose visitors before they finish filling it out on their phones? Have you incorporated APIs from other companies to make signing in to your site easier for mobile visitors?

If you're a Safari user, you can turn on the Developer menu in the Safari toolbar. This menu allows you to view your website as it appears on various operating systems and mobile devices. By taking a quick peek at how your website behaves for your visitors, you can adjust issues before you put the finished site out into the wild.

How you track your marketing campaigns targeted at a mobile audience is also key to your success. Building a mobile site helps. If you can't build an entire mobile site, build a landing page designed for your mobile visitors.

If you use a metrics service that makes this easy, using text messages can be helpful as well. You've seen this in action on reality shows like *American Idol,* where viewers are encouraged to text their vote to a certain number. This number is tracking the metrics of these votes as well as the conversions to website use and demographics.

In addition to the traditional ones like Google Analytics (see Figure 17-5), other services are designed specifically for mobile marketing campaigns. JitterJam (now Meltwater Engage), AdMob, Clickatell, Crowd Factory, and others all have ways to track mobile campaigns (and a couple also help you implement these campaigns).

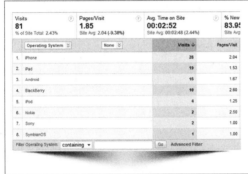

Figure 17-5: Google Analytics device filters.

Putting Your Metrics in Your Pocket

If you're a CEO who is always on the go, you might be interested to know that you can get many of your metrics delivered right to your phone or tablet for monitoring your marketing in real time, no matter where you are.

Google Analytics and other metrics services offer reports delivered by text or e-mail, it's true, but that's not really designed to be monitored on your phone. KISSmetrics also has features that allow you to see your metrics on the go, as do several of the metrics programs for your apps.

One new service, currently in beta, is Trendslide, shown in Figure 17-6. Designed only for iOS right now, this service brings your data from Oracle, SAP, Salesforce, Twitter, Facebook, Google Analytics, PayPal, and other services right to you on your mobile device.

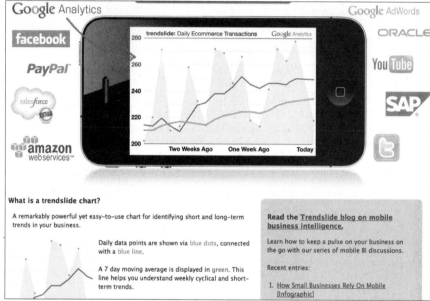

Figure 17-6: Trendslide mobile analytics solution.

Trendslide eliminates having to log in to several services to get a snapshot of how your business is doing when you're away or having to have your staff compile reports. It frees your staff up to do the real work of running your company and gives you the peace of mind you need while traveling. Trendslide is just the first of many services that will be emerging to bring your business metrics to you on the road.

Chapter 18

Exploring Cutting-Edge Metrics Ideas

In This Chapter

▶ Seeing what some top brands are doing with metrics

▶ Looking at up-and-coming social measurements

▶ Finding new things to measure

Social media metrics is all about enhancing the experience your customers have around your brand, whether you're Business to Business (B2B) or Business to Customer (B2C) targeted. It's also about increasing your sales by shortening the sales funnel and narrowing your marketing budget.

Social media metrics is about much more than just tracking the numbers. With a little elbow grease, you can track sentiment metrics, notes on books, people's likes, and other customer intelligence measurements.

Big brands get all the cool toys first, because they have the deepest pockets. That delay can be frustrating if you have to wait, but you can use their case studies to your advantage and learn from the metrics they measure. That gets you ready to maximize the metrics for yourself when you, too, get access to the sandbox.

Gaining Know-How from the Big Brands

In recent years, several companies have been innovating in the social media space, running marketing campaigns that cross the on- and offline boundaries and require some creative metrics skill to track.

Big data is more than a catchphrase — you're living in the big data age. This book is designed to help you get your feet wet tapping into the big data fire hose.

Ford

One of the first that comes to mind is Ford Motor Company, with a team led by Scott Monty. Ford first started thinking out of the box with its Ford Fiesta campaign in 2009 and has since repeated that campaign and followed up with many others of equal scale (see Figure 18-1).

Keyword	Google.com
ford vs chevy	-
ford mustang reviews	49
problems with ford mustang	116
issues with ford mustang	36
mustang vs camaro	-
does ford make a good car?	19
quality of ford vs. chevy	-
ford vs. chevrolet	-
what is the gas mileage for a ford mustang?	11
ford vs. toyota	166
ford vs chrysler	-
ford vs chevy trucks	192
ford vs dodge	-
ford vs chevy vs dodge	-
ford focus vs fiesta	8
ford focus vs honda civic	70
ford focus reviews	24
ford focus vs mazda 3	71
best ford car	1
best ford truck	1
best ford diesel engine	16
ford mustang 2011 vs 2012	7
2012 ford mustang vs 2012 chevy camaro	-
how to buy a ford mustang	4
how to buy a ford gt	15
is the ford edge 4 wheel drive?	3
is the ford escape a good car	31
is the ford fusion a good car	-
is the ford ranger a good truck	20

Figure 18-1: Ford Motors by the numbers.

Ford used standard metrics to track the stories generated by these campaigns online, but it also had layers of other metrics involved in making these campaigns successful. At one point, the nonsocial metrics technology of GPS tracking on cars came into play.

One of my favorite incidents from the initial Fiesta campaign was the Fiesta that was stolen in New York from its test driver and then left in a junkyard. Thanks to having an auto-tracking system on the car and the trackability of images and video online, the car was found quickly, and Ford was able to leverage the story for its brand.

Yahoo!

Another big brand, Yahoo! has been using social media metrics to measure how customers are using its services so that it can improve them. As a company that has struggled to retain market share, pinpointing its customers' pain points using social media is key to its recovery.

In its research, Yahoo! determined that it needed to first improve how it handled customer service requests online. Of its Twitter interactions in 2011, 36 percent were from people who forgot a password on their Yahoo! account or who had their account hacked, and 31 percent were from people unable to access their Yahoo! Mail or who discovered their account was sending spam.

Yahoo! also determined that it could redirect 13.7 percent of its Twitter interactions to the Y! Small Biz Twitter account and ease the work load on its customer service team. While Yahoo! hasn't done an out-of-the-box campaign like Ford (yet), it has been working on its metrics infrastructure to better track its campaigns so that it is ready to scale up.

Oracle and Starbucks

Brands like Oracle and Starbucks run white label, or gated, online communities to focus customer service on customers. Oracle is the more straightforward of these two examples, with an umbrella community housing 200 subcommunities and serving 210,000 customers. Oracle tracks customers on questions asked and answered, software use and usability, and general involvement in the community, among other things.

Starbucks is taking its metrics out into the wild by using its cups (augmented reality), mobile apps (payment app and augmented reality app), gated community (My Starbucks Idea), a site built around a rewards card with high incentives for repeat visits (Starbuck Rewards and Starbucks Gold), QR Codes in stores, partnerships with iTunes (free apps and free songs at the register), in-store merchandise sales, sales of the book written by its CEO, and more.

Starbucks has a huge amount of data to track. QR Codes, app downloads and use, rewards card use, in-store purchases, iTunes downloads, customer suggestions — it all needs to funnel metrics into complex databases and CMS systems, not to mention spreadsheets, to be tracked and used to increase sales. Starbucks and Apple both do this tracking well. Coupled with fantastic branding, these two companies rank consistently high in customer loyalty and new customer acquisition, and it's all thanks to their metrics tracking.

Target

Target came under fire while I was writing this book for how it tracks its customers from point of purchase throughout the life of their relationship with Target. Target assigns each person who shops with it a Customer ID and, over time, attaches that number to their personal information, credit cards, bank account information, phone number, and so on. Whether you first shop at Target in person or online, unless you use cash in person, Target's got you covered (see Figure 18-2).

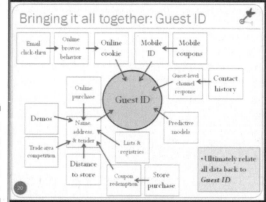

Figure 18-2: Target's Guest ID tracking system.

Target came under fire for the use of its data fire hose through its ad circulars and coupon mailers. Target has data-mining down to such a science that it can, in theory, tell when you're pregnant before you can just by the types of things you start to purchase. Creepy, right? Well, it becomes even creepier when you get a coupon mailer for baby items before you know you're pregnant. Target is that finely honed.

Because it got some flack for those more direct mailers, Target has gotten sneakier — it uses its data to pinpoint what you need and still sends you a mailer about it, featuring items that apply to what its data algorithm has indicated is your condition or need.

Target now just buries the targeted coupons under some random items, making you think that your whole block must have gotten a mailer, which makes you more comfortable using the coupons it sends, because you don't feel singled out. Fascinating, isn't it?

Taking Metrics to a New Level

I talk a lot about standard web metrics in this book, and future metrics are coming up in Chapter 19. In the following sections, I take a look at some up-and-coming things you can be measuring at the "new to this metrics thing" level.

Live chat and live help

Having a live help option inside your Facebook page or on your website (or both) makes people feel at home doing business with you. People like knowing that they can connect with the folks behind the business and actually talk to a person.

You can even measure live chat and live help (see Figure 18-3). Having live chat or live help means installing a plug-in or an application (app) or coding it in, and the software companies that offer these SaaS solutions include metrics (at least, the reputable ones do).

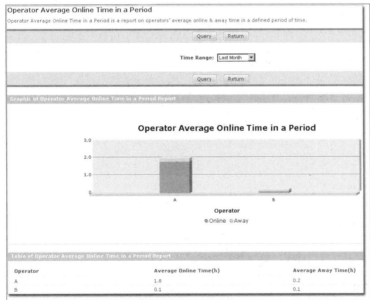

Figure 18-3:
Tracking live chat metrics.

The program you download should include a session history and IP tracking, at a minimum. (See the upcoming section for more on IP address filtering.) Then if the program's metrics don't go deeper, you can still use the IP tracking and session history to identify your visitors in your Analytics program and tag them to track their visits in future and see whether your session helped them.

For the live chat and live help apps that allow uploading of files and documents, you can also tag these files for tracking as well and have your forms feed into trackable systems. Use your live chat and live help to enhance your metrics, shorten your sales funnel, and improve your customer service.

Visitor flow

Visitor flow (how people move through your website) is a new tool in Google Analytics. You used to have to manually diagram this feature or program a spreadsheet of data to help create flow charts for the most traveled paths of visitors to your website, but now you can drill down to that in Google's Visitor Flow report, shown in Figure 18-4.

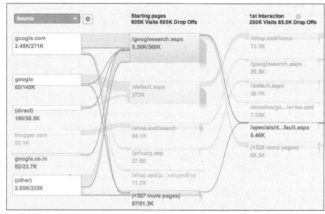

Figure 18-4: Google's new Visitor Flow report in Google Analytics.

Download tracking

The ability to track downloads is something else that's been available to folks in most Analytics platforms for a while. It's also something that many don't think to use to its fullest.

Download tracking applies to products you have on your site for download — and yes, you absolutely want to be tracking those. It also applies to general downloads on your site: images, text snippets, sounds, icons, and more.

In the past, tracking downloads has been used to catch people using your content without your permission, but it also gives you great insight into how people use your site in general and what they find most compelling about it. By paying attention to these numbers, you open up a new realm of possibility for your brand.

Idle session tracking

Tracking users' idle session time is a bit tricky. It's not an exact science to know when someone has simply left a tab in her browser open versus when he's struggling with something on your site.

Idle session time coupled with live chat, however, can bridge a customer service gap. Paying attention to the metrics behind idle session time tells you a lot about the behavior of your customer and potential customer and gives you the data you need to address any issues or to reach out.

IP address filtering

IP address filtering is helpful for many reasons unrelated to tracking live chat alone. It's pretty easy to implement and allows you to exclude addresses from certain IP ranges (such as your own IP) or pinpoint trouble spots.

To implement IP address filtering:

1. **Create a new profile inside your Analytics account that indicates the data is filtered by IP.**
2. **Make a new filter inside your Custom Reports that excludes the IP addresses you have listed.**

The reason for the separate profile is so that you still have your main profile collecting all data, unfiltered, so that you have a complete data set to work with in the event you want to stop IP filtering. The separate profile also helps you keep the data separate.

Making annotations

Did you know that you can make little notes to yourself all over your analytics? Well, you can. You can add special events, key dates for meetings or launches, and other campaign information and then use that information to pinpoint moments of change. Here's how:

1. **Go your Dashboard in Google Analytics.**

2. **Find any metrics graph with data you want to track.**

3. **Highlight the activity metrics you want to annotate.**

4. **Select Create a New Annotation and give the metric a title you can remember.**

   A little comment box displays your new note.

Branded versus nonbranded search traffic

You can track who is already familiar with your brand as opposed to who isn't. The section of your Analytics called Organic Search refers to nonpaid visits from search engine results pages. Some of these people already know your brand and typed your brand name rather than bookmark your URL. Some discovered you by searching for your keywords or their needs.

To track which is which:

1. **Make an Advanced Segment.**

   I discuss how to do this in Chapter 12.

2. **Include organic search visitors using the drop-down tool provided in Google Analytics and exclude any variant of your brand name using the AND modifier.**

   Variants include spelled wrong, extra spaces, and so on.

3. **Run comparison reports pitting the total number of each segment against the total number of organic searches that are branded to get the metrics on your reach.**

Identifying What Else You Can Measure

If you're wondering what else you can measure, just think outside the box. You hear this phrase all the time, but what does it mean for metrics? It means thinking of ways to measure the unmeasurable and better ways to track the typical metrics.

Some metrics you simply make a note of, pay attention to, and check regularly. They help judge some of the intangible values around your brand. Others you track in great detail via links, codes, landing pages, and other online metrics. Both hold value. Both integrate with each other well.

However you decide to think out of the box, make sure that you keep track of the unusual or intangible metrics you start to measure. These metrics may not plug easily in to your analytics reports, but they're invaluable tools in the sales process and marketing decision-making process.

Out-of-the-box measurements

If you put your mind to it, you can measure anything — some metrics are just harder to achieve and require more self-identification from the customer. Take yellow pages ads and billboards, for example.

Those rely on the customers indicating that they heard of your business through those mediums. That reliance on the customer means thinking outside the box and adding a layer of self-identification and tracking to the time between seeing the ad and making the call or stopping in.

Here are a few examples of thinking outside the box:

- ✔ Can you add a QR Code to a poster with a reward for scanning it? You can track QR Codes, as well as the reward use, which gives you even more data.

- ✔ Can you add a simple call-to-action to your billboard? "Tell us you saw us on Highway 9" will encourage the customer to self-identify, though adding an element of play or reward to it would net better results. For example, having someone check in to the billboard on foursquare or Facebook would be a fun way to snag those eyeballs in a way you can track.

- ✔ If you're on the radio, take live questions on Twitter or have a live chat open on your website that you check during the show. Catch your listeners, track them, and engage them outside of their speakers.

- ✔ If you have a radio ad, include your website, include a hashtag, and drive people to your site and your social sites where you can see how they use your product or engage your brand.

Take a cue from Target and begin keeping tabs on your customer from the first interaction. I don't know that every company needs to take it to the same invasive level as Target and other retailers do (what did you think those grocery rewards cards were for?), but the data is useful all the same.

Another metric that can help your business grow is customer feedback. Listen and measure customer suggestions and feature requests for your product. Your customers are talking to and about you and telling you what they want and need your product or service to do constantly on social media.

By listening to your customers, you can scale out new features quickly and continually and meet their needs in a timely fashion. This practice will help you with customer loyalty and customer satisfaction as well as customer acquisition.

Conversation about your brand

Paying attention to how much of the conversation is about your brand or a feature of your brand in your vertical is another key metric to track. For example, Toyota and Honda tend to dominate customer conversation online in the automotive vertical when it comes to discussions about price, but when it comes to conversations about family and brakes, it swings to Ford and Toyota instead.

Knowing where your strengths are in metrics related to your vertical tell you what you need to address for your brand. Ford may not want to compete in customer conversations on price, but if it did, it knows it's third in customer conversation for that metric and can work on it.

Resale cycles and values

Other unusual metrics to track include your products' *resale cycles* — the concept that a product is passed along through resale after a certain amount of time rather than kept until it has lived its product life span. Honda, for example, is a popular car in part because of its well-known resale value. Apple computers hold their value as well.

Resale value is another metric that helps you define the value people place on your product and how well it holds up over time. Resale value isn't a metric you can track in Google Analytics (well, actually, with the new product metric inside AdWords, and AdWords linking to Analytics, maybe you can soon), but it's one to pay attention to.

Chapter 19

Seeing into the Metrics Future

. . . .

. . . .

Affter you master the basics of social media metrics for your needs today, you're going to need to periodically consider what to measure next. Whether it's a current measurement that needs to evolve or a new metric you sense will be important in the future, you're going to need to be on top of it.

Perhaps your killer metric right now revolves around local business. The next evolution of your brand metrics may need to take that out to mobile metrics or perhaps to a metric not yet invented. Knowing when to start branching out is key.

How can you tell what comes next? This chapter is designed to help you figure it out.

Assessing Your Metrics

Getting in good metrics habits involves learning to assess your metrics on a weekly or monthly basis. This assessment is valuable for the things you're currently measuring, helps you fine-tune incoming data, and helps you use that data wisely because things change so fast online.

Adding in comparisons to past data helps you refine your metrics even more. By comparing where you've been to where you are, you can see whether the metrics you're tracking and the data analysis you're creating for your brand is working on an ongoing basis.

Even more important, value tracking and scope tracking of your metrics enables you to see gaps when they occur. These gaps reflect changes and allow you to address them in a timely manner.

For example, you may have very little mobile traffic at first, but it's grown into the mobile space over time. As that increase happens, you'll see a gap in the metrics coming in regarding mobile use: you'll be getting numbers but won't be tracking them as campaigns or goals yet. This gap is a chance to future-proof your metrics.

Knowing What New Things Deserve Measuring

What about new things to measure? How do you know where you need to go with your metrics in future?

Your current metrics can answer that question as well. As your customers start using new tools, new systems, new apps, and new techniques, they show up as outliers (see Figure 19-1) in your current metrics. (For more on outliers, see the next section.)

Figure 19-1:
A data outlier, flying above the curve of average.

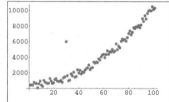

After you see a trend forming, you can begin to measure that metric. That trend may be a type of device, a location, a demographic you've never reached, or a new technology.

Let your data be your guide. Use your business sense and knowledge of your product to verify the benefit you see indicated and fine-tune the data.

Knowing What to Do with Outliers

An *outlier* is any data point that doesn't fit into your established average data pattern. By paying attention to your outliers, you can see where to position yourself by focusing on which outliers are repeating data and which ones start to multiply, indicating a trend.

There are two types of outliers in data:

- ✔ Outliers caused by errors in measurement or data.

- ✔ Outliers caused by the first indicator of long-tail changes in your measurement sets. (*Long-tail* is a marketing term referring to results shown over time.)

Outliers caused by errors

To deal with the first type of outlier (an error that you want to eliminate before it corrupts your data), you need to eliminate it. Eliminating the outlier requires several steps, the first of which is exporting your data to a spreadsheet:

1. **Sort your spreadsheet data by ascending order.**

2. **Locate your median number.**

   The median number of 3 and 4, for example, is 3.5.

3. **Find the point at which 25 percent of the metrics in your spreadsheet are larger.**

   This is called the *upper quartile,* or Q2.

4. **Find the point at which 25 percent of the metrics in your spreadsheet are smaller.**

   This is called the *lower quartile,* or Q1.

5. **Subtract Q1 from Q2.**

   The result is the *interquartile range.* You need this range to exclude the bad data.

6. **Multiply the IQ (interquartile range) by 1.5.**

7. **Add the results of Step 6 to the upper quartile and then subtract it from the lower quartile.**

   This step sets parameters.

8. **Mark any data outside this set of parameters as an outlier.**

9. **Multiply the IQ by 3.**

10. **Take the results of Step 9 and add it to the upper quartile and subtract it from the lower quartile.**

    The resulting number qualifies as an extreme outlier.

Extreme outliers are the data points that you should exclude from your data sets if you have bad data.

What about averages?

Averages are great for your present-day business metrics — judging what's going on now. Averages are the baseline you need to show growth (or a lack of growth). But it's the outlier data that tells you the interesting information you need to see where to step next.

Outliers caused by the first indicator of long-tail changes in your measurement sets

If you're experiencing the second type of outlier (the first indicator of a long-tail change), then you need to track it and create more metrics to figure out what it means to your brand and business model.

Instead of eliminating the data, you want to sort it into its own data set so that you can track it over time. This sorting lets you compare the data outliers to your business model and goals to see whether it's an increasing metric.

If you find that the metric is gathering steam, so to speak, then you know it's a future trend emerging and you can turn your future focus toward it and grow your business in a new direction.

Grabbing On to New Trends

What else can you do to foresee future metrics trends? Paying attention is the first hurdle — it's all about keeping your eyes open and watching how people access your product and brand and what's going on around you.

Say that you see outlier data that tells you new information that shows a trend: iPad 2 users within ten miles of your business are taking a growing interest in your web content. If this trend continues over time, you can make a few decisions relevant to the data:

- ✔ Create an iPad-specific mobile site that rewards iPad customers with special content and track its use with analytics.

- ✔ Create an actual iPad/iPhone app relevant to your business to turn iPad users (and iPhone users) into solid sales leads that you can track from the first point of interaction (download) using in-app metrics.

- ✔ Set up rewards systems you can track for iPad users.

As you can see, it's easy to think of two or three quick things to do to capitalize on your rising trends. By thinking creatively for any rising trends, your business will stay ahead of the curve. Do this every few months, and you'll be able to stay ahead of the game.

Using Current Metrics to Create New Business

You can also use your current metrics for future success. Big numbers to watch are your customer loyalty and referral metrics. These numbers can indicate future growth trends and allow you to capitalize on customer loyalty and referrals early.

The first of these metrics is your *net promoter score* (NPR). Your NPR answers the question, "How likely are you to refer our business to a friend/colleague?"

The second metric is your *referral rate,* or how fast your customers refer your business to others. This number ties in to your *viral coefficient,* or how viral your business, brand, content, or idea is in reality.

The *average number of referrals* tells you how many people you can expect repeat customers to refer over time. *Referral conversion rates* tell you how fast referrals are accepted, and the *repurchase rate metrics* tell you how fast and how often return customers purchase from you.

You can track all these metrics in two ways:

✔ Through your ecommerce section of your analytics on your site

✔ Through manual tracking of items, such as comment cards or rewards programs. Manual tracking can include importing data from an outside referral program into your analytics.

Utilizing these metrics, which you're already gathering, can help you figure out where you need to put the most effort in to grow in the future.

What's Coming Next

I say, "What's next?" but much of this technology is already here; it just hasn't trickled down into the hands of the average user yet. Here's what kind of "big data" is being tracked right now:

- **Lies:** That's right, sites like Match.com and OKCupid can already tell what people are most likely to lie about (like height or income, for example). Not only that, these sites can tell what each person might lie about because each person may fib about something different. Honesty metrics have gotten so good that soon they'll be able to apply the algorithm to larger text blocks, like a bio or About Me section that isn't just Q&A formatted. This will exponentially increase the accuracy rate of these sites.

- **Medical issues:** Science can already track your health, but soon it'll be able to predict health issues for each person based on data sets and input from other online sources about lifestyle. These sources will include nonhealth-related sites like Twitter and Facebook (and whatever site or app comes next where people over share).

- **Safety issues:** The government is already tracking keywords related to terrorism and other national security issues, including weighting them by sentiment analysis. This technology is likely to help your business before the other two will; it's data fire hose–based, and anyone with pockets deep enough can already tap into it. Heck, at this point, Twitter can already predict the stock market just by analyzing tweets in a given time frame. Imagine what that kind of information looks like at the next level.

- **Voice patterns:** Voice patterns and emotional recognition data are going to be huge. Siri (the iPhone voice-activated personal assistant) is a parlor trick to many people right now, but she is the first wave of a very interesting future. Your tone reflects so much about how you feel about any given topic, including if you're agitated with a brand when conducting searches for information about it. You'll have ways to measure voice patterns and emotions in the future, and those metrics will be huge.

- **Image recognition:** Many of today's metrics revolve around words and numbers. With the rise of visual data sets and interest sites and apps like visual-sharing tools Pinterest and Instagram, image metrics are going to be a necessary next step. Google has already begun using facial recognition in photos (much to some folks' dismay) and offers an image-based search, but it's still in early stages. Imagine what data this will bring to your doorstep once it is perfected.

I also cover some other metrics of the future in Chapter 18 when I take a look at what the big brands can track.

Part VII
The Part of Tens

The 5th Wave

By Rich Tennant

"Come on, Walt — we need a new profile picture for our company Facebook page."

In this part . . .

This part is the *For Dummies* series version of a top ten list. I take my ten favorite or ten best recommendations for a variety of metrics-related tools, tips, techniques, and topics and share them with you, one list at a time.

This list is ever-evolving — tools and techniques grow and change rapidly online — but it will get you started on your way to strong growth through excellent social media metrics.

Chapter 20

Ten Cool Ways to Use Metrics

Some nonbusiness and unconventional uses of metrics can be sources of insight for your business metrics. Studying what other people think can result in inspiration and out-of-the-box solutions.

Tracking things like food intake, weight, blog topics, exercise, phone calls, weather patterns, political unrest, crisis management, and more showcase useful skills and unique information. It also helps you get in the important mindset that you really *can* track and measure everything.

This chapter shows you how to think outside of the box and apply new data methods and data ideas to your business metrics.

Metrics of Fitness

Tracking fitness is a new metrics trend, and one that has obvious implications for any business that is focused on nutrition, exercise, weight loss, and activity. Being able to see the data behind your own fitness goals can be very addictive!

Services and devices like the Fitbit are one example of fitness data being placed in the hands of the consumer. For a $99 entry fee, anyone can buy a Fitbit and access its website for daily fitness tracking.

Fitbit (see Figure 20-1) allows you to track your daily activity (steps walked or run, miles covered, floors climbed, food eaten, mood, heart rate, sleep cycles, and more). Then Fitbit adds a layer of game theory to everything by allowing you to connect with friends who use the service to create a friendly competition and motivation through their leaderboard, as well as a social media layer with Facebook and Twitter integration (see Figure 20-2).

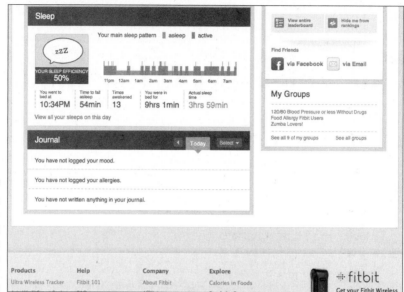

Figure 20-1:
Fitbit show-
cases that
this person
needs more
sleep!

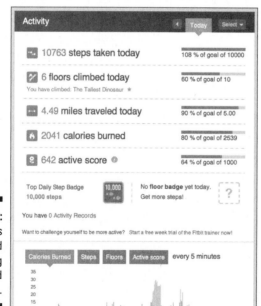

Figure 20-2:
Fitbit shows
you reached
goals using
badges and
charts.

The simple Fitbit device also works with your smartphone for tracking on the go, the Withings blood pressure monitor and scale (both Wi-Fi–enabled), and other brands of Wi-Fi fitness equipment. For the true data junkie, Fitbit also has an API where you can write your own program to integrate with Fitbit or pull your data out for measurement and tracking outside of its website (the most applicable for this purpose).

This kind of personal activity monitoring also has positive implications for any company that encourages telecommuting or that wants to lower health insurance costs by encouraging wellness overall — offering data on when your employees are at their computer and if they have been sitting there too long, among other things. Companies that encourage off-line time for activity have happier, more productive employees.

Note: Fitbit is one of many devices that track your activity somehow and feed the data back to a computer wirelessly. It is simply one that is both afford-able and accurate and that I can personally vouch for — that insomniac in Figure 20-1 was me during the final edit phase of this book!

Metrics of Health

Taking fitness tracking one step further (and often integrating with fitness trackers like the Fitbit) is an army of data-gathering devices that track blood pressure, weight, body mass, body fat, height, heart rate, body size (calipers), eye health, and more. Many of these devices send the data to your computer via Wi-Fi, Bluetooth, or USB connection, enabling you to track this via spreadsheet.

Think of how useful these metrics are for healthcare! Doctors can give more accurate diagnoses to patients and have a better success rate in their practice by getting a snapshot of the patients' daily wellbeing and habits! As Dr. House from TV says, everybody lies to their doctor. Fitness tracking removes a layer of vanity fibbing that all patients fall victim to.

If you provide a service like insurance, you can play with this type of data to reduce rates and offer more effective coverage. Researchers can broaden their studies to include data from everyday patients, or conduct research on data from individuals meeting varying qualifications.

One interesting thing about tracking your own health daily is the tendency to make better choices as you see the real numbers behind your blood pressure and other health metrics (see Figure 20-3). It removes the white coat syndrome excuse entirely, putting responsibility for your health back in your hands and giving you access to your own data and control over your future.

These are the kind of metrics that inspire innovation in social media and technology and the building of brand new business models.

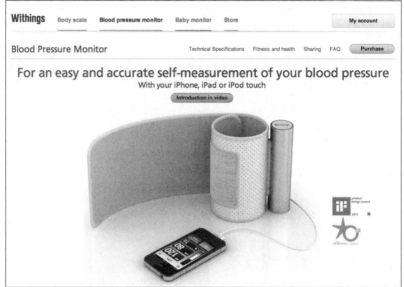

Figure 20-3:
Using
Withings
blood
pressure
cuff with
an iPhone.

Getting advanced: the metrics of personal brain scans made using smartphones truly puts medicine in your pockets (see Figure 20-4).

Figure 20-4:
Brain
scanning
tools with
smart-
phones.

Source: http://milab.imm.dtu.dk/eeg.

Metrics for E-Mails and Schedules

The concept of tracking your own data and using it to inspire or author cool new innovations has been around for a while. For example, Stephen Wolfram, founder of Wolfram | Alpha, a new kind of data-driven search engine, has been tracking his calendar and e-mail since 1989 (see Figure 20-5).

Figure 20-5:
What two-plus decades of e-mail data looks like.

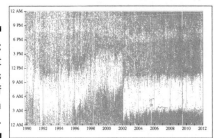

Source: http://blog.stephenwolfram.com/2012/03/the-personal-analytics-of-my-life.

Tracking your e-mail may seem counterintuitive, but think of what your e-mail use (and keystroke count, if you decide to track that also) over time can tell you: Sleep patterns (from before the era of tools like the Fitbit and offline sleep studies), travel patterns, your error rate when typing, your preferences for programs and tools and how they change over time, spikes in activity, and habits.

Add in schedule or calendar tracking over time, and you get a snapshot of your life which, paired with health and fitness data, can help you not only make personal changes but use the metrics to inspire others or create new business ideas. In fact, in Figure 20-6, you can see Stephen Wolfram's calendar tracking demonstrates that while many things have changed for him over time, the hour reserved for a meal with his family never wavers, showing he has clear priorities in spite of an incredibly busy schedule.

Figure 20-6:
Stephen Wolfram's calendar tracking graph.

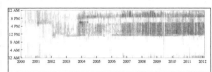

Stephen Wolfram is just one example of a new data-tracking trend in business and personal spheres called the Quantified Self (http://quantifiedself.com). Humans have a great need for input data and knowledge to make themselves and their businesses better, and this trend is growing at a sharp pace. In the next section, I talk a bit more about where some folks are taking this concept.

Metrics of the Quantified Self

One example of living a life based on metrics that stands out most for me is that of Nicholas Felton. He not only lives a life drenched in measurement and metrics, he makes money doing it through publication of *Personal Reports*.

He is one of the pioneers of the whole-metric solution to life and work known as the *Quantified Self movement.* He tracks the most minuscule of data, every piece of daily minutia: mood, cab rides versus subway rides, health data, time traveled each year, locations he's in, health data, computer use data, conversation data, and more.

From Felton's website, you can see the blurb he used to describe one of his reports (see Figure 20-7) and what he tried to learn with his daily data tracking and analytics (each of which sells for between $25 and $65, usually):

> *Philip K. Dick claimed that "a person's authentic nature is a series of shifting, variegated planes that establish themselves as he relates to different people; it is created by and appears within the framework of his interpersonal relationships."*
>
> *The Feltron 2010/2011 Biennial Report explores this notion by overlapping facets of Nicholas' behavior to visualize how his personality varies based on location and company.*

—Nicholas Felton

If the Quantified Self movement interests you in the ways you can apply it to your business metrics and decisions as well as your life and health, you can find out more about it (or meet others who are into this massive tracking of personal data over time and real life application of it) through the Quantified Self site at http://quantifiedself.com. Or you can jump right to the 400-plus apps geared toward gathering and measuring data of the self-found at http://quantifiedself.com/guide.

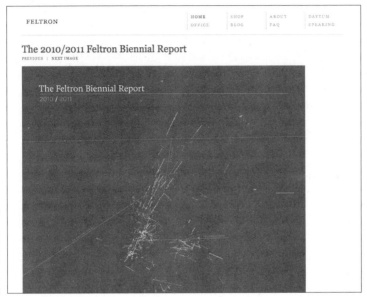

Figure 20-7:
The Feltron
Biennial
Report.

Metrics of Finance

Using metrics to track and optimize your personal and business finances is becoming essential in this age of mobile payments, credit cards, and online banking. As money becomes more and more intangible, it's easy for companies and people that don't pay close attention to it to falter and lose track.

Many applications and tools are designed to help you study the metrics of your money, many with social features to hold you accountable. Whether you need to collect data for personal or business use, there is something out there for you.

Mint.com by Intuit is possibly the best known of these monetary tools that have a strong metrics layer. Offering goals and reporting through visualizations, you can use Mint.com to figure out where your money is going. After you know the details, you can change your habits, create a budget, optimize spending across categories, and get more bang for your buck. You can also export data to correlate to other metrics you may be tracking in your spreadsheets.

MoneyBook is an iPhone-based money app that helps you track your money metrics on the go (see Figure 20-8). A key feature to note here (and one to look for in other apps) is the export to `.csv` function that allows you to send this data to spreadsheets so that you can get the full value of your data. This function is useful for taking a look at not only your money, but your expenses and other on-the-go information.

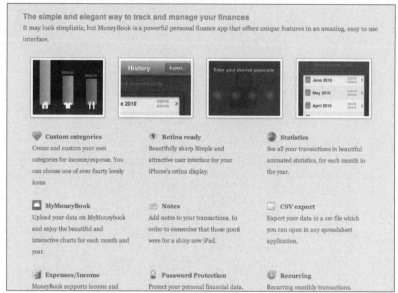

The simple and elegant way to track and manage your finances
It may look simplistic, but MoneyBook is a powerful personal finance app that offers unique features in an amazing, easy to use interface.

Custom categories
Create and custom your own categories for income/expense. You can choose one of over fourty lovely icons

Retina ready
Beautifully sharp Simple and attractive user interface for your iPhone's retina display.

Statistics
See all your transactions in beautiful animated statistics, for each month in the year.

MyMoneyBook
Upload your data on MyMoneybook and enjoy the beautiful and interactive charts for each month and year.

Notes
Add notes to your transactions. In order to remember that those 500$ were for a shiny new iPad.

CSV export
Export your data in a csv file which you can open in any spreadsheet application.

Expenses/Income
MoneyBook supports income and

Password Protection
Protect your personal financial data.

Recurring
Recurring monthly transactions.

Figure 20-8:
MoneyBook uses your iPhone for financial tracking.

There are apps for all phone types and all computer types, all of which give you a deeper understanding of the data surrounding your business and personal spending. Heck, there is even one that includes the often-overlooked Linux users: GnuCash! The data you glean from whatever app or program you choose will help you make better financial decisions and set and exceed your financial goals sooner.

This section isn't really intended to turn into a "best tools" recommendation session. I simply wanted to point you in the direction of a few examples of monetary tools that track the metrics of your money to get you started thinking of your finances as something you can measure, analyze, and improve. You can easily find more tools with a simple search using your favorite search engine.

Metrics of Travel

Whether you need to track geolocation data of your travels, fuel expenses, meals, other expenses, transportation type, or more, there is a way to do it. Some people use simple log books they keep in their car, some save receipts and write notes in them, and some use Evernote to take a snap and note of expenses or locations. Whatever your tool, tracking travel is incredibly useful (and in the case of the IRS in the United States, essential).

If you religiously track your miles and gas purchases, for example, you can see over time which gas providers offer better fuel by correlating data by brand over time. For example, if you consistently log more miles per gallon after every fill up from your local cash-only gas station but find that your mileage declines after a fill up from a national provider and no outlying data, such as city versus highway or old tires or other missed repairs, to change the outcome, then you now know to maximize your gas budget by avoiding those stations.

A trend lately is to use a tracking application on a mobile phone to track driving data and car repair data over time and then export it to (you guessed it) a spreadsheet for more analysis. Some apps that do that include GasBuddy, FuelFrog, and Road Trip, to name a few (see Figure 20-9).

As you begin to accumulate travel and travel expense data to analyze, you'll discover endless business applications. You can use those metrics and make your workforce more efficient, schedule fewer meetings at peak traffic times, shorten commutes (or eliminate them altogether by going to telecommuting), and more. And don't underestimate the power of having detailed data for tax prep — you'll probably discover that you have many more business write-offs, and clearer write-offs, than you thought.

Figure 20-9:
Apps like
Road Trip
help you
see travel
metrics on
the go.

Metrics for Energy Use

Whether you want to track your energy use at home or the office because you are a believer in the green movement or you simply hope to save some money in a tough economy, there are a variety of ways to do this now. Formerly, you had to rely on spotty data found on your utility bill and vague ideas like "keep the lights off when you leave a room" and hope that it worked. Not any more!

You can now track your whole house electricity use, specific appliances (you can even have them tweet to you, though that won't help you with metrics), your carbon footprint, your green energy scores, and more. Many of the energy-tracking tools also need a little help from gadgets you attach to appliances, house electrical systems, and such. Some also work better if you link up your utility company sites for double the data.

Both The Energy Detective (TED) and Wattvision (see Figures 20-10 and 20-11) track whole-house energy use. Wattvision adds an extra social layer by allowing you to share your house data and see how you fare against your neighbors as well. Again, you can export this data to spreadsheets so that you can use the metrics you get to achieve your goals.

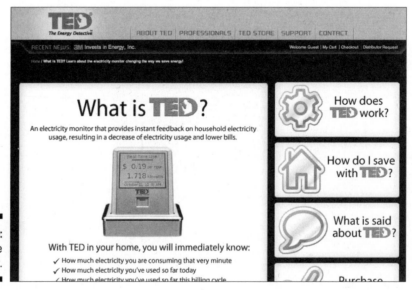

Figure 20-10: TED house tracker.

Figure 20-11:
Wattvision
house
tracker.

StepGreen and apps like it are made more for people who enjoy green causes. It lets you compete with your friends in supporting green actions (see Figure 20-12) and causes, showing you how you stack up in everything from turning lights off to sponsoring polar bears. This is mostly motivational, but can lead to surprising life decisions if tracked over time.

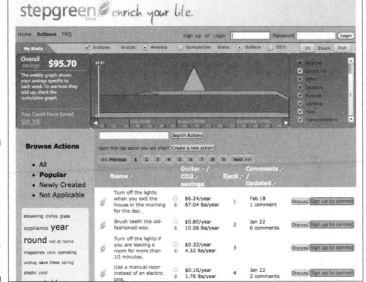

Figure 20-12:
Sample
actions
report taken
from a
StepGreen
user
account.

With the high number of incentives for green business today, you may want to think of applying these metrics to your business arsenal sooner rather than later.

Metrics for Productivity

Measuring productivity has never been easier. This is fantastic news for bosses who need to track employees or who wonder why they themselves are in the office until midnight every night. It's also helpful for people who work multiple jobs or who have to balance work and family.

Hundreds of applications can help you track everything from billable hours to daily activities. Two of my favorites are RescueTime and MeetingBurner, but I encourage you to do a web search and find the one that works for you and your staff (and don't forget the all important export your data feature).

RescueTime (see Figure 20-13) is a freemium service that tracks your computer use — all of it — and tells you where and how you can save time. It claims to save the average user about four hours a week in lost time and lost productivity after it analyzes your use patterns. That's huge!

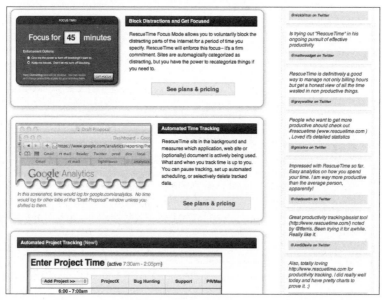

Figure 20-13: RescueTime even allows you to set your computer to focus mode when needed!

MeetingBurner (see Figure 20-14) brings metrics to your meetings by encouraging you to hold them webinar-style online. It then tracks and records every aspect from invite and agenda to topic rotation. This little app can reduce even the most painful weekly meetings by half simply by showing you in no uncertain terms where you lose time, focus, or productivity during each one.

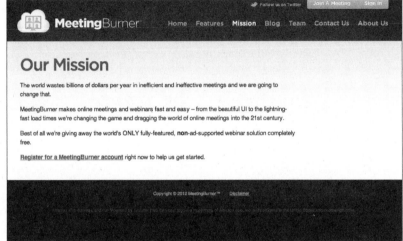

Figure 20-14:
Meeting-
Burner
trims the fat
from your
meeting or
presentation.

Whether you use simple to-do list software or complex CMS and CRM tools, tracking productivity will help you get more done in peak office time so that you can go home and enjoy your family, comfortable in the knowledge that the office is working at maximum efficiency.

Metrics for Learning

Continuing education is a hot topic being fueled by such venerable educational facilities as MIT and Stanford (both of whom are offering online courses free to the general public now). With the easy availability of tools for classrooms, teachers, students, and administrators, there is no excuse not to be measuring learning metrics.

While you can use open-source tools like Ushahidi to track learning as well as for crisis management, more people have access to online tools like Khan Academy, Udemy, and others. Each tool helps track limited metrics throughout the classes.

Codecademy is a unique way to learn to code, making it an interactive game. It offers metrics in the form of your stats in comparison with others. Then Lumosity offers a way to train your brain to be smarter and keep track of your stats.

You can also use tools like Daytum (see Figure 20-15) and trusty Microsoft Excel to record and track educational data. Daytum has a wide variety of stats you can track. Not surprisingly, Nicholas Felton is a Daytum user.

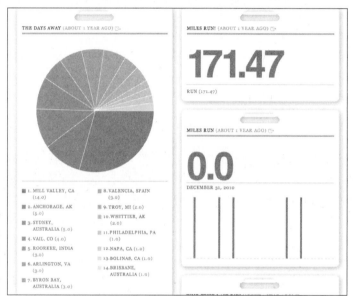

Figure 20-15: Felton's Daytum statistics.

Metrics for Relationships

Using location-based services to track proximity, mood applications to track the nuances of your mood and see how they affect dating and relationships for you, and motivation apps and services to get a handle on the data generated are all essential layers of tracking the metric of relationships.

Of all the cool metrics, this type is the most ethereal to gather data for. Whether you want to gather data on your moods using tools like AffectCheck (a Twitter mood measurement tool), get advice from a group of peers, download data from relationship sites to manually plug into spreadsheets and track dates and experiences with others, or something more, relationships are by nature subjective.

InMaps gives you visual representations of connections online at the business site LinkedIn (see Figure 20-16), a handy tool for monitoring data around business relationships. Morning Coach is an electronic personal evaluation system that is more in the personal, self-help category. Whichever way you decide to go with relationship data, it has application in both the business world (managing employees and clients) and personal realm.

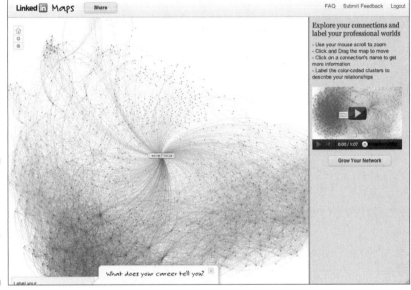

Figure 20-16:
InMaps'
data visu-
alizations
show how
you are
connected.

Chapter 21

Ten Useful Metrics Services

In This Chapter

▶ Figuring out which services can help you via self-serve reporting and consultation

▶ Finding out which services combine with tools or apps for greater metrics coverage

The difference between a service and a tool is the personal involvement that working with a service brings (usually a company that offers hands-on help with metrics or a company that also has a tool so you get the best of both worlds).

Tools are useful for the DIY approach or for automating metrics. Services work with you to figure out what metrics you need, print reports and white papers that the public can buy to educate themselves on metrics, or do your metrics analysis for you.

You can choose from hundreds of services. In this chapter, I'm simply high-lighting the ones that have been around for a while — tested by time — or are well known for their expertise in the metrics field.

If I miss a metrics service you love, let me know on Twitter by tweeting to the #SMM4D hashtag.

Forrester Research, Inc. and Altimeter Group

Forrester Research, Inc. (see Figure 21-1) and Altimeter Group (see Figure 21-2) are less about traditional metrics and analytics and more about analysis of big data and market research overall. These research firms spend every waking hour poring over huge data sets to help business of all sizes arm themselves with the knowledge it takes to solve problems and be better at what they do.

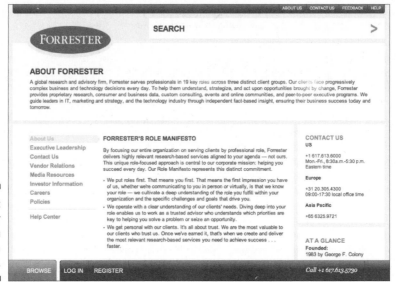

Figure 21-1:
Forrester
Research
offers data
analysis help.

Figure 21-2:
Altimeter
Group
offers data
analysis help.

Both companies help clients dig deeper into the problems they want to solve in two ways:

- First, via white papers, blog posts, and purchasable reports (some are free, and some clients can buy à la carte) to help them solve big problems when they don't have complex metrics of their own to work from.

- Second, by offering events and consulting to back up their reports and analysis.

If you're going to do a big project, a launch, scale up quickly in your vertical, or have a big problem to solve, chances are good that these companies will have data to help you find your way and succeed.

KD Paine & Partners

KD Paine isn't known as the Queen of Measurement for nothing. Author of several books on metrics (one is out this year) and owner of KD Paine & Partners (see Figure 21-3), she has made a career out of building a company that can help you measure the right metrics for social media and PR.

Her company offers a do-it-yourself solution for those on a tighter budget and layers on consulting to help you navigate the measurement waters for a little more.

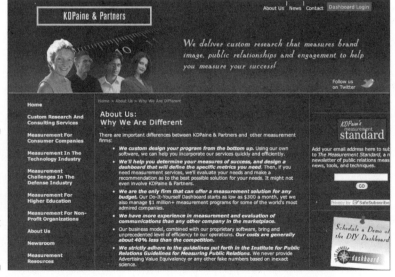

Figure 21-3:
KD Paine & Partners brings years of measurement knowledge to the table.

KD Paine is also working with the Institute for Public Relations Guidelines for Measuring Public Relations to create guidelines for measurement in her industry.

SEOmoz Pro plus Distilled

SEOmoz is a popular analytics blog and team that created a matching software solution to provide SEO and social metrics help. It has a variety of price points to suit any budget and years of experience tracking data.

Rather than provide the in-person backup themselves, it contracts out to partner Distilled to provide personal SEO and social metrics help to their SEOmoz Pro customers (see Figure 21-4). This partnership allows them to layer in the personal element while still being able to keep up with the fast moving world of SEO and metrics changes.

Distilled and SEOmoz also partner on events and training sessions, as well as the Friday White Board videos (see Figure 21-5). Distilled staff contribute regularly to the SEOmoz blog and publications.

Figure 21-4:
SEOmoz
goes pro.

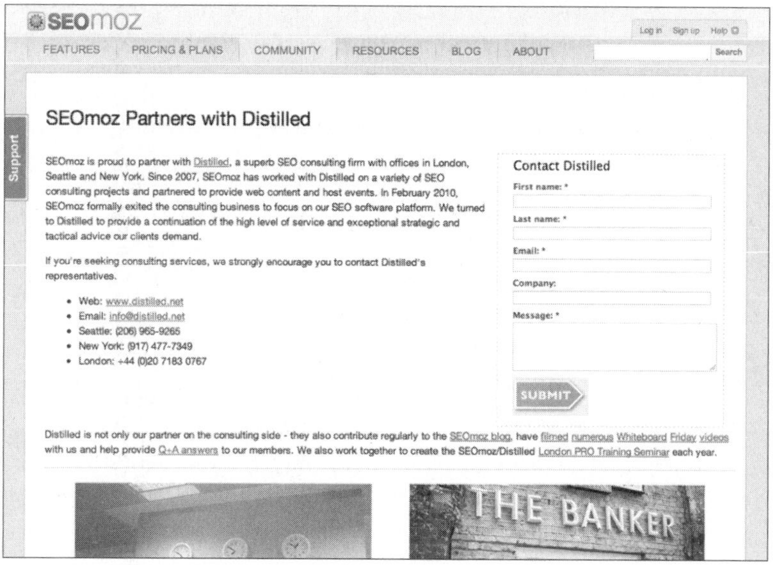

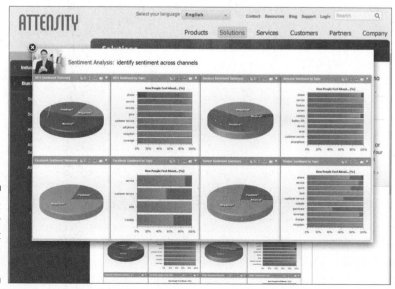

Figure 21-5:
SEOmoz
and Distilled
partner.

Attensity

Attensity (see Figure 21-6) is a combination Software as a Service (SaaS) and consulting firm. The Attensity has a Social Analytics Suite software solution that includes the modules Command Center, Analyze, and Respond.

Figure 21-6:
Attensity
sentiment
analysis
graphs.

Attensity also works to train customers in its LARA (Listen, Analyze, Relate, Act) method of thinking in regards to metrics and how that works in tandem with their metrics software data sets.

The software delivers your metrics in attractive charts and graphs that make it easy to report to the C-suite.

In addition to professional metrics services, Attensity offers training and support.

Localytics

Localytics (see Figure 21-7) is a company that specializes in mobile app metrics, a whole new dimension of social media metrics. Localytics has a do-it-yourself free as well as midlevel plans for those on a tight budget who need to track app metrics from download to use and conversion.

Localytics also has an enterprise-level plan that includes a personal metrics concierge service. Its program tracks metrics on apps across all mobile platforms (phone and tablet) and delivers the results in top-level ready reports.

Localytics also claims to integrate with your existing analytics for a more robust solution and includes in-app metrics, such as user pathing for more in-depth knowledge.

Figure 21-7: Localytics for mobile app metrics.

Localytics Enterprise is created for the needs of the most demanding app strategies. Take advantage of audience segmentation and filtering, user pathing, funnel analysis and full data export. One-on-one personal support from analytics specialists support you during the complete app product cycle.

Built for apps, Localytics provides complete off-line tracking and accurate location, carrier and device measurement. Integrate app analytics with your existing data warehouse, marketing and BI tools for enterprise-wide insights. Localytics is used by the largest and most successful apps on Android, iPhone, iPad, Windows Phone, HTML5 and Blackberry.

Mu Sigma

Offering predictive analytics and business intelligence to various verticals, Mu Sigma (see Figure 21-8) is an enterprise-level analytics and metrics service.

Figure 21-8: Mu Sigma solved business sales and retention problems with metrics.

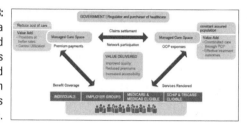

Mu Sigma specifically applies metrics to solving business challenges in sales, retention, customer behavior, and more inside each of the main verticals it serves, such as Financial Services, Insurance, or Automotive.

Mu Sigma is meant for business serving the larger verticals, but you can apply its case studies and white papers to any business looking to learn new metrics techniques and tips.

ForeSee

Foresee (see Figure 21-9) measures customer experience analytics, benchmarking the customer experience with your brand so that you can then make research-based decisions on marketing, sales, and more.

ForeSee offers research and white papers for your do-it-yourself efforts, or you can use its Satisfaction Analytics programs across varying channels (web, social, mobile, stores, and so on) to get brand-focused reports and metrics.

ForeSee also offers a tool called SessionReplay that lets you recreate and study the actual user experience on your site and in your store. By enabling you to identify problems in usability, Foresee helps you fine-tune your process and get better results.

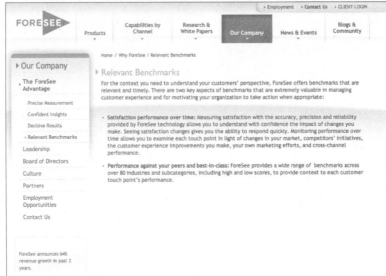

Figure 21-9:
ForeSee
tracks
experiences.

Yottamine

Yottamine (see Figure 21-10) is another predictive analytics product and consulting firm. Yottamine uses data mining, metrics, and analytics to assist you with model thinking about your business, your products, and your customer.

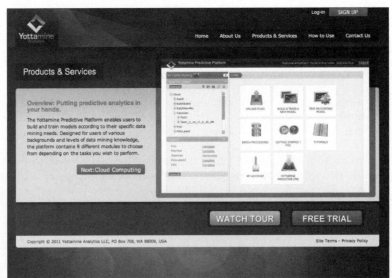

Figure 21-10:
Yottamine
predictive
analytics.

Yottamine has a specific focus in cloud data and offers a product that provides you with models you can use no matter what your familiarity with data mining is. It's not your typical metric set, but one that is useful for any business working in the cloud.

Salesforce

True, Salesforce isn't a company you typically think of as a metrics company. It's highly focused on the sales team vertical — or is it? In the last year or two, Salesforce (see Figure 21-11) has been on a development and acquisition binge, snapping up companies with strength in social media, metrics, analytics, and more.

One of these companies, Model Metrics, adds to the metrics Salesforce already offered for sales. Now you get website metrics, social metrics, and mobile metrics, all from within your sales tool.

With a new social layer for team communication, Salesforce is obviously positioning itself to be a player for the long haul.

If you've used Salesforce, you know that the software has quite a learning curve. Salesforce now has an array of business partners, local to you, that provide another layer of value to its customers by acting as the support staff, training team, and strategists for folks struggling to optimize Salesforce's robust platform.

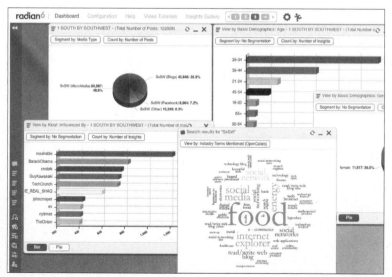

Figure 21-11: Salesforce brings tools like Radian6 to the user.

Salesforce's acquisition of Jigsaw, Jigsaw's integration into the new Data.com, and the recent purchase of analytics powerhouse Radian6 also combine to make Salesforce the tool to beat in the metrics service game.

Chapter 22

Ten Metrics Tools

In This Chapter

▶ Discovering tools you can use to monitor your metrics

▶ Figuring out which tools work best for your needs

*T*ools and services are a bit different. When we talk about tools, I mean those programs and Software as a Service (SaaS) solutions that help you measure your metrics. Services, on the other hand, are often tools and teams that measure your metrics for or with you with less involvement from you.

In this chapter, I cover a few tried-and-true tools you can use to measure metrics. Trust me when I say this list is far from complete!

What I've done is take the tools that have been around for a while or are used frequently and chosen ten that I thought would have the most impact on your metrics. I encourage you to do a search on your favorite search engine and see whether you can find additional solutions that may be a fit for your needs.

Additionally, things in the tech world move pretty fast. Once this book hits shelves, there will be at least one new tool worth investigating, possibly more. Half of the battle in conquering social media metrics is being aware of the new technology and knowing when it is appropriate for your business to try it out.

Google Analytics

The granddaddy of them all (and definitely the most well known), Google Analytics (see Figure 22-1) remains a heavy hitter in the social media metrics space. Google put metrics into the hands of everyone when it introduced Google Analytics. When Google started allowing users to link between services, it had a measurement powerhouse.

I talk a lot about using Google Analytics for your metrics in this book because of its exceptionally adaptable and customizable features. By giving you so many custom reporting and tracking features, Google Analytics makes it easy to customize the way you drill down into your data.

The most killer aspect of Google Analytics is, of course, that it's free. For folks on a budget, this is key. Add in the fact that Google layers in AdWords, YouTube, and other Google tools, and you have an easy-to-integrate tool.

The custom reports and export to Google Docs (where you can make those spreadsheets I talk about) features are also invaluable reasons to use Google Analytics.

Google Analytics is probably the analytics tool that I personally recommend most often (and certainly the one I use the most across the most sites and campaigns). It's certainly the most widely known and, one could argue, the most accessible.

One other thing I enjoy about Google Analytics is how many other third-party tools integrate with it. You can pull Google Analytics into a variety of plug-ins and applications and use it to get more layered, accurate results and take your metrics tracking out into the wild more easily.

Add in the export feature in reports, the e-mail notifications to help you keep your entire team in the loop and get feedback on your campaigns, advanced segmentation, and custom goal setting, and Google Analytics is still the reigning champ in the free analytics tools arena.

Figure 22-1:
Visualizing data in Google Analytics.

KISSmetrics

KISSmetrics is targeted analytics for people who sell things online. Whether you sell services or products, KISSmetrics tracks the conversion rate and a variety of other metrics on your sales site and pay portals.

KISSmetrics tracks the metrics by using events that you set up inside your KISSmetrics dashboard. These events correspond to the tracking code you install on your website.

These events are designed to be very specific. You can track simply who came to your homepage, but you'll get better metrics if you track who is clicking each button on that page, who uses your pay portals, and who fills out your forms.

This metrics program helps you track things like upsells as well and follow your A/B tests to see which versions of different landing pages bring you the most actual business or business leads that you can turn into new business.

One nice feature of KISSmetrics, if you have a product or app, is how it can track how your users are using it. You get data on installations and setups and where customers might drop off in your download or upgrade processes.

KISSmetrics offers a free version and paid versions that give you even more data. Figure 22-2 is from the free version, and you can see that even that version offers several options for events to track. You're limited only in your imagination.

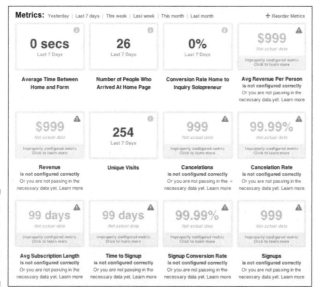

Figure 22-2: KISSmetrics offers visually pleasing data widgets.

Compete

There is some debate about the continuing usefulness of Compete and Compete Pro (see Figure 22-3) as metrics tools and how effective the data they provide is. These tools can be useful for comparison and ranking metrics and also offer some specific product solutions for things like ad impact, consumer behavior information, surveys, competitive intelligence, and opportunity identification.

Compete Pro, while not a tool I use, is a paid tool intended for agencies that starts out at $199 in pricing and goes up from there. If you want the benefits of deep analysis and don't have time to set up and monitor your own metrics in a tool like Google Analytics, this tool or one like it may solve your challenge. You may want to read all reviews first, however, to see if this is a tool that fits your needs and comfort level.

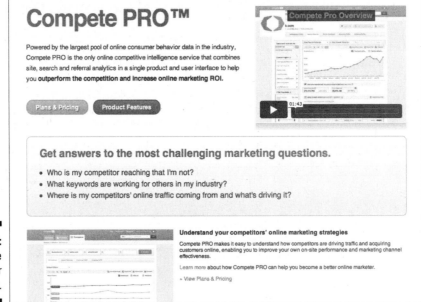

Figure 22-3:
Compete
Pro for
agencies.

Clicky

Clicky, shown in Figure 22-4, offers real-time analytics and tracked reports on how folks are using your website. You can view the reports by content type or page URL and see basic stats on real-time site use and other metrics.

In the Spy view (see Figure 22-5), you can see where the folks on your site are from and how they navigate the site. In fact, when your site is having an active day, turning on Clicky's Spy mode can give you valuable data on how people navigate your site, which in turn can tell you where you need improvement.

Figure 22-4: Clicky is a great metrics tool that I find useful.

Figure 22-5: Clicky Spy view.

Much like other analytics programs, Clicky also breaks out your site metrics into campaigns, platforms, links, visitors, goals, social media (with a report on Twitter, specifically, which is useful if you market heavily on Twitter), alerts, and other analytics.

Turning on the Big Screen (see Figure 22-6) gives you a Woopra-like view of your site's real time use without the lag time you can sometimes suffer with Woopra (though Woopra is also an interesting metrics tool in its own right for some applications — find out more at `http://Woopra.com`).

Figure 22-6:
The Clicky
Big Screen
view.

SocialBro

SocialBro, shown in Figure 22-7, is currently very social media-specific and geared strictly to Twitter use. It's a powerhouse of a tool for providing insights on a variety of Twitter metrics, however.

If you want to know what language your followers speak, where they're located, how many followers they have, which are influential among your contacts, and more, SocialBro is the tool you need (see Figure 22-8).

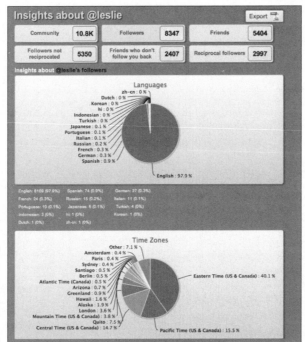

Figure 22-7: SocialBro tracks your social footprint.

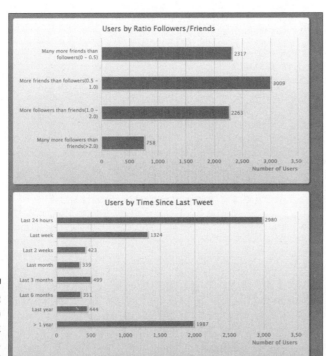

Figure 22-8: SocialBro helps track reach.

SocialBro also has a feature that tells you the best time to tweet and tools to make your hashtags and sales funnels work better. It offers a ton of data about your Twitter use and that of your followers (see Figure 22-9) that you can then use to make goals in your other analytics programs. You can also use that data in conjunction with campaigns and ads in analytics-rich tools like AdWords as well.

One interesting feature inside SocialBro is the slider. You can fine-tune your reports by weighting a variety of smaller metrics like time since last tweet and account age to get even more relevant results about your Twitter stream and how effective your tweets are.

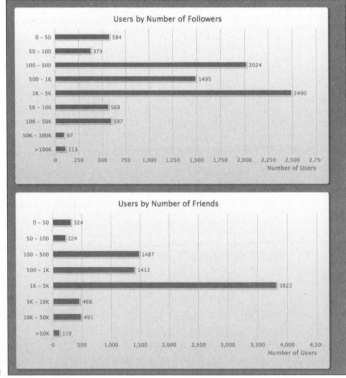

Figure 22-9:
SocialBro offers insights on your followers and friends.

AWStats

AWStats, shown in Figure 22-10, is a little technical to use and may be more appropriate for use by the person who actually mans your website and server. AWStats is a *log analyzer* that measures use of your website, streaming data, and ftp and mail server (see Figure 22-11). Some web hosts include this tool in your hosting package, but if yours doesn't, you can still install it and use it.

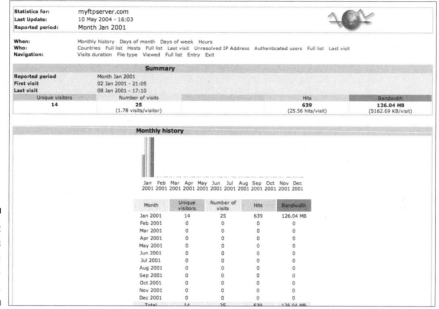

Figure 22-10:
AWStats gives you a more technical tool.

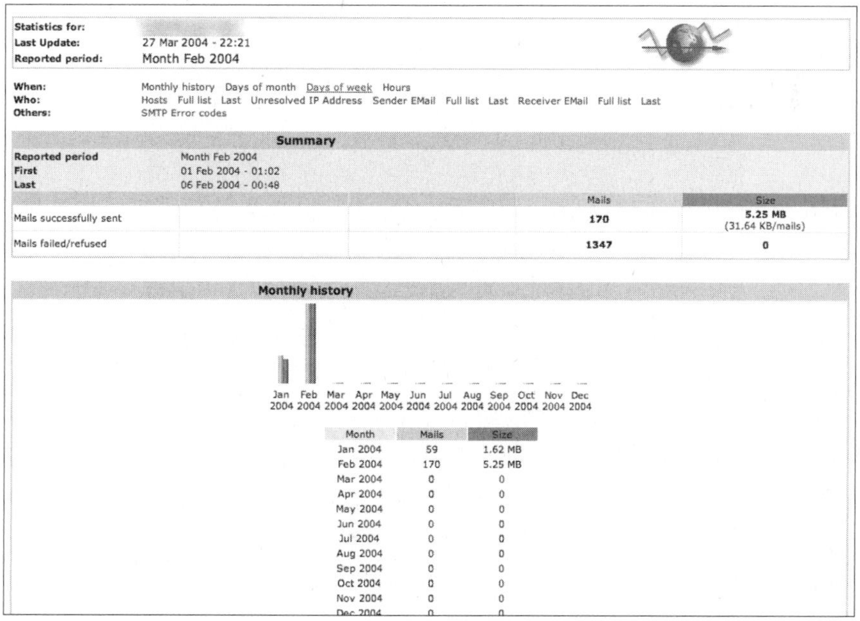

Figure 22-11:
AWStats for e-mail servers.

AWStats works via CGI or from the command line and captures all information from your use logs. It then gives this information to you in graphic-based web pages. Even if your web host includes AWStats in your hosting package, you will still need to do some configuring of this tool at the command line level to get the most out of it.

This tool tells you things that Google Analytics doesn't track, such as HTTPS error log data, worm attacks, robot information, rush hour data, and more. It's meant to give you metrics on the foundation of your website. AWStats helps you troubleshoot if your site is slow or if you need to be able to scale up your bandwidth for higher traffic times or similar issues.

Crazy Egg

Crazy Egg, shown in Figure 22-12, is a service that brings eye-tracking metrics to the everyday user. Normally you'd have to hire out to a lab that specializes in eye tracking and heat mapping at a high cost to get this data, but Crazy Egg offers similar data with plans starting at just $9 a month and up. All plans have the first month free.

Figure 22-12: Crazy Egg shows you heatmapping on your site.

Crazy Egg generates a variety of reports for your site:

- ✔ **Heatmap** tracks where folks click on your site.
- ✔ **Scrollmap** shows how far down a page people scroll to get information as well as the point of abandonment.
- ✔ **Overlay** shows you clicks by element.
- ✔ **Confetti** shows the clicks by segmentation.

While hiring out to a lab may give you more detailed eye metrics using cameras and other tools, Crazy Egg is the next best thing.

ThinkUp

ThinkUp, shown in Figure 22-13, is an open-source tool created by Gina Trapani and used by a variety of people and brands, including the White House, to track metrics. *Open source* means that the tool is free of charge to use and that other people can work on the code to customize it to their needs or add features. Other famous open-source tools include WordPress, the popular blogging platform.

ThinkUp captures your metrics from social networks like Google+, Twitter, Facebook, and more to see how that social traffic is driving users to your site and products. It creates an online report that you can either choose to keep private, only allowing your staff to log in and view the data, or make public. Making the data public allows you to share information gleaned from public outreach and campaigns or issues like those of the White House.

Figure 22-13:
ThinkUp is a tool even the White House uses.

Mint

Mint, which calls itself Have-A-Mint on its website to avoid being confused with the accounting program of the same name owned by Intuit, is a fully customizable PHP-based metrics solution. It delivers your metrics on sites made using PHP (like a WordPress blog, for example) in neat, easy-to-read widgets (see Figure 22-14).

Mint is limited only by your knowledge of PHP. It comes with many fantastic widgets out of the box, and a good PHP programmer can add in widgets customized to your business. Mint offers a variety of data views and interactions to make the experience of reading and studying your metrics more dynamic.

In Mint, the settings and features are called *pepper,* and the user-generated layers and options you can download for more reports are called the *pepper mill* (see Figure 22-15). Mint has a robust community that helps each other solve metrics issues and create better add-ons to the program. Mint is another type of open-source project.

Figure 22-14:
Mint's handy
widget view
of your data.

Figure 22-15:
Mint also
lets you add
more pepper
to your
metrics.

Mixpanel

Mixpanel, shown in Figure 22-16, tracks mobile and web data and focuses on the actions people are taking around your content, products, and apps. Mixpanel does this tracking in a variety of ways, including segmentation, database analysis, dynamic bucketing, and more.

One nice feature for visual thinkers is Mixpanel's reporting tools, which the company touts as eliminating the need for spreadsheet software like Excel. I'm not ready to give up my spreadsheets just yet, but the reporting tools do provide lovely visuals of your data in ways that you can manipulate to tell you the information you need in a format you can include on reports and in presentations.

Mixpanel also lets you build funnels to track drop rates, retention issues, signups, and points of conversion. It offers a nice array of tools for folks who have a mobile app or site and a website with landing pages.

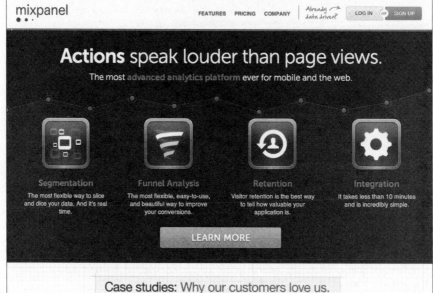

Figure 22-16:
Mixpanel
can help
you track
mobile as
well as
web data.

Index

• B •

• *C* •

• M •

• O •

Apple & Mac

iPad 2 For Dummies,
3rd Edition
978-1-118-17679-5

iPhone 4S For Dummies,
5th Edition
978-1-118-03671-6

iPod touch For Dummies,
3rd Edition
978-1-118-12960-9

Mac OS X Lion
For Dummies
978-1-118-02205-4

Blogging & Social Media

CityVille For Dummies
978-1-118-08337-6

Facebook For Dummies,
4th Edition
978-1-118-09562-1

Mom Blogging
For Dummies
978-1-118-03843-7

Twitter For Dummies,
2nd Edition
978-0-470-76879-2

WordPress For Dummies,
4th Edition
978-1-118-07342-1

Business

Cash Flow For Dummies
978-1-118-01850-7

Investing For Dummies,
6th Edition
978-0-470-90545-6

Job Searching with Social
Media For Dummies
978-0-470-93072-4

QuickBooks 2012
For Dummies
978-1-118-09120-3

Resumes For Dummies,
6th Edition
978-0-470-87361-8

Starting an Etsy Business
For Dummies
978-0-470-93067-0

Cooking & Entertaining

Cooking Basics
For Dummies, 4th Edition
978-0-470-91388-8

Wine For Dummies,
4th Edition
978-0-470-04579-4

Diet & Nutrition

Kettlebells For Dummies
978-0-470-59929-7

Nutrition For Dummies,
5th Edition
978-0-470-93231-5

Restaurant Calorie Counter
For Dummies,
2nd Edition
978-0-470-64405-8

Digital Photography

Digital SLR Cameras &
Photography For Dummies,
4th Edition
978-1-118-14489-3

Digital SLR Settings
& Shortcuts
For Dummies
978-0-470-91763-3

Photoshop Elements 10
For Dummies
978-1-118-10742-3

Gardening

Gardening Basics
For Dummies
978-0-470-03749-2

Vegetable Gardening
For Dummies,
2nd Edition
978-0-470-49870-5

Green/Sustainable

Raising Chickens
For Dummies
978-0-470-46544-8

Green Cleaning
For Dummies
978-0-470-39106-8

Health

Diabetes For Dummies,
3rd Edition
978-0-470-27086-8

Food Allergies
For Dummies
978-0-470-09584-3

Living Gluten-Free
For Dummies,
2nd Edition
978-0-470-58589-4

Hobbies

Beekeeping
For Dummies,
2nd Edition
978-0-470-43065-1

Chess For Dummies,
3rd Edition
978-1-118-01695-4

Drawing For Dummies,
2nd Edition
978-0-470-61842-4

eBay For Dummies,
7th Edition
978-1-118-09806-6

Knitting For Dummies,
2nd Edition
978-0-470-28747-7

Language &
Foreign Language

English Grammar
For Dummies,
2nd Edition
978-0-470-54664-2

French For Dummies,
2nd Edition
978-1-118-00464-7

German For Dummies,
2nd Edition
978-0-470-90101-4

Spanish Essentials
For Dummies
978-0-470-63751-7

Spanish For Dummies,
2nd Edition
978-0-470-87855-2

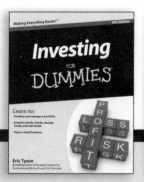

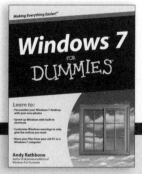

Math & Science

Algebra I For Dummies,
2nd Edition
978-0-470-55964-2

Biology For Dummies,
2nd Edition
978-0-470-59875-7

Chemistry For Dummies,
2nd Edition
978-1-1180-0730-3

Geometry For Dummies,
2nd Edition
978-0-470-08946-0

Pre-Algebra Essentials
For Dummies
978-0-470-61838-7

Microsoft Office

Excel 2010 For Dummies
978-0-470-48953-6

Office 2010 All-in-One
For Dummies
978-0-470-49748-7

Office 2011 for Mac
For Dummies
978-0-470-87869-9

Word 2010
For Dummies
978-0-470-48772-3

Music

Guitar For Dummies,
2nd Edition
978-0-7645-9904-0

Clarinet For Dummies
978-0-470-58477-4

iPod & iTunes
For Dummies,
9th Edition
978-1-118-13060-5

Pets

Cats For Dummies,
2nd Edition
978-0-7645-5275-5

Dogs All-in One
For Dummies
978-0470-52978-2

Saltwater Aquariums
For Dummies
978-0-470-06805-2

Religion & Inspiration

The Bible For Dummies
978-0-7645-5296-0

Catholicism For Dummies,
2nd Edition
978-1-118-07778-8

Spirituality For Dummies,
2nd Edition
978-0-470-19142-2

Self-Help & Relationships

Happiness For Dummies
978-0-470-28171-0

Overcoming Anxiety
For Dummies,
2nd Edition
978-0-470-57441-6

Seniors

Crosswords For Seniors
For Dummies
978-0-470-49157-7

iPad 2 For Seniors
For Dummies, 3rd Edition
978-1-118-17678-8

Laptops & Tablets
For Seniors For Dummies,
2nd Edition
978-1-118-09596-6

Smartphones & Tablets

BlackBerry For Dummies,
5th Edition
978-1-118-10035-6

Droid X2 For Dummies
978-1-118-14864-8

HTC ThunderBolt
For Dummies
978-1-118-07601-9

MOTOROLA XOOM
For Dummies
978-1-118-08835-7

Sports

Basketball For Dummies,
3rd Edition
978-1-118-07374-2

Football For Dummies,
2nd Edition
978-1-118-01261-1

Golf For Dummies,
4th Edition
978-0-470-88279-5

Test Prep

ACT For Dummies,
5th Edition
978-1-118-01259-8

ASVAB For Dummies,
3rd Edition
978-0-470-63760-9

The GRE Test For
Dummies, 7th Edition
978-0-470-00919-2

Police Officer Exam
For Dummies
978-0-470-88724-0

Series 7 Exam
For Dummies
978-0-470-09932-2

Web Development

HTML, CSS, & XHTML
For Dummies, 7th Edition
978-0-470-91659-9

Drupal For Dummies,
2nd Edition
978-1-118-08348-2

Windows 7

Windows 7
For Dummies
978-0-470-49743-2

Windows 7
For Dummies,
Book + DVD Bundle
978-0-470-52398-8

Windows 7 All-in-One
For Dummies
978-0-470-48763-1